Credits

W9-CEU-148

Acquisitions Editor
Aaron Black

Project Editor
Maureen S. Tullis

Copy Editor
Scott D. Tullis

Manager, Content Development &
Assembly
Mary Beth Wakefield

Vice President, Professional
Technology Strategy
Barry Pruett

Editorial Assistant
Jessie Phelps

Project Coordinator
Joel Jones

Proofreader
Debbye Butler

About the Author

Paul McFedries is a full-time technical writer. Paul has been authoring computer books since 1991 and has more than 85 books to his credit. Paul's books have sold more than four million copies worldwide. These books include the Wiley titles *iPad Portable Genius, Third Edition; Macs Portable Genius, Second Edition; MacBook Air Portable Genius, Fourth Edition; Switching to a Mac Portable Genius,* Second Edition; *Teach Yourself VISUALLY Complete Mac Pro; Teach Yourself VISUALLY OS X Yosemite*; and *The Facebook Guide for People Over 50*. Paul is also the proprietor of Word Spy (www.wordspy.com), a website that tracks new words and phrases as they enter the English language. Paul encourages everyone to drop by his personal website at www.mcfedries. com, or to follow him on Twitter at www.twitter.com/paulmcf and www.twitter.com/wordspy.

Acknowledgments

Another year, another iPhone, and another edition of iPhone Portable Genius. I enjoy working on this book so much that I almost look forward to writing the new book more than using the new phone (almost!). Why? For starters, it's just pure fun to write about what's new and noteworthy in the new iPhone, particularly the lesser-known features that can make your life easier and more efficient. More than that, however, I get to work with a great bunch of professionals at Wiley. There's a list of all the people who contributed to the making of this book a couple of pages back, and I extend a hearty thanks to all of them for their hard work and competence. A few of those people I had the pleasure of working with directly, including Acquisitions Editor Aaron Black, Project Editor Maureen Tullis, and Copy Editor Scott Tullis. Many thanks to each of you for the skill, professionalism, sense of humor, and general niceness that made my job infinitely easier and made this a better book.

This book is dedicated to my beautiful wife, Karen,
who is wise, funny, and smart, even in texts.

Contents
at a Glance

Contents

chapter 1

chapter 2

chapter 3

How Do I Connect My iPhone to a Network?   56

chapter 4

How Can I Get More Out of
the Phone App? 74

chapter 5

How Can I Make the Most of
iPhone Web Surfing? 96

chapter 6

chapter 12

How Do I Manage My Ebook
Library? 254

chapter 13

How Do I Keep My Life in
Sync with iCloud? 270

chapter 14

How Do I Fix My iPhone?   286

Introduction

The iPhone is a success not because over 750 million of them have been sold (or, I should say, not *only* because over 750 million of them have been sold; that's a *lot* of phones!), but because the iPhone, in just a few years, has reached the status of a cultural icon. Even people who don't care much for gadgets in general and cell phones in particular know about the iPhone. And for those of us who do care about gadgets, the iPhone elicits a kind of technological longing that can be satisfied in only one way: by buying one (or, in my case, by buying all nine versions!).

Part of the iconic status of the iPhone comes from its gorgeous design and remarkable interface, which makes all the standard tasks — surfing, emailing, texting, scheduling, and playing — easy and intuitive. But just as an attractive face or an easygoing manner can hide a personality of complexity and depth, so too does the iPhone hide many of its most useful and interesting features.

When you want to get beyond the basics of iPhone and solve some of its riddles, you might consider making an appointment with the Genius Bar at your local Apple Store. More often than not, the on-duty genius gives you good advice on how to get your iPhone to do what you want it to do. The Genius Bar is a great thing, but it isn't always a convenient thing. In some cases, you may even need to leave your iPhone for a while (No!) to get the problem checked out and, hopefully, resolved.

What you really need is a version of the Genius Bar that's easier to access, more convenient, and doesn't require tons of time or leaving your iPhone in the hands of a stranger. What you really need is a portable genius that enables you to be more productive and solve problems — wherever you and your iPhone happen to be.

Welcome, therefore, to iPhone 6s Portable Genius. This book is like a mini Genius Bar all wrapped up in an easy-to-use, easy-to-access, and eminently portable format. In this book, you learn how to get more out of your iPhone by accessing all the really powerful and timesaving features that aren't obvious at a casual glance. In this book, you learn about all the amazing new features found in the iPhone 6s and in iOS 9. In this book, you learn how to prevent iPhone problems from occurring and (just in case your preventative measures are for naught) how to fix many common problems.

This book is for iPhone users who know the basics but want to take their iPhone education to a higher level. It's a book for people who want to be more productive, more efficient, more creative, and more self-sufficient (at least as far as the iPhone goes). It's a book for people who use their iPhone every day but would like to incorporate it into more of their day-to-day activities. It's a book I had a blast writing, so I think it's a book you'll enjoy reading.

What's New in This Edition

This is the *iPhone 6s Portable Genius* so, of course, it covers all the new features that come with Apple's latest phones, the iPhone 6s and the iPhone 6s Plus. These new features include 3D Touch, which adds a new dimension (literally) to interacting with your iPhone by enabling you to press down on the screen: A light press activates the Peek feature, while a more vigorous press activates the Pop feature. I also cover the interesting new Camera feature called Live Photos, which magically takes a series of photos for a second and half not only after you press the Shutter button, but *before*, as well. The result is a three-second long animated photo — with sound! — that you can set in motion by pressing the screen. I also tell you about the other new capabilities of the iSight camera, what's new with the FaceTime HD camera, and the updated video recording specs of the iPhones 6s and 6s Plus.

Please note that although this edition of the book has "6s" in the title, with the exception of the iPhone 6s-specific features I mentioned above, everything in the book applies just as well to older iPhones. (And in cases where you need a specific iPhone version to run a certain feature, I let you know.) This is particularly true if you've upgraded your phone operating system to iOS 9, which runs on every iPhone from the 4s and up. In the book I take you through all the major new and improved features of iOS 9. These include (but are by no means limited to) the following:

- Keyboard improvements, including the new Shift key behavior and the new switch for toggling character preview on and off.

- The new app switcher, which you use to switch from one running app to another without having to use the Home screen, as well as the new "Back to" feature that makes it easy to return to the app that launched the current app.

- The Maps app's addition of transit info for many major cities worldwide, as well as the new Nearby feature, which you can use to discover coffee shops, restaurants, and more that are near your location.
- New passcode and parental restrictions features.
- Answering phone calls on other devices.
- Working with the iCloud app.
- Mail's new swipe options.

All in all, it's an iPhone feast. Enjoy!

How Do I Start Using My iPhone?

When you first look at your iPhone, you notice its sleek, curvaceous design, and then you notice what might be its most remarkable feature: It's nearly button-free! Unlike your garden-variety smartphone bristling with keys and switches and ports, your iPhone has very few physical buttons. This makes for a stylish, possibly even sexy, design, but it also leads to an obvious problem out of the box: How do you work the darn thing? This chapter solves that problem by giving you the grand tour of your iPhone. You learn about the few physical buttons on the phone, and then I show you the real heart of the iPhone, the remarkable touchscreen.

Using the Home Button

The starting point for most of your iPhone excursions is the Home button, which is the circular button on the face of the phone at the bottom, as shown in Figure 1.1. The Home button has six main functions:

The Home button

1.1 Press the Home button to (among other things) leave standby mode or to return to the Home screen.

- When the iPhone is in standby mode, pressing the Home button wakes the iPhone and displays the unlock screen.

- When the unlock screen is displayed, leave your thumb (or whichever finger you've trained) on the Home button to unlock your iPhone using your fingerprint (assuming you have Touch ID configured; see Chapter 2).

- When the iPhone is running, pressing the Home button returns the iPhone to the Home screen.

- Pressing and holding the Home button invokes Siri, which enables you to control many iPhone features using voice commands. (If Siri is turned off, pressing and holding the Home button invokes Voice Control, Siri's predecessor.)

- Double-pressing the Home button displays the multitasking bar, which enables you to quickly switch between your running apps.

- On the iPhone 6 or 6s, double-tapping the Home button (that is, lightly tapping the button rather than firmly pressing it) slides the current screen's contents down about halfway, making it easier to access items at or near the top if you're using the phone one-handed. To push the screen back up, double-tap the Home button once again or tap in the blank area above the screen contents (you can also wait about eight seconds and the screen will restore itself automatically).

Genius

To disable the Home button double-tap feature, tap Settings, tap General, tap Accessibility, and then tap the Reachability switch to Off.

If your iPhone is in standby mode, press the Home button to display the Slide to Unlock screen, shown in Figure 1.2. (The iPhone displays this screen for up to about eight seconds, and if you don't do anything the phone just drops back into standby mode.) Place your finger on the left side of the screen and slide it to the right side of the screen. This either unlocks the iPhone and displays the Home screen or, if you configured a passcode during setup, it prompts you to enter that code.

Working with the Sleep/Wake Button

If your iPhone is on but you're not using it, the phone automatically goes into standby mode after one minute. This is called Auto-Lock and it's a handy feature because it saves battery power when your iPhone is just sitting there. However, you can also put your iPhone into standby mode at any time by using the Sleep/Wake button. You find this button either on the right side of your phone (if you have an iPhone 6 or later) or at the top of your phone (for all earlier models). It's the dash-shaped button (see Figure 1.3) and, as you see in this section, it actually has three main functions: sleeping and waking, powering on and off, and handling incoming calls.

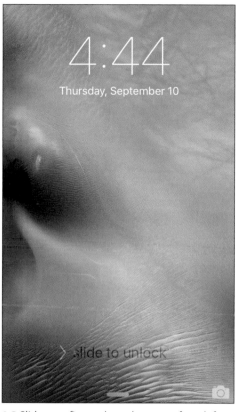

1.2 Slide your finger along the screen from left to right to unlock your iPhone.

1.3 On an iPhone 6 or later, the Sleep/Wake button appears on the right side.

The Sleep/Wake button

Sleeping and waking the iPhone

If you're currently using your iPhone, you put the phone in standby mode by pressing the Sleep/Wake button once. You can still receive incoming calls and texts, but the screen powers down, which drops the power consumption considerably. Tap the Sleep/Wake button again to wake your iPhone. This is just like pressing the Home button: You're prompted with the Slide to Unlock screen, and you slide your finger from the left side of the screen to the right to unlock the phone (or enter your passcode).

Genius

Press the Sleep/Wake button to put your phone in standby whenever you're not using the screen. This not only conserves battery power but also prevents accidental screen taps. If you have a program such as the Music app running, it continues to run even while the phone is in standby.

Powering the iPhone on and off

You can also use the Sleep/Wake button to turn off your iPhone so that it uses no power. This is a good idea if your battery is getting low and you don't think you'll be able to charge it any time soon. You can still periodically check your messages or make an outgoing call when needed, but as long as you turn the phone off when you're done, you minimize the chance that your battery will drain completely. You might also want to turn off your iPhone if you won't be using it for a few days.

Follow these steps to turn off your iPhone:

1. **Press and hold the Sleep/Wake button for three seconds.** The slide to power off slider appears on the screen.

Note

If you change your mind and decide to leave your iPhone on, tap Cancel at the bottom of the screen. Note, too, that the slide to power off screen automatically cancels itself if you do nothing for 30 seconds.

2. **Use your finger to drag the slider all the way to the right.** The iPhone shuts down after a few seconds.

When you're ready to resume your iPhone chores, press and hold the Sleep/Wake button until you see the Apple icon. The iPhone powers up and then a few seconds later displays the unlock screen.

Silencing or declining a call

The Sleep/Wake button has another couple of tricks up its electronic sleeve, and these features give you quick ways to handle incoming calls:

- **Silence an incoming call.** Press the Sleep/Wake button once. This temporarily turns off the ringer, which is great in situations where you don't want to disturb the folks around you. You still have the standard four rings to answer, should you decide to. If you don't answer, your iPhone sends the call to your voicemail.

- **Decline an incoming call.** Press the Sleep/Wake button twice. This sends the call directly to voicemail, which is useful in situations where you don't want the ringing to disturb your neighbors and you don't want to answer the call. Note that, in this case, you don't have the option of answering the call.

Working with the Ring/Silent Switch

When a call comes in and you press the Sleep/Wake button once, your iPhone silences the ringer. That's great if you're in a meeting or a movie, but the only problem is that it may take you one or two rings before you can tap Sleep/Wake, and by that time the folks nearby are already glaring at you.

To prevent this phone faux pas, you can switch your iPhone into silent mode, which means it doesn't ring, and it doesn't play any alerts or sound effects. When the sound is turned off, only alarms that you've set using the Clock application will sound. The phone will still vibrate unless you turn this feature off as well.

You switch the iPhone between ring and silent modes using the Ring/Silent switch, which is located on the left side of the iPhone, near the top (assuming you're holding the phone in portrait mode, where the Home button appears at the bottom), as shown in Figure 1.4.

Use the following techniques to switch between silent and ring modes:

- **Put the phone in silent mode.** Flick the Ring/Silent switch toward the back of the phone. You see an orange stripe on the switch, the iPhone vibrates briefly, and the screen displays a bell with a slash through it.

- **Resume normal ring mode.** Flick the Ring/Silent switch toward the front of the phone. You no longer see the orange stripe on the switch and the iPhone displays a bell on the screen.

The Ring/Silent switch   Volume Down   Volume Up

1.4 Use the Ring/Silent switch to toggle your phone between ring and silent modes.

Operating the Volume Controls

The volume controls are on the left side of the iPhone (again, when you're holding the phone in portrait mode), right below the Ring/Silent switch (see Figure 1.4). The button closer to the top of the iPhone is Volume Up, and you press it to increase the volume; the button closer to the bottom of the iPhone is Volume Down, and you press it to decrease the volume. As you adjust the volume, a speaker appears on-screen with filled-in dashes representing the volume level.

You use these buttons to control the volume throughout your iPhone:

- If you're on a call, the volume controls adjust your speaker volume.
- If you're using the Music app, the volume controls adjust the music volume.
- In all other situations, the volume controls adjust the output of sounds such as alerts and effects.

Getting to Know the Rest of the iPhone

Except for the touchscreen, there are a number of other physical features of your iPhone that you need to be familiar with.

For starters, the bottom panel of your iPhone has four features (see Figure 1.5):

● **Headset jack.** The headset jack is located at the left of the bottom panel of the iPhone. This is where you plug in the EarPods that came with your iPhone to listen to music or a phone call. You can also use this jack to plug in any other headset or headphones that use a 3.5mm stereo audio jack.

● **Microphone.** This feature is also located at the bottom of your phone, to the right of the headset jack. This is where the iPhone picks up your voice for phone conversations, recording voicemail, and anything else that requires you to speak.

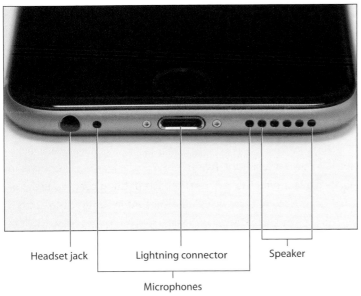

Headset jack   Lightning connector   Speaker

Microphones

1.5 The bottom panel of your iPhone houses the headset jack, microphone, Lightning connector, and speaker.

● **Lightning connector.** This feature is on the bottom panel of the phone, between the speaker and microphone. This is where you connect the cord to either charge your iPhone or hook it up to a computer.

● **Speaker.** This is located at the bottom of your phone, on the right side of the bottom panel. This is where the sound is broadcast when you turn on the speakerphone or listen to music.

Genius

Because the speaker is at the bottom of the phone, you may have trouble hearing it. In that case, turn the iPhone so that the bottom panel is facing you, which should give you better sound quality.

The front of the iPhone holds the Home button, as you've seen, but it also has four other features near the top (see Figure 1.6):

- **Front camera.** This is one of the two cameras on the iPhone, and you use this one to take pictures of yourself (and perhaps a nearby friend or loved one) or to conduct FaceTime video calls.

- **Front microphone.** This second (and amazingly tiny) microphone is used for noise cancellation when you're on a call. This microphone picks up the ambient sounds around you and the iPhone then cancels them out, so the person you're talking to can hear you more clearly.

- **Proximity sensor.** When you're on a phone call, this sensor (which is behind the screen and so can't be seen) determines when your head is near the iPhone, and it then turns off the screen to prevent you from accidentally tapping the screen with your cheekbone.

- **Ambient light sensor.** This sensor (also behind the screen) monitors the surrounding light and automatically turns up the screen brightness when there's a lot of light and turns down the screen brightness if it's dark.

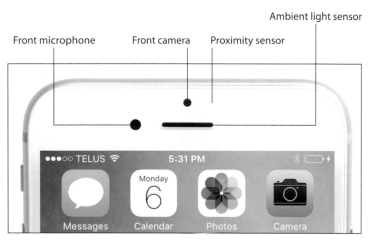

1.6 The front of the iPhone holds the front camera and a couple of sensors.

The back of the iPhone is home to three more features (see Figure 1.7):

- **Rear camera.** This is the second of the two iPhone cameras. This one has much higher resolution, so you'll use it to take most of your iPhone photos.

- **Rear microphone.** Yes, a third microphone! This one is also used for noise cancellation, particularly with video recording through the rear camera.

- **LED flash.** This is the flash used by the rear camera in low-light situations.

Rear microphone

Rear camera   LED flash

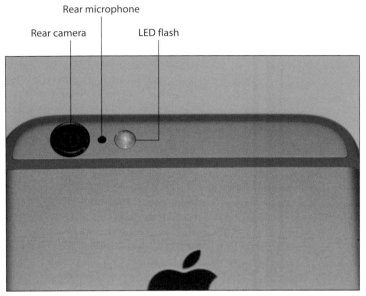

1.7 The back of the iPhone is where you'll find the rear camera and its LED flash.

Finally, the right panel is also home to the SIM card tray, which holds the Nano-SIM card provided by your cellular company. To open the tray, push a SIM removal tool or a pin into the hole on the cover. This ejects the tray, as shown in Figure 1.8.

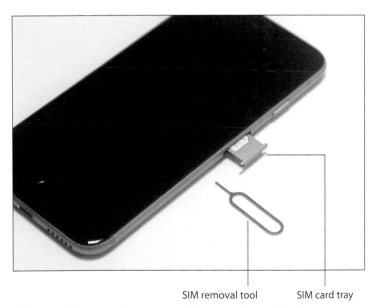

SIM removal tool   SIM card tray

1.8 Push a SIM removal tool or pin into the hole to eject the tray.

Operating the Touchscreen

I can't get enough of the touchscreen on the iPhone, and I think it's the phone's best feature, by far. You can zoom in and out, scroll through lists, drag items here and there, and even type messages. Amazingly, the touchscreen requires no external hardware to do all this. You don't need a stylus or digital pen, and you don't need to attach anything to the iPhone. Instead, the touchscreen requires just your finger (or, for some operations, a couple of fingers).

Navigating the touchscreen

There are a few maneuvers that you need to be familiar with to successfully use the touchscreen in all its glory. Take some time to try these out now. I'll refer to these gestures throughout the rest of the book, so play around and make sure you understand them.

- **Tap.** This means that you use your finger to quickly press and release the screen where desired. This gesture is what you use to initiate just about any action on the iPhone. This opens applications, activates options, enters text boxes, and much more.

- **Press.** This means that you apply pressure to the screen to activate the 3D Touch feature of the iPhone 6s or 6s Plus. A light press on a screen object (such as a Home screen icon) activates that object's Peek feature, which either gives you a sneak peek of the object or displays commands that you can run on the object. If you then release the screen, iOS takes you back to where you were. Otherwise, a slightly harder press on the screen object activates the object's Pop feature, which takes you into the object's app.

- **Double-tap.** This is what it sounds like: two quick taps with your finger. In applications such as Photos or Safari, it zooms in on images or chunked parts of web pages. A second double-tap zooms back out.

- **Swipe and flick.** To swipe means to drag your finger across the screen. You use this technique to scroll through lists, drag items to different spots, and unlock the iPhone. Flicking is just an exaggerated swipe. This rapidly scrolls through lists. Flick your finger up and down (or sometimes left and right) on the screen and the iPhone rapidly scrolls through the list. The faster the flick, the faster the scroll. Touch the screen to stop the scrolling process.

- **Spread and pinch.** You use these techniques to zoom in on or out of the screen. To spread means to move two fingers apart, and you use it to zoom in; to pinch means to move two fingers closer together, and you use it to zoom out. This is especially useful when viewing web pages because the text is often too small to read. Spread to zoom in on the text, making it readable, and pinch to return to the full screen for easy scrolling and navigation.

Searching your iPhone

Parkinson's Law of Data pithily encapsulates an inescapable fact of digital life: "Data expands to fill the space available for storage." With each new iteration of the iPhone, the space available for storage keeps getting larger: from 4GB in the original phone to 128GB in a top-of-the-line iPhone 6s Plus. So, following Parkinson's Law, we keep adding more data to our iPhones: music, photos, videos, email messages, Safari bookmarks, and on and on.

That's cool because it means you can bring more of your digital world with you wherever you go, but there's another law that quickly comes into play; call it McFedries' Law of Digital Needles in Electronic Haystacks: "The more data you have, the harder it is to find what you need." Fortunately, iOS rides to the rescue by adding welcome search features to the iPhone.

If you use a Mac, then you probably know how indispensable the Spotlight search feature is. It's just a humble text box, but Spotlight enables you to find *anything* on your Mac in just a blink or two of an eye. It's an essential tool in this era of massive hard drives. (Windows users get much the same functionality with Start screen or Start menu searches.)

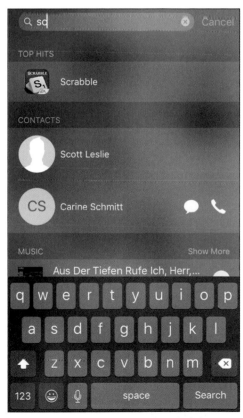

The size of your iPhone hard drive might pale in comparison to your desktop's drive, but you can still pack an amazing amount of stuff into that tiny package, so you really need a way to search your entire iPhone, including email, contacts, calendars, bookmarks, apps, and much more. And, best of all, Spotlight on the iPhone is just as easy to use as Spotlight on the Mac:

1. **Tap the Home button to return to the Home screen.**

2. **Flick down on the screen.** The iPhone displays the Search iPhone box at the top of the screen.

3. **Enter your search text.** Your iPhone immediately begins displaying items that match your text as you type, as shown in Figure 1.9.

4. **Tap Search to see the complete results.** If you see the item you're looking for, tap it to open it.

1.9 Flick down on the Home screen and then type your search text.

Spotlight looks for a wide variety of items not only on your iPhone, but also on the Internet, iTunes, the App Store, and more. If you find you're getting too many results, you can configure Spotlight to search only selected sources, and you can also change the order in which Spotlight returns the results. Tap Settings, tap General, and then tap Search. In the Search screen, tap the switch to Off beside each data type that you don't want to see in the search results.

Typing on the keyboard

You can type on your iPhone, although don't expect to pound out the prose as easily as you can on your computer. The on-screen keyboard (see Figure 1.10) is a bit too small for rapid and accurate typing, but the iPhone does typing better than any other touchscreen phone out there.

1.10 Trust the touchscreen even though the keys may be small.

To use the keyboard, tap into an area that requires text input, and the keyboard appears automatically. Tap the keys that you want to enter. As you touch each key, a magnified version of the letter pops up. If you touch the wrong key, slide your finger over to the correct one. The keyboard does not enter a key until your finger comes off the screen.

Special keys

The keyboard has a few specialty keys that allow you to do some tricks:

- **Shift.** This key is a little upward-pointing arrow. Tap this key once to engage shift. The letter keys change to uppercase and the Shift key changes to a black arrow on a white background. The next letter you type will be a capital letter, at which point the Shift key returns to normal automatically (and the letter keys return to their lowercase versions).

If you prefer the old keyboard where the keys always appear as uppercase letters, tap Settings, tap General, tap Accessibility, tap Keyboard, and then tap the Show Lowercase Keys switch to Off.

- **123.** Tap this key (it shows as .?123 if you don't have Siri enabled) to display the numeric keyboard, which includes numbers and most punctuation marks. The key then changes to ABC. Tap this key to return to the standard keyboard.

- **#+=.** This key appears within the numeric keyboard. Tap this key to enter yet another keyboard that contains more punctuation marks as well as a few symbols that aren't used very frequently.

- **Backspace.** This key is shaped like a left-pointing arrow with an X inside it. This key deletes at three different speeds. The first speed deletes in response to a single tap, which deletes just a single letter. The second speed deletes in response to being held. If you hold the delete key, it begins moving backward through letters and won't stop after a single letter. The third speed kicks in if you hold the delete key long enough. This deletes entire words.

- **Return.** This key moves to the next line when you're typing text. However, this key often changes names and functions, depending on what you're doing. For example, you saw earlier (see "Searching your iPhone") that this becomes the Search key when you invoke the Search screen.

Editing text

Everyone asks me how you're supposed to move throughout the text to edit it. The only obvious option is to delete all the way back to your error, which is impractical to say the least. The solution is, of course, in the touchscreen, which enables you to zoom in on the specific section of text you want to edit. Follow these steps:

1. **Press and hold your finger on the line you want to edit.** iPhone displays the text inside a magnifying glass, and within that text you see the cursor (you might need to angle your iPhone just so to see the cursor).

2. **Slide your finger along the line.** As you slide, the cursor moves through the text in the same direction.

3. **When the cursor is where you want to begin editing, remove your finger.**

Understanding predictive typing

As you type, the iPhone often tries to predict which word you want to use, and in iOS 8 it displays its suggestions in a bar that appears just above the keyboard. (In earlier versions, a single suggestion appears in a little bubble underneath the current word.) This is called *predictive typing* and the suggestions you see depend on the context of your writing. You have three ways to handle these suggestions:

- To accept the highlighted suggestion, tap the spacebar or any punctuation.

- To use another suggestion, tap it.

- To keep your typing as is, tap the suggestion that appears in quotation marks.

The suggestion feature also shows up with misspelled words. The iPhone guesses the correct word and provides a suggestion. If the suggestion is the word you want, tap it to accept it.

Selecting and copying noneditable text

How you select and then either cut or copy text depends on whether that text is editable or noneditable.

The simplest case is noneditable text, such as you get on a web page. In that scenario, when the text you want to use is on the screen, tap and hold anywhere within the text. After a second or two, your iPhone selects the text and displays blue selection handles around it, as shown in Figure 1.11. If necessary, tap and drag the selection handles to select more or less of the text, and then tap Copy.

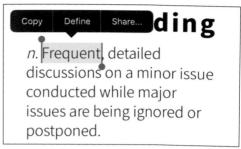

1.11 For text you can't edit, tap and hold within the text to select it, and then tap Copy to copy it.

Selecting and then cutting or copying editable text

If the text is editable, such as the text in a note, an email message you're composing, or any text box, then the process is more involved, but only ever so slightly:

1. **Tap and hold anywhere within the text.** After a short pause for effect, your iPhone displays a couple of buttons above the text, as shown in Figure 1.12 (if you've previously copied some text, you'll also see a Paste button; more on this follows).

2. **Tap one of the following options:**

   - **Select.** Tap this button if you only want to select some of the text. Your iPhone displays blue selection handles around the word you tapped.

   - **Select All.** Tap this button if you prefer to select all the text. The iPhone displays the buttons shown in Figure 1.13; if you don't need to adjust the selection, skip to Step 4.

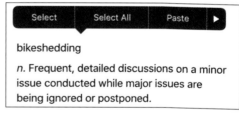

1.12 For editable text, tap and hold within the text to see these options.

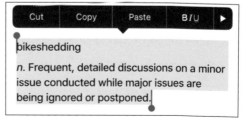

1.13 Select your text and then choose what you want to do with it.

3. **Tap and drag the selection handles to select the text you want to work with.** The iPhone displays a new set of buttons above the text, as shown in Figure 1.13.

4. **Tap the action you want iPhone to take with the text:**

   - **Cut.** Tap this button to remove the text and store it in the memory of your iPhone.

   - **Copy.** Tap this button to store a copy of the text in the memory of your iPhone.

Genius

If you have an iPhone 6 Plus, rotate it into landscape mode to see an extended keyboard that includes dedicated buttons for Cut (the scissors icon), Copy (the letter A in a square), and Paste (a glue bottle).

Pasting text

With your text cut or copied and residing snugly in the memory of your iPhone, you're ready to paste the text. If you want to paste the text into a different app, open that app. Position the cursor where you want the text to appear, tap the cursor, and then tap Paste, as shown in Figure 1.14. Your iPhone dutifully adds the cut or copied text.

Copying and pasting a photo

If you want to make a copy of a photo, such as an image shown on a web page, the process is more or less the same as copying noneditable text:

1.14 Tap the cursor, and then tap Paste to place your cut or copied text in the app.

1. **Tap and hold the photo.** After a second or two, your iPhone displays a pop-up menu of image options.

2. **Tap Copy.** The iPhone copies the photo into its memory.

3. **Open the app where you want the copy of the photo to appear.**

4. **Position the cursor where you want the photo to appear, and then tap the cursor.**

5. **Tap Paste.** The iPhone pastes the photo.

Undoing a paste

The addition of the Cut, Copy, and Paste commands makes the iPhone feel even more like a computer. That's good, but it also means that you can make the same pasting errors that you can with your regular computer. For example, you might paste the text or photo in the wrong spot, or once you've performed the paste you might realize that you selected the wrong data.

Frustrating? Yes. A big problem? Nope! Slap your forehead lightly in exasperation, and then perform one of the coolest iPhone tricks: Shake it. Your iPhone displays the options shown in Figure 1.15. Tap Undo Paste to reverse your most recent paste, and then move on with your life.

1.15 Reverse an imprudent paste by shaking the iPhone and then tapping Undo Paste.

Genius

To undo on the iPhone 6 Plus, rotate into landscape mode and tap the Undo key (the semi-circular arrow pointing to the left).

Running Your iPhone from the Control Center

As you read the rest of this book, you'll see that your iPhone is rightly called a "Swiss Army phone" because it's positively bristling with useful tools. However, unlike the easy-to-access tools in a typical Swiss Army knife, the tools on your iPhone aren't always so readily accessible. Most features and settings require several taps, which doesn't sound like much, but it can get old fast with features you use frequently.

Fortunately, iOS aims to solve that problem by offering the Control Center. This is a special screen that offers one-flick access to a dozen of the most useful features on your iPhone. By "one-flick access" I mean just this: From any iPhone screen, flick your finger up from the bottom of the screen. This displays the Control Center, as shown in Figure 1.16, which also points out what each icon and control represents. Most of these features are covered elsewhere in the book, so I won't go into the details here. To hide the Control Center, either tap the Home button or tap the downward-pointing arrow that appears at the top of the Control Center screen.

Airplane Mode Do Not Disturb Brightness

Wi-Fi Bluetooth Orientation Lock

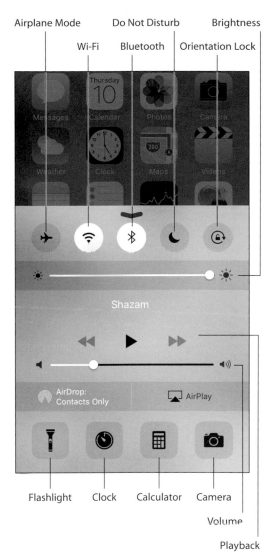

Flashlight Clock Calculator Camera

Volume

Playback

1.16 Flick up from the bottom of any screen to come face-to-face with the Control Center.

How Do I Configure My iPhone?

The iPhone is justly famous for its stylish design and its effortless touch-screen. However, although good looks and ease of use are important for any smartphone, it's what you do with that phone that's important. The iPhone helps by offering a lot of features, but chances are those features aren't set up to suit the way you work. Maybe your most-used Home screen icons aren't at the top of the screen where they should be, or perhaps your iPhone goes to sleep too soon. This chapter shows you how to configure your iPhone to solve these and many other annoyances so the phone works the way you do.

Customizing the Home Screen

The Home screen is your starting point for all things iPhone, and what could be simpler? Just tap the icon you want, and the app loads lickety-split. Ah, but things are never so simple, are they? In fact, there are a couple of hairs in the Home screen soup:

- The icons in the top row and the left column are a bit easier to find and a bit easier to tap.

- When you have more than 24 icons on the iPhone 6 or later (or 20 icons on the iPhone 5 or 5s, or 16 on earlier iPhones), they extend onto a second (or third or fourth) Home screen. If the app you want isn't on the main Home screen, you must first flick to the screen that has the app's icon (or tap its dot) and then tap the icon. Note, however, that even when your icons extend onto multiple Home screens, the four icons in the iPhone Dock appear on every Home screen, so they're always available.

You can make the Home screen more efficient by moving your four most-used icons to the iPhone Dock and by moving your other often-used icons to the top row or left column of the main Home screen. You can do all of this by rearranging the Home screen icons as follows:

1. **Display the Home screen.**

2. **Tap and hold any Home screen icon.** When you see the icons wiggling, release your finger.

3. **Tap and drag the icons into the positions you prefer.** To move an icon to a previous screen, tap and drag it to the left edge of the current screen. To move it to a later screen, tap and drag it to the right edge of the current screen. Next, wait for the new screen to appear and then drop the icon where you want it.

4. **Rearrange the existing Dock icons by dragging them left or right to change the order.**

5. **To replace a Dock icon, first tap and drag the icon off the Dock to create some space.** Then tap and drag any Home screen icon into the Dock.

6. **Press the Home button.** Your iPhone saves the new icon arrangement.

Creating an app folder

The best way to make the main Home screen more manageable is to reduce the total number of icons you have to work with. This isn't a problem when you're just starting out with your iPhone, because out of the box it comes with only a limited number of apps. However, the addictive nature of the App Store almost always means that you end up with screen after screen of apps. In fact, the iPhone lets you use a maximum of 11 screens. If you fill each screen to the brim — that's 24 apps per screen on the iPhone 6 or later — you end up with a total of 268 icons (including the four Dock icons; the iPhone 5 can have up to 224 icons and earlier iPhone versions can have up to 180 icons). That's a lot of icons.

Now, when I tell you to reduce the number of icons on the Home screens, I don't mean that you should delete apps. Too drastic! Instead, you can take advantage of a great feature called *app folders*. Just like a folder on your hard drive that can store multiple files, an app folder can store multiple app icons. You can store nine apps per page and create multiple pages. This enables you to group related apps together under a single icon, which not only reduces your overall Home screen clutter but can also make individual apps easier to find.

Here are the steps to follow to create and populate an app folder:

1. **Navigate to the Home screen that contains at least one of the apps you want to include in your folder.**

2. **Tap and hold any icon until you see all the icons wiggling.**

3. **Tap and drag an icon that you want to include in the folder, and drop it on another icon that you want to include in the same folder.** Your iPhone creates the folder and displays a text box so that you can name it. The default name is the underlying category used by the apps, as shown in Figure 2.1. If the apps are in different categories, your iPhone uses the category of the app you dragged and dropped.

2.1 Drop one app icon on another to create an app folder.

4. **Tap inside the text box to edit the name, if you feel like it, and tap Done when you finish.**

5. **Press the Home button.** Your iPhone saves your new icon arrangement.

Use the following techniques to work with your app folders:

- **To add another app to the folder, tap and drag the app icon and drop it on the folder.**

- **To launch an app, tap the folder to open it and tap the app.**

- **To rename a folder or rearrange the apps within a folder, tap the folder to open it.** Then tap and hold any app icon within the folder. You can then edit the folder name, or drag and drop the apps within the folder.

- **To remove an app from a folder, tap the folder to open it.** Tap and hold any app icon within the folder, then drag it out of the folder.

Adding a Safari web clip to the Home screen

Do you have a web page that you visit all the time? If so, you can set up that page as a bookmark in the iPhone Safari browser, but there's an even faster way to access it: Add it to the Home screen as a web clip icon. A *web clip* is a link to a page that preserves that page's scroll position and zoom level. For example, suppose a page has a form at the bottom. To use that form, you have to navigate to the page, scroll to the bottom, and then zoom in to see it better. However, you can perform all three actions — navigate, scroll, and zoom — automatically with a web clip.

Follow these steps to save a page as a web clip icon on the Home screen:

1. **Use the Safari browser on your iPhone to navigate to the page you want to save.**

2. **Scroll to the portion of the page you want to see.**

3. **Pinch and spread your fingers over the area you want to zoom in on until you can comfortably read the text.**

4. **Tap the Share icon (the arrow) at the bottom of the screen.** iPhone displays a list of actions.

5. **Tap Add to Home Screen.** iPhone prompts you to edit the web clip name.

6. **Edit the name as needed.** Names up to about 10 to 14 characters display on the Home screen without being broken. The fewer uppercase letters you use, the longer the name can be. For longer names, iPhone displays the first and last few characters (depending on the locations of spaces in the name) separated by an ellipsis (...). For example, if the name is My Home Page, it appears in the Home screen as My Ho...Page.

7. **Tap Add.** iPhone adds the web clip to the Home screen and displays the Home screen. If your main Home screen is already filled to the brim with icons, iPhone adds the web clip to the first screen that has space available.

Genius

To delete a web clip from the Home screen, tap and hold any Home screen icon until the icon dance begins. Each web clip icon displays an X in the upper left corner. Tap the X of the web clip you want to remove. When iPhone asks you to confirm, tap Delete, and then press the Home button to save the configuration.

Resetting the default Home screen layout

If you make a bit of a mess of your Home screen, or if someone else is going to be using your iPhone, you can reset the Home screen icons to their default layout. Follow these steps:

1. **On the Home screen, tap Settings.** The Settings app appears.

2. **Tap General.** The General screen appears.

3. **Scroll down and tap Reset.** The Reset screen appears.

4. **Tap Reset Home Screen Layout.** iPhone warns you that the Home screen will be reset to the factory default layout.

5. **Tap Reset Home Screen.** iPhone resets the Home screen to the default layout, but it doesn't delete the icons for any apps you've added.

Working with App Notifications

A lot of apps take advantage of an IOS feature called *notifications,* which enables them to send messages and other data to your iPhone. For example, the Facebook app displays an alert on your iPhone when a friend sends you a message. Similarly, the Foursquare app, which lets you track where your friends are located, sends you a message when a friend checks in at a particular location.

If an app supports notifications, then the first time you start it, your iPhone usually displays a message like the one shown in Figure 2.2, asking if you want to allow notifications for the app. Tap OK if you're cool with that; if you're not, tap Don't Allow.

"Flickr" Would Like to Send You Notifications

Notifications may include alerts, sounds, and icon badges. These can be configured in Settings.

| Don't Allow | OK |

2.2 Your iPhone lets you allow or disallow notifications for an app.

There are actually four kinds of notifications:

- **Sound.** This is a sound effect that plays when some app-related event occurs.

- **Alert.** This is a message that pops up on your iPhone screen. You must then tap a button to dismiss the message before you can continue working with your current app.

- **Banner.** This is a message that appears at the top of the screen. Unlike an alert, a banner allows you to keep using your current app and disappears automatically after a few seconds. If you prefer to switch to the app to view the message, tap the banner.

● **Badge.** This is a small, red icon that appears in the upper right corner of an app icon. The icon usually displays a number, which might be the number of messages you have waiting for you on the server.

Displaying the Notification Center

If you miss an alert or banner, or if you see a banner but ignore it, you can still eyeball your recent notification messages by displaying the Notification Center. This is a feature that combines all your recent alerts and banners in one handy location. So, not only can you see the most recent alert, but you can also see the last few so you don't miss anything.

Even better, displaying the Notification Center is a snap — just swipe down from the top of the screen and then tap Notifications. The Notification Center displays your recent messages sorted by app. From here, you can either tap an item to switch to that app or swipe up from the bottom of the screen to hide the Notification Center.

Handling notifications within the Notification Center

Tapping a notification opens the associated app so that you can work with the item. For example, if the notification concerns a recently received email message, you might want to tap the notification to open Mail and read or delete the message. However, for simple actions (such as deleting an email), opening the app feels like overkill. Fortunately, the Notification Center can often save you a tap or two by enabling you to handle some notifications directly within the Notification Center.

You do this by swiping left on a notification. This reveals one or more buttons that you can tap to handle the notification. For example, if you swipe left on an email message, you see two buttons: Mark as Read and Trash (see Figure 2.3).

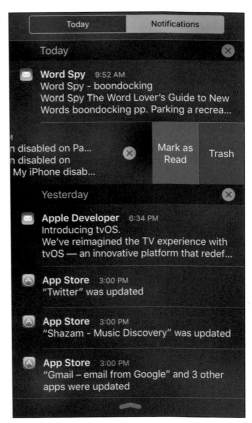

2.3 Swipe left on a notification to reveal one or more buttons that enable you to handle the item from within the Notification Center.

Customizing notifications

For each app, your iPhone also lets you toggle individual notification types (sounds, alerts, and badges), switch between banner and alert messages, or remove an app from the Notification Center altogether. You can also configure app notifications to appear in the Lock screen (with the Lock screen displayed, swipe down from the top of the screen to see the Notification Center). This is handy because you can see your notifications without having to unlock your iPhone.

Here's how to configure app notifications:

1. **On the Home screen, tap Settings.** The Settings app appears.

2. **Tap Notification Center.** The Notification Center screen appears.

3. **Tap the app you want to customize.** The app notification settings appear. Figure 2.4 shows the settings for the Reminders app. Note that not all apps support all possible settings.

4. **To remove the app from the Notification Center, tap the Allow Notifications switch to Off.**

5. **To set the maximum number of app messages that appear on the Notification Center, tap Show in Notification Center and then tap the number of messages.**

6. **If the app supports sounds, use the Sounds switch to toggle this type of notification On or Off.**

7. **If the app supports badges, use the Badge App Icon switch to toggle this type of notification On or Off.**

8. **Use the Show on Lock Screen switch to toggle whether the app's notifications appear in the iPhone Lock screen.**

9. **In the Alert Style section, tap the style you prefer for message notifications.** Tap None to turn off alerts, or tap the style you want: Banners or Alerts.

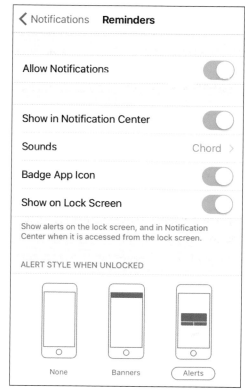

2.4 Use each app's notification settings to control notifications on your iPhone.

10. **If you prefer to see alerts only from people you know, tap Show Alerts from My Contacts.**

11. **Tap Notifications to return to the Notification Center screen.**

12. **Repeat Steps 3 to 11 to customize each app.**

Configuring Do Not Disturb settings

The Notification Center is a truly useful tool that helps you see what's going on in your world at a glance and gives you a heads-up about activities, incoming messages, app happenings, and more. The Notification Center is a great innovation, but it's also a distracting one with its banners, alerts, and sounds. If you're in a meeting, at a movie, or going to sleep, you certainly don't want your iPhone disturbing the peace. Most people handle this by activating Airplane mode, which turns off all the antennas on the iPhone. That ensures you're distraction-free for a while, but it suffers from a major drawback: Without any working antennas, your iPhone can't communicate with the world, so it doesn't download messages or perform any other online activities. That might be what you want, but it's less than optimum if you're expecting something important.

iOS solves this conundrum by offering Do No Disturb mode, which silences all iPhone distractions — including Notification Center alerts and phone calls — but keeps your iPhone online so that it can continue to receive data. That way, when you're ready to get back to the action, all your new data is already on your iPhone, so you can get back up to speed quickly.

You can get even more out of Do Not Disturb by configuring it to suit the way you work. Here are the steps to follow:

1. **Tap Settings to open the Settings app.**

2. **Tap Do Not Disturb.** The Do Not Disturb screen appears.

3. **To set a time to automatically activate and deactivate Do Not Disturb, tap the Scheduled switch to On.** You then tap the From/To control; use From to set the start time and use to set the end time, then tap Do Not Disturb.

4. **If you want to allow certain calls even when Do Not Disturb is activated, tap Allow Calls From and then tap whom you want to get through: Everyone, No One, Favorites (that is, anyone in the Phone app's Favorites list), or a particular contact group.**

5. **If you want Do Not Disturb to allow a call through when the same person calls twice within three minutes, leave the Repeated Calls switch in the On position.** If you don't want to allow this exception, tap the Repeated Calls switch to Off.

6. **If you want Do Not Disturb to handle calls and notifications normally (that is, non-silently) when your iPhone is unlocked, tap the Only While iPhone is Locked option.**

Note

To turn on Do Not Disturb outside of the scheduled time, tap Settings, tap Do Not Disturb, and then tap the Manual switch to On.

More Useful iPhone Configuration Techniques

You've seen quite a few handy iPhone customization tricks so far, but you're not done yet — not by a long shot. The next few sections take you through a few more heartwarmingly useful iPhone customization techniques.

Changing the name of your iPhone

When you first configure your iPhone, one of the chores you perform is giving it a custom name. This might sound frivolous, but there's a good reason to give your iPhone a unique name. First, in Chapter 7, I explain that when you sync your iPhone, iTunes automatically creates a backup of the iPhone data. Each backup is identified by the name of the iPhone and the date the backup was performed. If you're in an environment where the same copy of iTunes is used to sync multiple iPhones, giving each iPhone its own name enables you to differentiate between multiple iPhone backups.

Of course, feel free to rename your iPhone for the sake of giving it a cool or snappy name if the mood strikes. Here's how:

1. **In the iPhone Home screen, tap Settings.** The Settings screen appears.
2. **Tap General.** The General settings appear.
3. **Tap About.** The About page appears.
4. **Tap Name.** The Settings app displays a text box with the current name of your iPhone inside.
5. **Edit the name as you see fit.**

Turning sounds on and off

Your iPhone is often a noisy little thing that makes all manner of rings, beeps, and boops, seemingly at the slightest provocation. Consider a short list of the events that can give the lungs of your iPhone a workout:

- Incoming calls
- Incoming and outgoing email messages

29

- Incoming text messages
- New voicemail messages
- Outgoing tweets and Facebook posts
- Calendar and reminder alerts
- Locking and unlocking the phone
- Tapping the keys on the on-screen keyboard

What a racket! None of this may bother you when you're on your own, but if you're in a meeting, at a movie, or anywhere else where extraneous sounds are unwelcome, you might want to turn off some (or all) of the iPhone sound effects.

First, you should know that when a call comes in and you press the Sleep/Wake button once, your iPhone silences the ringer. That's a sweet and useful feature, but the problem is that it may take you one or two rings before you can dig out your iPhone and press Sleep/Wake. By that time, folks nearby are already glaring at you.

To prevent this faux pas, you can switch your iPhone into silent mode, as I describe in Chapter 1, which means it doesn't ring and it doesn't play any alerts or sound effects. When the sound is turned off, the only alarms that are audible are the ones you've set using the Clock app. The phone still vibrates unless you also turn this feature off. If silent mode is a bit too drastic, you can control exactly which sounds your iPhone utters by following these steps:

1. **On the Home screen, tap Settings.** The Settings app appears.

2. **Tap Sounds.** The Sounds screen appears.

3. **The two switches in the Vibrate section determine whether your iPhone vibrates when the phone rings or is in silent mode.** Vibrating probably isn't all that important in ring mode, so feel free to change this setting to Off. The exception is if you reduce and/or lock the ringer volume (see Steps 4 and 5), in which case setting Vibrate on Ring to On might help you notice an incoming call. Vibrating in silent mode is a good idea, so On is a good choice for the Vibrate on Silent setting.

4. **In the Ringer and Alerts section, drag the volume slider to set the volume of the ringtone that plays when a call comes in.**

5. **To lock the ringer volume, tap the Change with Buttons switch to Off.** This means that pressing the volume buttons on the side of the iPhone will have no effect on the ringer volume.

Genius

Locking the ringer volume is a good idea because it prevents one of the major iPhone frustrations: missing a call because the ringer volume has been muted accidentally (for example, by your iPhone getting jostled in a purse or pocket).

6. **To set a different default ringtone, tap Ringtone to open the Ringtone screen.** Tap the ringtone you want to use (iPhone plays a preview), and then tap Sounds to return to the Sounds screen.

7. **For each of the other events in the list (from Text Tone to AirDrop), tap the event and then tap the sound you want to hear.** You can also tap None to turn off the event sound.

8. **To turn off the sound that your iPhone makes when you lock and unlock it, tap the Lock Sounds switch to Off.**

9. **To turn off the sound that your iPhone makes each time you tap a key on the virtual keyboard, tap the Keyboard Clicks switch to Off.**

Genius

One of the truly annoying iPhone sound effects is the clicking sound made by each key when using the on-screen keyboard. If it doesn't make you batty after five minutes, it will certainly drive anyone within earshot to thoughts of violence. So I strongly recommend tapping the Keyboard Clicks setting to Off. There, that's better.

Customizing the keyboard

Although you can type on your iPhone, don't expect to pound out the prose as easily as you can on your computer. The on-screen keyboard is a bit too small for rapid and accurate typing, but it's still a far sight better than any other phone out there, mostly because the keyboard was thoughtfully designed by the folks at Apple. It even changes depending on the app you use. For example, the regular keyboard features a spacebar at the bottom. However, if you're entering an email address in the Mail app, the keyboard that appears offers a smaller spacebar and uses the extra space to show an at sign (@) key and a period (.) key, two characters that are part of any email address. Nice!

Another nice innovation you get with the iPhone keyboard is Auto-Capitalization. If you type a punctuation mark that indicates the end of a sentence — for example, a period (.), a question mark (?), or an exclamation mark (!) — or if you press Return to start a new paragraph, the iPhone automatically activates the Shift key, because it assumes you're starting a new sentence.

On a related note, double-tapping the spacebar activates a keyboard shortcut: Instead of entering two spaces, the iPhone automatically enters a period (.) followed by a space. This is a welcome bit of efficiency because otherwise you'd have to tap the Number key (123) to display the numbers and punctuation marks, tap the period (.), and then tap the spacebar.

Genius

Typing a number or punctuation mark normally requires three taps: tapping Number (123), tapping the number or symbol, and then tapping ABC. Here's a faster way: Use one finger to tap and hold the Number key to open the numeric keyboard, use a second finger to tap the number or punctuation symbol you want, and then release the Number key. This types the number or symbol and returns you to the regular keyboard.

For many people, one of the keys to quick iPhone typing is to clear the mind and just tap away without worrying about accuracy. In many cases, you'll actually be rather amazed at how accurate this willy-nilly approach can be. Why does it work? The secret is the Auto-Correction feature on your iPhone, which eyeballs what you're typing and automatically corrects any errors. For example, if you tap *hte,* your iPhone automatically corrects this to *the.* Your iPhone displays the suggested correction before you complete the word (say, by tapping a space or a comma), and you can reject the suggestion by tapping the typed text that appears with quotation marks in the predictive typing bar. If you find you never use the predictive suggestions, you can turn them off to save a bit of screen real estate.

One thing the iPhone keyboard doesn't seem to have is a Caps Lock feature that, when activated, enables you to type all-uppercase letters. To do this, you need to tap and hold the Shift key, and then use a different finger to tap the uppercase letters. However, the iPhone actually does have a Caps Lock feature: Double-tap Shift to turn Caps Lock on (which is indicated on the Shift key with a horizontal bar under the arrow), then tap Shift to turn Caps Lock off.

Another of the iPhone's keyboard innovations is a feature called *character preview*, which displays a pop-up version of each character as you tap it. This is great for iPhone keyboard rookies because it helps them be sure they're typing accurately, but veterans often find it distracting. Some even complain that it's a security risk because the letters pop up even when you're typing a password! That might be why Apple chose to turn off character preview by default in iOS 9, but you can turn it back on if you miss it.

Finally, your iPhone also supports multiple keyboard layouts. This is great if you need to type in another language, but your iPhone also comes with an Emoji keyboard (which is enabled automatically in iOS 9) so that you can punctuate your writing with colorful and fun icons.

To change the settings for any of these keyboard features, follow these steps:

1. **On the Home screen, tap Settings.** The Settings app appears.

2. **Tap General.** The General screen appears.

3. **Tap Keyboard.** The Keyboard screen appears.

4. **Use the Auto-Capitalization, Auto-Correction, Enable Caps Lock, Predictive, Character Preview, and "." Shortcut switches to toggle these features off and on.**

5. **To add an extra keyboard layout, tap Keyboards to open the Keyboards screen, tap Add New Keyboard, and then tap the keyboard layout you want to add.**

Note When you're using two or more keyboard layouts, the keyboard sprouts a new key to the left of the spacebar (it looks like a stylized globe). Tap that key to run through the layouts (the names of which appear briefly in the spacebar).

Creating text shortcuts

The Auto-Correction keyboard feature that I mentioned earlier can speed up your typing chores a tad because Auto-Correction displays predictive suggestions whenever it recognizes the word you're currently typing. When the suggestion appears as the default in the predictive typing bar, tap a word-ending character, such as a space, comma, or period, and your iPhone automatically fills in the rest of the word.

Still, this is only marginally useful for speeding up typing because Auto-Correction plays it safe and usually waits until you have only a character or two left before it displays the suggested word. If you really want to shift your iPhone typing into a higher gear, you need to take advantage of the text shortcuts feature. If you've ever created a keyboard macro or used the AutoText feature in Microsoft Word, you'll know exactly what's happening here. A *text shortcut* is a short sequence of characters (usually just two or three) that represents a longer phrase. When you type the shortcut characters, your iPhone displays the phrase (much the same way that Auto-Correction does) and you then type a word-ending character to replace the shortcut characters with the entire phrase.

Note When your iPhone displays the longer phrase, it also includes an X at the end, which you can tap to tell iPhone not to enter the phrase. This is just like Auto-Correction, but remember that the two features aren't the same. If you turn off Auto-Correction, as I describe earlier in this chapter, you can still use text shortcuts.

These phrases can be dozens or even hundreds of characters long, so if you have phrases or boilerplates that you use all the time, your iPhone typing fingers will thank you for saving them a ton of wear and tear. Here are the steps to follow to create a text shortcut:

1. **If you have the phrase you want to use somewhere on your iPhone, copy it.** This saves some time later when you create your shortcut.

2. **On the Home screen, tap Settings.** The Settings app appears.

3. **Tap General.** The General screen appears.

4. **Tap Keyboard.** The Keyboard screen appears.

5. **Tap Shortcuts and then tap Add New Shortcut (the + icon).** The Shortcut screen appears.

6. **If you copied the phrase earlier, paste it into the Phrase text box.** Otherwise, type the phrase.

7. **Use the Shortcut text box to type the characters you want to use to represent the phrase.** The shortcut must be at least two characters long.

8. **Tap Save.** Your iPhone saves the text shortcut.

Note

To remove a text shortcut, display the Keyboard screen, tap Edit, tap the red button to the left of the shortcut you want to remove, tap Delete, and then tap Done.

Configuring Siri

Controlling a computer with just voice commands has been a mainstream dream ever since the first *Star Trek* series. OS X and Windows offer speech-recognition features, but few people use them because they're difficult to configure and are more often than not frustrating to use. Third-party speech recognition programs are more powerful, but they tend to be expensive and still don't work all that well.

The dream of voice control remains unfulfilled on desktop machines, but on the iPhone (that is, on every model since the iPhone 4s), voice control is a reality that comes in the form of the Siri app. Siri replaced the Voice Control feature from the iPhone 3Gs and 4, which was limited to placing phone calls and controlling the Music app with voice commands. Siri is one of the slickest iPhone features because it goes well beyond this by also giving you voice control over web searching, your appointments, your contacts, your reminders, map navigation, text messages, and notes. In iOS 9, Siri has been beefed up with lots of new features that enable you to make unit conversions (such as converting kilometers to miles), get more detailed weather forecasts, and even access information in some third-party apps.

First, make sure that Siri is activated by tapping Settings in the Home screen, tapping General, tapping Siri, and then tapping the Siri switch to On. While you're here, you might want to tap the Allow "Hey Siri" switch to On, which make it even easier to start Siri. Also, you should also tell Siri who you are, so that when you use references such as "home" and "work," Siri knows what you're talking about. In the Siri screen, tap My Info, and then tap your item in the Contacts list.

You crank up Siri by using any of the following techniques:

- Saying "Hey Siri" (assuming you enabled this feature in the Siri settings; for this to work, your iPhone must be connected to a power source, although this restriction has been lifted for the iPhone 6s and 6s Plus).
- Pressing and holding the Home button.
- Pressing and holding the Mic button on your iPhone headphones.
- Pressing and holding the Mic equivalent on a Bluetooth headset.

In each case, wait until you hear a two-tone beep and you see the Siri screen.

Siri is often easier to use if you define relationships within it. So, for example, instead of saying "Call Sandy Evans," you can simply say "Call mom." You can define relationships in two ways:

- **Within the Contacts app.** Open the Contacts app, tap your contact item, tap Edit, tap Add Related Name, and then tap the relationship you want to use. Tap the blue More icon to open the All Contacts list and then tap the person you want to add to the field.
- **Within Siri.** Say "*Name* is my *relationship*," where *Name* is the person's name as given in your Contacts list, and *relationship* is the connection, such as *wife, husband, spouse, partner, brother, sister, mother,* or *father*. When Siri asks you to confirm, say "Yes."

Genius

You'll often ask Siri to locate nearby businesses, such as coffee shops or gas stations. However, for this to work, Siri must have access to the location services on your iPhone. Open the Settings app, tap Privacy, tap Location Services, tap Siri, and then tap While Using the App (which means that Siri can access your location only while you're using it).

Signing in to your Facebook account

Much ink — both real and virtual — has been spilled in the past few years describing the techno-logical juggernaut that is Facebook, with its hundreds of millions of users (probably more than a billion by the time you read this). While the world's pundits and talking heads can't seem to say enough about Facebook's impact on the world, the rest of us just use it day in and day out to stay in touch with friends, family, colleagues, and college buddies. On your iPhone, this usually involves accessing the Facebook app. That's fine, but it has long seemed odd that all your Facebook friends and events are separate from your other iPhone contacts and calendars, and that performing sim-ple social tasks such as sharing a link or a photo required a few extra hoops to jump through.

However, iOS also comes with Facebook support built right in to the system. You can integrate your Facebook friends with the Contacts app, see Facebook events in the Calendar app, easily post links, photos, and other content to your Facebook Timeline, and even send simple status updates without having to load the Facebook app.

Here's how to sign in:

1. **On the Home screen, tap Settings.** The Settings app appears.

2. **Tap Facebook.** The Facebook screen appears.

3. **Type your Facebook username or email address in the User Name text box.**

4. **Type your account password in the Password text box.**

5. **Tap Sign In.** A screen appears with information about signing in to Facebook.

6. **Tap Sign In.** Your iPhone connects to your Facebook account. It also prompts you to install the free Facebook iPhone app, so tap Later or Install, as you prefer.

7. **If you don't want the Calendar app to display your Facebook events, tap the Calendar switch to Off.**

8. **If you don't want the Contacts app to display your Facebook friends, tap the Contacts switch to Off.**

Genius Facebook events are added to your iPhone as a separate calendar, so you can also toggle them on and off within the Calendar app. Tap Calendar in the Home screen, and then tap Calendars to display a list of your calendars. Scroll down to the Facebook section and then tap Facebook Events to toggle that calendar on and off. You can also tap Birthdays to toggle Facebook birthdays on and off.

Using Siri to update Facebook

With Siri activated and configured and your iPhone signed in to your Facebook account, it's time to combine these tools and use Siri to compose and send a Facebook status update. Here's how it works:

1. **Use any of the methods I mentioned earlier to launch Siri.**

2. **Say "Post to Facebook."** Siri responds with "OK...what would you like to say?"

3. **Dictate your message.** Siri processes the speech and then displays the text in the Facebook dialog, as shown in Figure 2.5. Note that the message is editable, so if you see an error or want to insert missing punctuation, tap inside the message to make your changes.

4. **Say "Post."** Siri posts the status update to your Facebook account.

2.5 Siri is happy to pass along your status update to Facebook.

Signing in to your Twitter account

Twitter, that 140-characters-or-less phenomenon, started off by asking you the not-so-musical question, *What are you doing?* It's a question that seems crafted to elicit nothing but the most trivial of replies: I just woke up; I'm having toast for breakfast; I'm in a boring meeting; I just finished dinner; I'm going to bed. But Twitter users took that original question and broadened it into a world of new questions: What are you reading? What great idea did you just come up with? What are you worried about? What interesting person did you just see or hear? What great information did you stumble upon on the web? What hilarious video would you like to share? Which is why, a few years ago, Twitter itself changed the original question from *What are you doing?* to *What's happening?*

Of course, what's most likely happening is that you're working or playing with your iPhone, and you've got something to share with your Twitter followers: a link, a photo, a video, or what have you. Sharing such things has never been easier because Twitter is baked right into your iPhone. Once you sign in to your Twitter account using the Settings app, you can tweet stuff directly from apps such as Safari and Photos.

Here's how to sign in:

1. **On the Home screen, tap Settings.** The Settings app appears.

2. **Tap Twitter.** The Twitter screen appears.

3. **Type your Twitter account name in the User Name text box.**

4. **Type your account password in the Password text box.**

5. **Tap Sign In.** Your iPhone connects to your Twitter account. It also prompts you to install the free Twitter iPhone app, so tap Later or Install, as you prefer.

Genius

If you have multiple Twitter accounts, you can add more by displaying the Twitter screen, tapping Add Account, typing the account username and password, and then tapping Sign In.

Using Siri to send a tweet

Earlier I showed you how to use Siri to post a Facebook status update, so it will come as absolutely no surprise that you can also use Siri to tweet. Follow these steps:

1. **Use any of the methods I mentioned earlier to launch Siri.**

2. **Say "tweet."** Siri asks if it can use your Twitter account.

3. **Tap Yes.** Siri responds with "OK...what would you like to say?"

4. **Dictate your message.** Siri processes the speech and then displays the text in the Twitter dialog.

5. **Say "Send."** Siri posts the tweet to your Twitter account.

Controlling your privacy

Third-party apps occasionally request permission to use the data from another app. For example, an app might need access to your contacts, your calendars, your photos, or your Twitter and Facebook accounts. You can always deny these requests, of course, but if you've allowed access to an app in the past, you might later change your mind and decide you'd prefer to revoke that access. Fortunately, iOS offers a Privacy feature that enables you to control which apps have access to your data. Here's how it works:

1. **On the Home screen, tap Settings to open the Settings app.**

2. **Tap Privacy.** The Privacy screen appears.

3. **Tap the app or feature for which you want to control access.** Your iPhone displays a list of third-party apps that have requested access to the app or feature.

4. **To revoke a third-party app's access to the app or feature, tap its switch to Off.**

Resetting the iPhone

If you've spent quite a bit of time in the Settings app, your iPhone probably doesn't look much like it did fresh out of the box. That's okay, though, because your iPhone should be as individual as you are. However, if you've gone a bit too far with your customizations, your iPhone might feel a bit alien and uncomfortable. That's okay, too, because there's an easy solution to the problem: You can erase all your customizations and revert the iPhone to its default settings.

A similar problem that comes up is when you want to sell or give your iPhone to someone else. Chances are you don't want the new owner to see your data — contacts, appointments, email and text messages, favorite websites, music, and so on — and it's unlikely the other person wants to wade through all that stuff anyway (no offense). To solve this problem, you can erase not only your custom settings but also all the content you've stored on the iPhone.

Caution

If you have any content on your iPhone that isn't synced with iTunes — for example, iTunes music you've recently downloaded or an App Store program that you've recently installed — you lose that content if you choose Reset All Content and Settings. First sync your iPhone with your computer to save your content, and then run the reset.

The Reset app handles these scenarios and a few more to boot. Here's how it works:

1. **On the Home screen, tap Settings.** The Settings app appears.

2. **Tap General.** The General screen appears.

3. **Scroll to the bottom and tap Reset.** The Reset screen appears.

4. **Tap one of the following reset options:**

   - **Reset All Settings.** Tap this option to reset your custom settings to the factory default settings.

   - **Erase All Content and Settings.** Tap this option to reset your custom settings and remove any data you've stored on the iPhone.

   - **Reset Network Settings.** Tap this option to delete your Wi-Fi network settings. This is often an effective way to solve Wi-Fi problems.

- **Reset Keyboard Dictionary.** Tap this option to reset your keyboard dictionary. This dictionary contains a list of the keyboard suggestions that you've rejected. Tap this option to clear the dictionary and start fresh.

Note

The keyboard dictionary contains those words that your iPhone thought were errors, but you then tapped to use them as is (that is, they're the predictive typed strings that you accepted). For example, if you type "logophile," iPhone suggests "loophole" instead. If you tap the "logophile" predictive typed string to accept it, the word "log-ophilie" is added to the keyboard dictionary.

- **Reset Home Screen Layout.** Tap this option to reset your Home screen icons to their default layout.

- **Reset Location & Privacy.** Tap this option to wipe out the location preferences for your apps. A location warning is the dialog you see when you start a GPS-aware app for the first time. When you start one of these, your iPhone asks if the app can use your current location, and you then tap either OK or Don't Allow.

5. **When the iPhone asks you to confirm, tap the red button.** Note that the name of this button is the same as the reset option. For example, if you tapped the Reset All Settings option in Step 4, the confirm button is called Reset All Settings. iPhone resets the data.

Protecting Your iPhone

These days, an iPhone is much more than just a phone. You use it to surf the web, send and receive email and text messages, manage your contacts and schedules, find your way in the world, and much more. This is handy, for sure, but it also means that your iPhone is jammed with tons of information about you. Even though you might not store the nuclear launch codes on your iPhone, chances are what is on it is pretty important to you. Therefore, you should take steps to protect your iPhone, and that's what the next few sections are all about.

Locking your iPhone with a passcode

When your iPhone is asleep, the phone is locked in the sense that tapping the touchscreen or pressing the volume controls does nothing. This sensible arrangement prevents accidental taps when the phone is in your pocket, or rattling around in your backpack or handbag. To unlock the phone, you press either the Home button or the Sleep/Wake button, drag across the screen, and you're back in business.

Unfortunately, this simple technique means that anyone else who gets his or her mitts on your iPhone can also be quickly back in business — *your* business! If you have sensitive or confidential information on your phone, or if you want to avoid digital joyrides that run up massive roaming or data charges, you need to truly lock your iPhone.

You do that by specifying a passcode that must be entered before anyone can use the iPhone. The new default in iOS 9 is a six-digit passcode, but you can change that to either a simple four-digit passcode, or to a custom code that is longer and more complex and uses any combination of numbers, letters, and symbols. Follow these steps to set up your passcode:

1. **On the Home screen, tap Settings.** The Settings app appears.

2. **Tap Touch ID & Passcode to open the Touch ID & Passcode screen.** On the iPhone 5c or 5, tap Passcode Lock, instead.

3. **Tap Turn Passcode On.** The Set Passcode screen appears.

4. **If you prefer to use something other than a six-digit passcode, tap Passcode Options and then tap the type of passcode you want to use.**

5. **Tap your passcode.** For security, the characters appear in the passcode box as dots.

6. **If you're entering a custom passcode, tap Next.** Your iPhone prompts you to reenter the passcode.

7. **Tap your passcode again.**

8. **If you're entering a custom passcode, tap Done.**

Caution
You really, really need to remember your iPhone passcode. If you forget it, you're locked out of your own phone. The only way to get back in is to use iTunes to restore the data and settings to your iPhone from an existing backup (as described in Chapter 14).

With your passcode now active, iOS enables the following passcode-related settings on the Touch ID & Passcode screen:

- **Turn Passcode Off.** If you want to stop using your passcode, tap this button and then enter the passcode. This is for security (otherwise an interloper could just shut off the passcode).

- **Change Passcode.** Tap this button to enter a new passcode. Note that you must first enter your old passcode before you can enter the new one.

- **Require Passcode.** This setting determines how much time elapses before the iPhone locks the phone and requests the passcode. The default setting is Immediately, which means you see the Enter Passcode screen as soon as you finish dragging Slide to Unlock. The other options are After 1 minute, After 5 minutes, After 15 minutes, After 1 hour, and After 4 hours. Use one of the latter if you want to be able to work with your iPhone for a bit before getting locked out. For example, the After 1 minute option is good if you want to quickly check email without having to enter your passcode.

- **Voice Dial.** When this setting is On, you can voice dial a call when your iPhone is locked.

- **Allow Access When Locked.** When the settings in this section are On, you can use these features — Today, Notifications View, Siri, Passbook, Reply with Message, and Wallet — even when your iPhone is locked. If you change a setting to Off, you can no longer use that feature when your iPhone is locked.

- **Erase Data.** When this setting is On, your iPhone will self-destruct — er — I mean erase all its data when it detects ten incorrect passcode attempts. Ten failed passcodes almost always means that some nasty person has your phone and is trying to guess the passcode. If you have sensitive or private data on your phone, setting it to erase automatically is a good idea.

With the passcode activated, when you bring the iPhone out of standby, you drag across the screen as usual, and then the Enter Passcode screen appears. Type your passcode (and tap Done if it's a complex passcode) to unlock the iPhone.

Note

If an emergency arises and you need to make a call for help, you probably don't want to mess around with entering a passcode. Similarly, if something happens to you, another person who doesn't know your passcode may need to use your iPhone to call for assistance. In both cases, you can temporarily bypass the passcode by tapping the Emergency button on the Enter Passcode screen.

Unlocking your iPhone with a fingerprint

Protecting your iPhone with a passcode is just good sense in this age of so-called "iCrime," where thieves routinely go "Apple picking" by snatching iPhones and other Apple devices from the unwary. With a passcode acting as a digital barrier between the crook and your iPhone, at least your personal data is safe from prying eyes. Yes, a passcode is a smart safety precaution, but it's not always a convenient one. First, having to tap that four (or more) character code many times during the day adds a small but nevertheless unwelcome annoyance to using the iPhone. Second, because iOS, perhaps unwisely, highlights each character as you type your passcode, it's at least theoretically possible that some shoulder-surfing snoop could discern your code.

But that's the price of living in the big city, right? Not necessarily. If you have an iPhone 5s or later, help is but a fingertip (or thumbtip) away. I speak, of course, of Touch ID, the fingerprint sensor built into the Home button of the latest iPhones. By teaching the device your unique fingerprint, you can unlock your phone merely by leaving your finger or thumb resting on the Home button. That's right: No more passcode tapping to get to your Home screen. As an added bonus, you can use the same fingerprint to approve purchases you make in the iTunes Store, the App Store, the iBooks Store, and even some third-party apps, so you no longer have to enter your Apple ID password.

Here's how to set up Touch ID:

1. **On the Home screen, tap Settings.** The Settings app appears.

2. **Tap Touch ID & Passcode and then type your passcode (if you have one) to open the Touch ID & Passcode screen.**

3. **Tap Add a Fingerprint.** The Touch ID screen appears.

4. **Lightly rest your thumb — or whatever finger you most often use to press the Home button when you're unlocking your iPhone — on the Home button.**

5. **Repeatedly lift and place your finger as Touch ID learns your fingerprint pattern.**

6. **When you see the Adjust Your Grip screen, tap Continue.**

7. **Once again, repeatedly lift and place your finger, this time emphasizing the edges of the finger.**

8. **When you see the Complete screen, tap Continue.** If you haven't yet specified a pass-code, your iPhone prompts you to do so now.

9. **Tap your passcode and then tap it again when you're asked to confirm.** Settings returns you to the Touch ID & Passcode screen.

10. **If you want to use your fingerprint to unlock your iPhone, tap the iPhone Unlock switch to On.**

11. **If you want to use your fingerprint to approve iTunes Store, App Store, and iBooks Store purchases, tap the App and iTunes Store switch to On, then enter your Apple ID password.**

12. **To specify another fingerprint, repeat Steps 3 to 8.**

Here's how you use Touch ID:

- **Unlock your iPhone.** Use your fingerprint-scanned finger to tap the Home button to wake the phone, then leave the same finger resting on the Home button until the Home screen appears.

- **Make a purchase.** In the iTunes Store, the App Store, or the iBooks Store, tap the price of the item you want to buy, and then tap the Buy button. When the Touch ID dialog appears, rest your finger on the Home button until the purchase is approved.

Configuring your iPhone to sleep automatically

You can put your iPhone into standby mode at any time by pressing the Sleep/Wake button once. However, if your iPhone is on but you're not using it, it automatically goes into standby mode after two minutes. This is called Auto-Lock and it's a handy feature because it saves battery power (and prevents accidental taps) when your iPhone is just sitting there. It's also a crucial feature if you've protected your iPhone with a passcode lock, as I describe earlier, because if your iPhone never sleeps, it never locks, either.

To make sure your iPhone sleeps automatically, or if you're uncomfortable with the default Auto-Lock interval, you can make it shorter or longer (or turn it off altogether). Here are the steps to follow:

1. **On the Home screen, tap Settings.** The Settings app appears.
2. **Tap General.** The General screen appears.
3. **Tap Auto-Lock.** The Auto-Lock screen appears.
4. **Tap the interval you want to use.** You have seven choices: 30 seconds, 1 Minute, 2 Minutes, 3 Minutes, 4 Minutes, 5 Minutes, or Never.

Backing up your iPhone

When you sync your iPhone with your computer, iTunes automatically creates a backup of your current iPhone data before performing the sync. Note, however, that iTunes doesn't back up your entire iPhone, which makes sense because most of what's on your phone — music, photos, videos, apps, and so on — is already on your computer. Instead, iTunes backs up only data unique to the iPhone, including your call history, text messages, web clips, network settings, app settings and data, and Safari history and cookies.

However, what if you've configured iTunes not to sync your iPhone automatically? Is there a way to back up your iPhone without performing a sync? You bet there is:

1. **Connect your iPhone to your computer.**

2. **Open iTunes, if it doesn't launch automatically.**

3. **If your iPhone asks whether you trust this computer, tap Trust and, on your computer, click Continue.**

4. **In the Devices list, click your iPhone.**

5. **Click the Summary tab.**

6. **Click Back Up Now.** iTunes backs up the iPhone data.

If you have an iCloud account, you can also control where your iPhone gets backed up: to your computer or to iCloud. To configure this, connect your iPhone to your computer and then click your iPhone when it appears in the Devices list. In the Summary tab's Automatically Back Up section, select either iCloud or This Computer.

You can then follow these steps to back up your data to iCloud directly from your iPhone:

1. **Connect your iPhone to a Wi-Fi network.** iPhone-to-iCloud backups don't work if your iPhone is running using a cellular network connection.

2. **Tap Settings to launch the Settings app.**

3. **Tap iCloud.**

4. **Tap Backup.**

5. **Check that the iCloud Backup switch is On.** If not, tap the switch to On and then tap OK when iCloud confirms the setting. This tells your iPhone to make automatic backups whenever it is locked, connected to a Wi-Fi network, and plugged in to a power source.

6. **Tap Back Up Now.** Your iPhone backs up its data to your iCloud account.

Configuring parental controls

If your children have access to your iPhone, or if they have iPhones of their own, then you might be a bit worried about some of the content they might be exposed to on the web, on YouTube, or in iTunes. Similarly, you might not want them installing apps or giving away their current location.

For all those and similar parental worries, you can sleep better at night by activating the parental controls on your iPhone. These controls restrict the content and activities that kids can see and do. Here's how to set them up:

1. **On the Home screen, tap Settings.** The Settings app appears.

2. **Tap General.** The General screen appears.

3. **Tap Restrictions.** The Restrictions screen appears.

4. **Tap Enable Restrictions.** iPhone displays the Enable Restrictions screen, which you use to specify a four-digit code that you can use to override the parental controls. (Note that this code is not the same as the passcode lock that I discuss earlier in this chapter.)

5. **Tap the four-digit restrictions passcode and then retype the code.** iPhone returns you to the Restrictions screen and enables all the controls, as shown in Figure 2.6.

6. **In the Allow section, for each app or task, tap the On/Off switch to enable or disable the restriction.**

7. **Under Allowed Content, tap Ratings For and then tap the country with the ratings you want to use.**

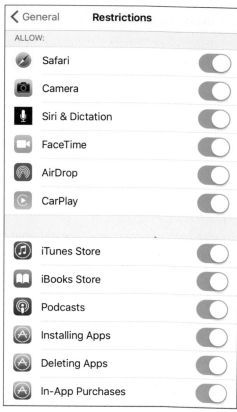

2.6 Use the Restrictions screen to configure the parental controls you want to use.

8. **For each of the content controls — Music & Podcasts, Movies, TV Shows, Books, Apps, Siri, and Websites — tap the control and then tap the highest rating you want your children to use.**

9. **If you don't want your children to make changes to certain settings, tap the corresponding setting types in the Privacy section and then tap Don't Allow Changes.**

10. **If you don't want your children to make changes to the current mail, calendar, or contacts account settings, tap Accounts under Allow Changes, and then tap Don't Allow Changes.**

11. **If you don't want your children to adjust the maximum volume limit you've set (as explained in Chapter 8), tap Volume Limit, and then tap Don't Allow Changes.**

12. **In the Game Center section, tap the On/Off switches to enable or disable multi-player games, and to enable or disable adding friends.**

Locating and protecting a lost iPhone

If there's a downside to using a smartphone (particularly one as smart as the iPhone), it's that you end up with a pretty large chunk of your life on that phone. Initially, that may sound like a good thing, but if you happen to lose your phone, you've also lost that chunk of your life. Plus, assuming you haven't configured your iPhone with a passcode lock, as described earlier, you've opened a gaping privacy hole because anyone can now delve into your data.

If you've been syncing your iPhone with your computer regularly, then you can probably recover most, or even all, of that data. However, I'm sure you'd probably rather find your iPhone because it's expensive and there's just something creepy about the thought of some stranger flicking through your stuff.

The old way of finding your missing iPhone consisted of scouring every nook and cranny that you visited before losing it, and calling up various lost-and-found departments to see if anyone turned it in. The new way to find your iPhone is via an app called Find My iPhone. (You can also use this feature through your iCloud account, if you have one.) Find My iPhone uses the GPS sensor embedded inside your iPhone to locate the device. You can also use Find My iPhone to play a sound on your iPhone, remotely lock it and send a message, or, in a real pinch, remotely delete your data. The next few sections provide the details.

Note   You might think that a fatal flaw with Find My iPhone is that someone who has your iPhone can easily turn off the feature and disable it. Fortunately, that's not the case because your iPhone comes with a feature called Activation Lock, which means that a person can turn off Find My iPhone only by entering your Apple ID password.

Activating Find My iPhone

Find My iPhone works by looking for a particular signal that your iPhone beams out into the ether. This signal is turned off by default, so you need to turn it on if you ever plan to use Find My iPhone. Here are the steps to follow:

1. **Add your iCloud account, if you haven't done so already, as described in Chapter 13.** When you add the account, be sure to tap OK when iCloud asks if it can use your location.

2. **On the Home screen, tap Settings.** The Settings app appears.

3. **Tap iCloud.** Your iCloud account settings appear.

4. **Tap Find My iPhone.** The Find My iPhone screen appears.

5. **Tap the Find My iPhone switch to On.** Your iPhone asks you to confirm.

6. **Tap Allow.** Your iPhone activates the Find My iPhone feature.

Genius

Your lost iPhone might just be lying somewhere where no one can find it. In that case, the danger is that the iPhone battery will die before you have a chance to locate it using Find My iPhone. To make this less likely, be sure to activate the Send Last Location switch. This configures your iPhone to send you the phone's last known location as soon as it detects that its battery is nearly done.

With Find My iPhone now active on your iPhone, you can use the Find My iPhone app or iCloud to locate it at any time. The next two sections show you how to do this.

Locating your iPhone using the Find My iPhone app

Follow these steps to see your lost iPhone on a map using the Find My iPhone app:

1. **On an iPhone, iPad, or iPod touch that has the Find My iPhone app installed, tap the app to launch it.** Find My iPhone prompts you to sign in with your Apple ID.

2. **Type your Apple ID and password.** Note that you must use the same Apple ID as the one you used to activate the Find My iPhone setting on your iPhone.

3. **Tap Go.** The app signs in to your Apple account.

4. **Tap All to open the list of devices, then tap your lost iPhone.** The Find My iPhone app locates the iPhone on a map, as shown in Figure 2.7.

5. **To see if the location has changed, tap the Refresh Location button (the circular arrow).**

Locating your iPhone using iCloud

Follow these steps to see your lost iPhone on a map using iCloud:

1. **Log in to your iCloud account.**

2. **Click Find My iPhone and, if prompted, enter your iCloud password.** The iCloud Find My iPhone application appears.

3. **Click All Devices.** iCloud displays the My Devices list.

4. **Click your iPhone in the list.** iCloud locates your iPhone on a map.

5. **To see if the location has changed, click the location and then click the Refresh Location button (the circular arrow).**

2.7 In the list of devices, tap your iPhone to locate it on a map.

Getting an email message when your iPhone comes online

Find My iPhone is only useful if you can, you know, *find* your iPhone. That won't happen if your iPhone is powered off or not connected to the Internet. You could keep refreshing the list of devices, but it could be hours before your iPhone comes online. To avoid a constant vigil, you can tell Find My iPhone to send an email message to your iCloud account as soon as your iPhone comes online:

1. **Display the My Devices list.**

2. **Tap or click your iPhone in the devices list.** Find My iPhone displays information about your iPhone.

3. **If Find My iPhone has no location data for your iPhone, select Notify When Found.**

Playing a sound on your iPhone

If you misplace your phone, the first thing you should try is calling your number using another phone so you can (hopefully!) hear it ringing. That might not work, however, because your phone might have Ring/Silent switched to silent mode, it might be in Airplane mode, or you might not have another phone handy. In any case, you only get so many rings before the call goes to voicemail, so unless you locate your phone right away, calling your number isn't always the best solution.

Your next step when looking for a lost iPhone is to use Find My iPhone to play a sound on your phone. This sound plays even if your iPhone is in silent mode or Airplane mode, and it plays loudly even if your iPhone has its volume turned down or muted. Here's how it works:

1. **Display the My Devices list.**

2. **Tap or click your iPhone in the list.** Find My iPhone locates your iPhone on a map.

3. **Tap or click Play Sound.** Find My iPhone begins playing the sound on your iPhone and it also displays the alert shown in Figure 2.8.

4. **When you find your iPhone (fingers crossed), tap the alert to silence the sound.**

2.8 Find My iPhone also displays this alert on your iPhone.

Locking the data on your lost iPhone

If you can't find your iPhone right away by playing a sound, your next step should be to ensure that some other person who finds the phone can't rummage around in your stuff. You do that by putting your iPhone into lost mode, which remotely locks the iPhone using the passcode that you set earlier. (Sorry, if you didn't protect your iPhone with a passcode, you can't remotely lock your phone.) You can also provide a phone number where you can be reached and send a message for whomever finds your iPhone. Follow these steps to put your iPhone into lost mode:

1. **Display the My Devices list.**

2. **Tap or click your iPhone in the list.** Find My iPhone locates your iPhone on a map.

3. **Tap or click Lost Mode.** Find My iPhone asks you to confirm you want to enable lost mode.

4. **Tap or click Turn On Lost Mode.** Find My iPhone displays the Lost Mode dialog, which prompts you for a phone number where you can be reached.

5. **Type your phone number and then tap or click Next.** Find My iPhone prompts you to type a message that will appear on the iPhone along with the phone number.

6. **Type the message and then tap or click Done.** Find My iPhone remotely locks the iPhone and displays the message, as shown in Figure 2.9.

Deleting the data on your lost iPhone

If you can't get the other person to return your iPhone and it contains sensitive or confidential data — or just that big chunk of your life I mentioned earlier — you can use the Find My iPhone app or the iCloud Find My iPhone feature to take the drastic step of remotely wiping all the data from your iPhone. Here's what you do:

1. **Display the My Devices list.**

2. **Tap or click your iPhone in the list.** Find My iPhone locates your iPhone on a map.

2.9 After you remotely lock your lost iPhone, Find My iPhone displays your message on the lock screen.

3. **Tap or click Erase iPhone.** Find My iPhone asks you to confirm.

4. **Tap or click Erase iPhone.** Find My iPhone prompts you for your Apple ID password.

5. **Type your password and then tap or click Next.** Find My iPhone asks you to enter an optional phone number where you can be reached, which will appear on the iPhone after it has been erased.

6. **Type your phone number, and then select Next.** Find My iPhone prompts you to type a message that will appear on the iPhone along with the phone number, after it has been erased.

7. **Type the message, and then tap or click Done.** Find My iPhone remotely wipes all data from the iPhone.

Enhancing Your iPhone with Apps

Your iPhone is an impressive, eyebrow-raising device right out of the box. It does everything you want it to do — or so you think, until you find out about some previously unknown feature and wonder how you ever lived without it. It's hard to imagine that anyone would, or even could, improve the iPhone. However, as you see in this section, the App Store can make your iPhone more convenient, more productive, and more, well, anything!

Syncing apps

You can get apps directly on your iPhone by tapping App Store on the Home screen. You can also get apps indirectly by using your computer to open iTunes and then clicking the iTunes Store command. After you download an app or two into iTunes, they won't do you much good just sitting there. To actually use the apps, you need to get them on your iPhone. Here's how:

1. **Connect your iPhone to your computer.** iTunes opens and accesses the iPhone.

2. **In iTunes, click your iPhone in the Devices list.**

3. **Click the Apps tab.**

4. **In the app list, click Install beside each app that you want to sync.**

5. **Click Apply.** iTunes syncs the iPhone using your new app settings.

Genius

For convenience, you can configure iTunes to automatically sync to your iPhone any new apps you add to your computer. You do this by selecting the Automatically Install New Apps check box, which appears just below the app list.

Multitasking apps

Your iPhone is capable of multitasking, which enables you to run multiple apps at the same time. This is useful if, say, you're playing a game and an email message comes in. You can switch to the message, read it, respond to it, and then resume your game right where you left off.

At its most basic, multitasking on the iPhone means that whenever you run an app and then switch to another app, your iPhone keeps the first app running in the background. In most cases, the first app does nothing while it's in the background — it doesn't take any processor time away from your current app and it doesn't use battery power. This means that you're free to open as many apps as you like. However, if the first app is performing some task and you switch to another app, the first app continues to perform the task in the background.

To get a firm grip on how iPhone multitasking works, you need to understand the three modes an app can have on the iPhone:

- **Closed State.** This mode means the app is completely shut down. If you reboot your iPhone (by turning it off and then back on), all your apps are then in the Closed State.

- **Suspended State.** If you launch an app, then press the Home button to return to the Home screen, usually your iPhone places the running app into the Suspended State. This means the app remains loaded into memory, but it's not running, it's not using up processor time, and it's not draining the battery. However, the app still maintains its current conditions, so that when you return to it, the app resumes where you left off.

- **Background State.** If you launch an app, start some process such as playing music, and then press the Home button to return to the Home screen, your iPhone puts the app into the Background State, which means it keeps the app's process running in the background. When you return to the app, either you see the process still running or it has been completed.

I should note, as well, that the vast majority of apps go into the Suspended State when you switch to another app. However, if you launch an app and your iPhone doesn't have enough free memory available, the iPhone starts putting suspended apps into the Closed State to free up memory.

So how do you switch from one app to another? Double-click the Home button (that is, press the Home button twice in succession) to reveal the multitasking screen, which displays the running apps, as shown in Figure 2.10. Flick left or right to bring the app thumbnail into view and then tap the app to switch to it.

2.10 Double-tap the Home button to see the running apps.

Genius When you double-click the Home button, if you take too long between each press, you won't see the multitasking screen. If that's a persistent problem for you, you can slow down the Home-click speed. Tap Settings, tap General, tap Accessibility, tap Home Button, and then tap Slow. iOS vibrates the phone and flashes the Slow option at the new Home-click speed. If you still have trouble, try using the Slowest speed instead.

Genius To help you navigate the list of running apps, shut down any apps you won't be using for a while. Double-tap the Home button to display the multitasking screen, and then drag any app you want to shut down up to the top of the screen.

Using Siri to launch an app

Having a big iPhone 6, 6 Plus, 6s, or 6s Plus screen is great, but it sure does display a lot of icons on the Home screen. And if you've been busy with the App Store, you might have quite a few such screens to scroll through, so finding the app you want to use might devolve into a uniquely modern exercise in frustration. Siri can help you to avoid such a fate, because it lets you launch any app on your iPhone by using any of the following verbs: "launch," "run," "open," or "start," followed by the name of the app. Here are some examples:

- "Launch Safari."
- "Run Photos."
- "Open Settings."
- "Open Wi-Fi Settings."
- "Start Notes."

How Do I Connect My iPhone to a Network?

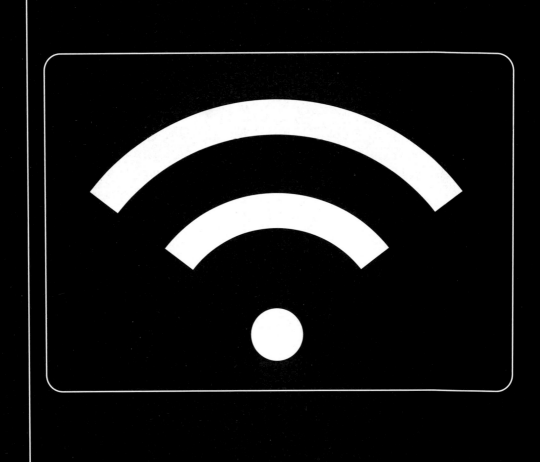

As a stand-alone device, your iPhone works just fine, thank you, because you can make calls, listen to music, take pictures, record and edit video, work with your contacts and calendars, take notes, play games, and much more. But your iPhone was made to connect: to surf the web, exchange email and text messages, watch YouTube videos, navigate with maps, and on and on. To do all that, your iPhone must first connect to a network, and that's what this chapter is all about. I show you how to make, monitor, and control network connections, set up your iPhone as an Internet hub, and more.

Connecting to a Wi-Fi Network

Connections to a cellular network are automatic and occur behind the scenes. As soon as you switch on your iPhone, it checks for an LTE signal. If it finds one, it connects to the network and displays the LTE icon in the status bar, as well as the connection strength (the more bars, the better). If your current area doesn't do the LTE thing, your iPhone tries to connect to the slower 3G network. If that works, you see the 3G icon in the status bar and the connection strength. If there's no 3G network in sight, your iPhone tries to connect to a slower EDGE network instead. If that works, you see the E icon in the status bar (plus the usual signal strength bars). If none of that works, you see No Signal, so you might as well go home.

Making your first connection

Things aren't automatic when it comes to Wi-Fi connections, at least not at first. As soon as you try to access something on the Internet — a website, your email, a map, or whatever — your iPhone scours the surrounding airwaves for Wi-Fi network signals. If you've never connected to a Wi-Fi network, or if you're in an area that doesn't have any Wi-Fi networks that you've used in the past, you see the Select a Wireless Network dialog, as shown in Figure 3.1. If you don't see this dialog, you can still connect to a wireless network; see the section about how to stop Wi-Fi network prompts, later in this chapter.

Select a Wireless Network

GCSS 🔒 📶

Krusty 🔒 📶

LogophiliaB 🔒 📶

Cancel

3.1 If you're just starting out on the Wi-Fi trail, your iPhone displays a list of nearby networks.

This dialog displays a list of the Wi-Fi networks that are within range. For each network, you get three tidbits of data:

- **Network name.** This is the name that the administrator has assigned to the network. If you're in a coffee shop or similar public hotspot and you want to use that network, look for the name of the shop (or a variation on the name).

- **Password-protection.** If a Wi-Fi network displays a lock icon, it means that it's protected by a password, and you need that password to make the connection.

- **Signal strength.** This icon gives you a rough idea of how strong the wireless signals are. The stronger the signal (the more bars you see, the better the signal), the more likely you are to get a fast and reliable connection.

Follow these steps to connect to a Wi-Fi network:

1. **Tap the network you want to use.** If the network is protected by a password, your iPhone prompts you to enter it.

2. **Use the keyboard to type the password.**

Caution

Because the password box shows dots instead of the actual text for added security, this is no place to demonstrate your iPhone speed-typing prowess. Keep it slow and steady and note that the iPhone displays the actual character you type for about a second before changing it to a dot, so you can check your typing as you go.

3. **Tap Join.** The iPhone connects to the network and adds the Wi-Fi network signal strength icon to the status bar.

To connect to a commercial Wi-Fi operation — such as those you find in airports, hotels, and convention centers — you almost always have to take one more step. Usually, the network prompts you for your name and credit card data so you can be charged for accessing the network. If you're not prompted right away, you will be as soon as you try to access a website or check your email. Enter your information and then enjoy the Internet in all its (expensive) Wi-Fi glory.

Connecting to known networks

Your iPhone remembers any Wi-Fi network to which you connect. So, if the network is one that you use all the time — for example, your home or office — your iPhone makes the connection without so much as a peep as soon as that network comes within range. Thanks!

Connecting to a hidden Wi-Fi network

Each Wi-Fi network has a network name — often called the Service Set Identifier, or SSID — that identifies the network to Wi-Fi–friendly devices, such as your iPhone. By default, most Wi-Fi networks broadcast the network name so that you can see it and connect to it. However, some Wi-Fi networks disable network name broadcasting as a security precaution. The idea here is that if an unauthorized user can't see the network, he or she can't attempt to connect to it. (However, some devices can still pick up the network name when authorized computers connect to it, so this is not a foolproof security measure.)

You can still connect to a hidden Wi-Fi network by entering the connection settings by hand. You need to know the network name, its security and encryption types, and the network password. Here are the steps to follow:

1. **On the Home screen, tap Settings to open the Settings app.**

2. **Tap Wi-Fi.** You see the Wi-Fi Networks screen.

3. **Tap Other.** Your iPhone displays the Other Network screen, as shown in Figure 3.2.

4. **Type the network name in the Name text box.**

5. **Tap Security to open the Security screen.**

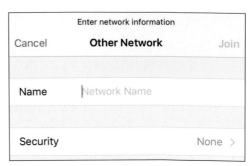

3.2 Use the Other Network screen to connect to a hidden Wi-Fi network.

6. **Tap the type of security the Wi-Fi network uses: None, WEP, WPA, WPA2, WPA Enterprise, or WPA2 Enterprise.** If you're not sure, most secure networks use WPA2.

7. **Tap Back to return to the Other Network screen.** If you chose WEP, WPA, WPA2, WPA Enterprise, or WPA2 Enterprise, your iPhone prompts you to type the password.

8. **Type the password in the Password text box.**

9. **Tap Join.** The iPhone connects to the network and adds the Wi-Fi network signal strength icon to the status bar.

Stopping incessant Wi-Fi network prompts

The Select a Wireless Network dialog is a handy convenience if you're not sure whether a Wi-Fi network is available. However, as you move around town, you may find that dialog popping up all over the place as new Wi-Fi networks come within range (although iOS is smart enough not to prompt when you're moving quickly — such as when driving). This constant tapping of the Cancel button can wear down your finger to the bone. However, you can just tell your iPhone to shut up already with the Wi-Fi prompting. Here's how:

1. **On the Home screen, tap Settings.** The Settings app appears.

2. **Tap Wi-Fi.** iPhone opens the Wi-Fi Networks screen.

3. **Tap the Ask to Join Networks switch to Off.** Your iPhone no longer prompts you with nearby networks. Whew!

Okay, I hear you ask, if I'm no longer seeing the prompts, how do I connect to a Wi-Fi network if I don't even know it's there? That's a good question, and here's a good answer:

1. **On the Home screen, tap Settings.** Your iPhone displays the Settings app.

2. **Tap Wi-Fi.** The Wi-Fi Networks screen appears, and the Choose a Network list shows you the available Wi-Fi networks.

3. **Tap the network you want to use.** If the network is protected by a password, your iPhone prompts you to enter it.

4. **Use the keyboard to tap the password.**

5. **Tap Join.** The iPhone connects to the network and adds the Wi-Fi network signal strength icon to the status bar.

Sending a file from your Mac to your iPhone

In Chapter 7, "How Do I Synchronize My iPhone?," you learn how to transfer data between your iPhone and your Mac. However, if you just want to pass along a single file from your Mac to your phone, the sync procedure is overkill. Instead, if your Mac is running OS X Yosemite or later and your iPhone is running iOS 8 or later, and your Mac and iPhone are connected to the same Wi-Fi network, you can use a tool called AirDrop to send a file directly from your Mac to your phone. Here's how it works:

1. **On your Mac, open Finder and click AirDrop in the sidebar.** You can also click Go ⇨ AirDrop or press ⌘+Shift+R. You should see an icon for your iPhone in the AirDrop window.

Note If you don't see your iPhone, make sure it has AirDrop turned on. Swipe up from the bottom of the screen to display the Control Center, tap AirDrop, and then tap Contacts Only. If you still don't see your iPhone on your Mac, tap Everyone, instead.

2. **Open a second Finder window (click File ⇨ New Finder Window) and use it to locate the file you want to send to your iPhone.**

3. **Drag the file from the Finder window and drop it on your iPhone icon in the AirDrop window, as shown in Figure 3.3.** If the sender is in your Contacts, your iPhone alerts you that a file is incoming, as shown in Figure 3.4; if the sender isn't in your Contacts, your iPhone asks you to confirm the transfer.

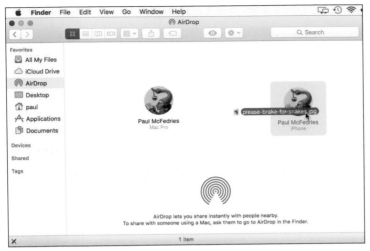

3.3 Drag the file into the AirDrop window and drop it on your iPhone's icon.

4. **If your iPhone asks you to confirm the transfer, tap Accept.** Your iPhone initiates the transfer and either saves or displays the file.

Forgetting a Wi-Fi network

Having the iPhone remember networks you've joined is certainly convenient, except, of course, when it's not. For example, if you have a couple of networks nearby that you can join, you might connect to one and then realize that the other is

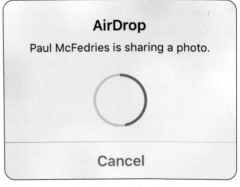

3.4 If your sender is in your Contacts, your iPhone lets you know that a file transfer is underway.

better in some way (for example, it's faster or cheaper). Unfortunately, there's a good chance your iPhone will continue to connect to the network you don't want every time it comes within range, which can be a real hassle. Rather than threatening to throw your iPhone in the nearest trash can, you can tell it to forget the network you don't want to use. Here's how it's done:

1. **On the Home screen, tap Settings.** The Settings app appears.

2. **Tap Wi-Fi.** The iPhone opens the Wi-Fi Networks screen.

3. **Tap the blue More Info icon to the right of the network you want to forget.** Your iPhone displays the network's settings screen.

4. **Tap Forget this Network.** Your iPhone asks you to confirm.

5. **Tap Forget.** Your iPhone discards the login data for the network and no longer connects to the network automatically.

Turning off the Wi-Fi antenna

The Wi-Fi antenna on your iPhone is constantly on the lookout for nearby Wi-Fi networks. That's useful because it means you always have an up-to-date list of networks to check out and it makes the iPhone location services (such as the Maps app) more accurate, but it also takes its toll on the iPhone battery. If you know you won't be using Wi-Fi for a while, you can save some battery juice for more important pursuits by turning off the Wi-Fi antenna. Here's how:

1. **On the Home screen, tap Settings.** The Settings app appears.

2. **Tap Wi-Fi.** The Wi-Fi Networks screen appears.

3. **Tap the Wi-Fi switch to Off.** Your iPhone disconnects from your current network and hides the Choose a Network list.

When you're ready to resume your Wi-Fi duties, return to the Wi-Fi Networks screen and tap the Wi-Fi switch to On.

Genius

You can also toggle the Wi-Fi antenna off and on by swiping up from the bottom of the screen to open the Control Center and then tapping the Wi-Fi icon.

Setting Up Your iPhone as an Internet Hub

Here's a scenario you've probably tripped over a time or two when roaming around with both your iPhone and your notebook computer along for the ride. You end up at a location where you have access to just a cellular network, with no Wi-Fi in sight. This means that your iPhone can access the Internet (using the cellular network), but your notebook can't. That's a real pain if you want to do some work involving Internet access on the computer. To work around this problem, you can use a nifty feature called Personal Hotspot, which enables you to configure your iPhone as a kind of Internet hub or gateway device — something like the hotspots that are available in coffee shops and other public areas. To do this, you connect your iPhone to your notebook (either directly via a USB cable or wirelessly via Wi-Fi or Bluetooth), and your notebook can then use the cellular Internet connection of your iPhone to get online. This is often called Internet tethering.

Even better, you can connect up to five devices to your iPhone, so you can also share your iPhone Internet connection with desktop computers, tablets, other cellphones, and pretty much anything else that can connect to the Internet.

This sounds too good to be true, but it's real, I swear. The downside (you just knew there had to be a downside) is that some providers will charge you extra for tethering. This is slowly changing (for example, AT&T in the United States offers tethering on many of its smartphone plans), but you should read the fine print on your contract to be sure.

Activating the Personal Hotspot

Your first step down the Personal Hotspot road is to activate the feature. Here's how it's done:

1. **On the Home screen, tap Settings.** The Settings app appears.
2. **Tap Personal Hotspot.** iPhone opens the Personal Hotspot screen.
3. **Tap the Personal Hotspot switch to On.**
4. **Tap Wi-Fi Password, type a password, and then tap Done.**

Connecting to the hotspot using Wi-Fi

With Personal Hotspot enabled, follow these steps to allow a device such as a Mac, a PC, or an iPad to use your iPhone Internet connection via Wi-Fi:

1. **On the device, display the list of nearby wireless networks.**

2. **In the network list, click the one that has the same name as your iPhone.** Your device prompts you for the Wi-Fi password.

3. **Type the Personal Hotspot Wi-Fi password and then click OK.** Under the status bar, your iPhone displays Personal Hotspot: 1 Connection, as shown in Figure 3.5.

3.5 When you successfully set up a connection to the Personal Hotspot, the iPhone displays a banner showing you how many current connections you have.

Keeping an Eye on Your Data Usage

If you're using your iPhone with a plan that comes with a maximum amount of monthly data and you exceed that monthly cap, you'll almost certainly pay big bucks for the privilege. To avoid that, most cellular providers are kind enough to send you a message when you approach your cap. However, if you don't trust that process, or if you're just paranoid about these things (justly, in my view), then you can keep an eye on your data usage yourself. Your iPhone keeps track of the cellular network data it has sent or received, as well as the roaming data it has sent or received if you've used your iPhone out of your coverage area.

First, take a look at your most recent bill from your cellular provider and, in particular, look for the dates the bill covers. For example, the bill might run from the 24th of one month to the 23rd of the next month. This is important because it tells you when you need to reset the usage data on your iPhone.

Now follow these steps to check your cellular data usage:

1. **On the Home screen, tap Settings.** The Settings app appears.

2. **Tap Cellular to open the Cellular screen.**

3. **In the Cellular Data Usage section, read the Current Period and Current Period Roaming values.**

4. **If you're at the end of your data period, tap Reset Statistics at the bottom of the screen to start with fresh values for the new period.**

Controlling Network Data

Your iPhone gives you fairly precise control over your network data. For example, you can toggle just the LTE data, all cellular data, data for individual apps, data roaming, or all your iPhone antennas. The next few sections provide the details.

Turning off LTE

Using the LTE cellular network is a real pleasure because it's so much faster than a 3G connection (which in turn is much faster than a molasses-in-January EDGE connection). If LTE has a downside, it's that it uses up a lot of battery power. That's true even if you're currently connected to a Wi-Fi network, because the LTE antenna is constantly looking for an LTE signal. If you'll be on your Wi-Fi network for a while, or if your battery is running low and you don't need an LTE cellular connection, you should turn off the LTE antenna to reduce the load on your iPhone battery. Here's how:

1. **On the Home screen, tap Settings.** The Settings app appears.

2. **Tap Cellular.** The Cellular screen opens.

3. **Tap Voice & Data.** The Voice & Data screen opens.

4. **Tap 3G. Your iPhone turns off the LTE antenna in favor of the lower-power 3G antenna.**

Turning off cellular data

If you've reached the limit of your cellular data plan, you almost certainly want to avoid going over the cap because the charges are usually prohibitively expensive. As long as you have a Wi-Fi network in range, or you're disciplined enough not to surf the web or cruise YouTube when there's no Wi-Fi in sight, you'll be okay. Still, accidents can happen. For example, you might accidentally tap a link in an email message or text message, or someone in your household might use your phone without knowing about your restrictions.

To prevent these sorts of accidents (or if you simply don't trust yourself when it comes to YouTube), you can turn off cellular data altogether, which means your iPhone accesses Internet data only if it has a Wi-Fi signal. Follow these steps to turn off cellular data on your iPhone:

1. **On the Home screen, tap Settings.** The Settings app appears.

2. **Tap Cellular.** The Cellular screen opens.

3. **Tap the Cellular Data switch to Off.**

Controlling cellular data usage

Rather than turning off cellular data completely, as I described in the previous section, you can take a more targeted approach. For example, if you're a bit worried about going over your cellular plan's data ceiling, it makes sense to avoid relatively high-bandwidth items, such as FaceTime and iTunes, but not relatively low-bandwidth content, such as iCloud documents and the Safari reading list.

You could just police this yourself but, hey, you're a busy person and you might forget the next time a FaceTime call comes in and you're in a cellular-only neighborhood. I say leave the details to your iPhone by configuring it to not allow certain content types over a cellular connection. Here's how:

1. **On the Home screen, tap Settings.** The Settings app appears.

2. **Tap Cellular.** The Cellular screen opens.

3. **In the Use Cellular Data For section, tap the switch to Off for each type of content you want to ban from cellular (see Figure 3.6).**

Turning off data roaming

Data roaming is an often-convenient cell phone feature that enables you to make calls — and, with your iPhone, surf the web, check and send email, and exchange text messages — when you're outside of your normal coverage area. The downside is that, unless you've got a fixed-rate roaming package from your cellular provider, roaming charges are almost always eye-poppingly expensive. You're often talking several dollars per minute or megabyte, depending on where you are and what type of service you're using. Not good!

Unfortunately, if you have the Data Roaming feature on your iPhone turned on, you may incur massive roaming charges even if you never use your phone! That's because your

Settings	Cellular
USE CELLULAR DATA FOR:	
App Store 75.1 MB	
Calendar 460 KB	
Chrome 1.6 MB	
Clock	
Contacts 249 KB	
Evernote 1.8 MB	
Facebook 3.1 MB	
FaceTime	
Find iPhone 229 KB	
Gmail 4.3 MB	
Google Maps 14.0 MB	
iBooks	
iTunes Store	

3.6 You can configure your iPhone to not use certain types of content over the cellular network.

iPhone still performs background checks for things like incoming email messages and text messages, so a week in some far-off land could cost you hundreds of dollars without even using your phone.

To avoid this insanity, turn off the Data Roaming feature on your iPhone when you don't need it. Follow these steps:

1. **On the Home screen, tap Settings.** The Settings app appears.

2. **Tap Cellular.** The Cellular screen appears.

3. **Tap the Data Roaming switch to Off.**

Switching your iPhone to Airplane mode

When you board a flight, aviation regulations in most countries are super strict about cell phones — no calls in and no calls out. In fact, most of those regulations ban wireless signals of any kind. This means your iPhone is a real hazard to sensitive airline equipment because it transmits Wi-Fi and Bluetooth signals, even if there are no Wi-Fi receivers or Bluetooth devices within 30,000 feet of your current position.

Your pilot or friendly flight attendant will suggest that passengers simply turn off their phones. Sure, that does the job, but darn it, you've got an iPhone, which means there are plenty of things you can do outside of its wireless capabilities, such as listen to music or an audiobook, watch a show, view photos, and much more.

So how do you reconcile the no-wireless-and-that-means-you regulations with the multitude of no-wireless-required apps on your iPhone? You put your iPhone into a special state called Airplane mode. This mode turns off the transceivers — the internal components that transmit and receive wireless signals — for the phone, Wi-Fi, and Bluetooth features. With your iPhone now safely in compliance with federal aviation regulations, you're free to use any app that doesn't rely on wireless transmissions.

There are two methods you can use to activate Airplane mode:

- **On the Home screen, tap Settings and then tap the Airplane Mode switch to On.**
- **Swipe up from the bottom of the screen to open the Control Center, and then tap the Airplane Mode button.**

Note If a flight attendant sees you playing around with your iPhone, he or she may ask you to confirm that the phone is off. (One obviously iPhone-savvy attendant even asked me if my phone was in Airplane mode.) Showing the Airplane icon should be sufficient.

Your iPhone disconnects your cellular network and your wireless network (if you have a current connection). Notice, as well, that while Airplane mode is on, an Airplane Mode icon appears in the status bar in place of the Signal Strength and Network icons (see Figure 3.7).

Pairing Your iPhone to Bluetooth Devices

Your iPhone is configured to use a wireless technology called Bluetooth, which enables

Airplane Mode icon

3.7 When your iPhone is in Airplane mode, an Airplane Mode icon appears in the status bar.

you to make wireless connections to other Bluetooth-friendly devices. Most Macs come with Bluetooth built in, and they use it to connect to a wide range of devices, including mice, keyboards, cell phones, printers, digital cameras, other Macs, and even the new iPhone-compatible game controllers that were about to come to market as this book went to press. Your iPhone can, at the very least, connect to a Bluetooth headset on which you can listen to phone conversations, music, and movies without wires and without disturbing your neighbors.

In theory, connecting Bluetooth devices should be criminally easy: You bring them within 33 feet of each other (the maximum Bluetooth range), and they connect without further ado. In practice, however, there's usually at least a bit of further ado (and sometimes plenty of it). This usually takes one or both of the following forms:

- **Making the devices discoverable.** Unlike Wi-Fi devices that broadcast their signals constantly, most Bluetooth devices broadcast their availability — that is, they make themselves *discoverable* — only when you say so. This makes sense in many cases because you usually only want to connect a Bluetooth component, such as a headset, with a single device. By controlling when the device is discoverable, you ensure that it works only with the device you want it to.

- **Pairing the iPhone and the device.** As a security precaution, many Bluetooth devices need to be *paired* with another device before the connection is established. Usually, the pairing is accomplished by entering a multidigit *passkey* — your iPhone calls it a

PIN — that you must then enter into the Bluetooth device (assuming, of course, that it has some kind of keypad). In the case of a headset, the device comes with a default passkey that you must enter into your iPhone to set up the pairing.

Making your iPhone discoverable

So your first order of Bluetooth business is to ensure that your iPhone is discoverable by activating the Bluetooth feature. It is usually on by default, but follow these steps to make sure your iPhone is discoverable:

1. **On the Home screen, tap Settings.** The Settings app appears.

2. **Tap Bluetooth.** The Bluetooth screen appears.

3. **Tap the Bluetooth switch to On, as shown in Figure 3.8.**

Also notice in Figure 3.8 that the status bar now shows the Bluetooth logo to the left of the Battery Status icon, which tells you that Bluetooth is up and running on your phone.

Bluetooth icon

3.8 Use the Bluetooth screen to make your iPhone discoverable.

Pairing your iPhone with a Bluetooth keyboard

The iPhone virtual keyboard is an ingenious invention, but it's not always a convenient one, particularly when you need to type fast or type a lot. Fortunately, iOS supports connections to a Bluetooth keyboard that, while paired, disables the on-screen keyboard. Follow these steps to pair your iPhone with a Bluetooth keyboard:

1. **On the Home screen, tap Settings.** The Settings app appears.

2. **Tap Bluetooth.** The Bluetooth screen appears.

3. **If the keyboard has a separate switch or button that makes the device discoverable, turn on that switch or press that button.** Wait until you see the keyboard appear in the Bluetooth screen.

4. **Tap the name of the Bluetooth keyboard.** Your iPhone displays a passkey, as shown in Figure 3.9.

5. **On the Bluetooth keyboard, type the passkey and press Return or Enter.** Your iPhone pairs with the keyboard and returns you to the Bluetooth screen, where you now see Connected beside the keyboard.

Bluetooth Pairing Request

Enter the code "3819" on "Microsoft Bluetooth Mobile Keyboard 6000", followed by the return or enter key.

Cancel

3.9 Your iPhone displays a passkey, which you then type on the Bluetooth keyboard.

Pairing your iPhone with a Bluetooth headset

If you want to listen to music, headphones are a great way to go because the sound is often better than with the built-in iPhone speakers (and no one else around is subjected to Radical Face at top volume). Similarly, if you want to conduct a hands-free call, a headset (a combination of headphones for listening and a microphone for talking) makes life easier because you can put the phone down and make all the hand gestures you want (provided you aren't driving, of course). Add Bluetooth into the mix, and you've got an easy and wireless audio solution for your iPhone.

Follow these general steps to pair your iPhone with a Bluetooth headset:

1. **On the Home screen, tap Settings.** The Settings app appears.

2. **Tap Bluetooth.** The Bluetooth screen appears.

3. **If the headset has a separate switch or button that makes the device discoverable, turn on that switch or press that button.** Wait until you see the correct headset name appear in the Bluetooth screen.

4. **Tap the name of the Bluetooth headset.** Your iPhone should pair with the headset automatically, and you should see Connected in the Bluetooth screen. If you see this, you can skip the rest of these steps. Otherwise you see the Enter PIN screen.

5. **Enter the headset's passkey in the PIN box.** See the headset documentation to get the passkey (it's often 0000).

6. **Tap Done.** Your iPhone pairs with the headset and returns you to the Bluetooth screen, where you now see Connected beside the headset name.

Selecting a paired headset as the audio output device

After you pair a Bluetooth headset, your iPhone is usually smart enough to start blasting your tunes through the headset instead of the phone's built-in speaker. If that doesn't happen, follow these steps to choose your Bluetooth headset as the output device:

1. **Swipe up from the bottom of the screen to open the Control Center.**

2. **Tap the AirPlay icon that appears below the playback controls (to the right of the AirDrop section).** The AirPlay screen appears, as shown in Figure 3.10.

3. **Tap your paired Bluetooth headset.** Your iPhone starts playing the song through the headset.

3.10 Use the AirPlay screen to select your paired Bluetooth headset.

Unpairing your iPhone from a Bluetooth device

If you no longer plan to use a Bluetooth device, you should unpair it from your iPhone. Follow these steps:

1. **On the Home screen, tap Settings.** The Settings app appears.

2. **Tap Bluetooth.** The Bluetooth screen appears.

3. **Tap the blue More Info icon to the right of the Bluetooth device name.**

4. **Tap Forget this Device.** Your iPhone unpairs the device.

Out of the Phone App?

The iPhone is chock-full of great apps that enable you to surf the web, send and receive email messages, listen to music, take photos, organize your contacts, schedule appointments, and much, much more. These features put the *smart* in its status as a *smartphone*, but let's not forget the *phone* part! So, while you're probably familiar with the basic steps required to make and answer calls, the powerful phone component in your iPhone is loaded with amazing features that can make the cell phone portion of your life easier, more convenient, and more efficient. This chapter takes you through these features.

Understanding Cellular Speeds

When we need data, I suspect most of us connect our iPhones to a nearby Wi-Fi network. Of course, there are plenty of us who are more mobile and need data while we're out and about and can't always rely on finding a convenient Wi-Fi hotspot. Older versions of the iPhone supported EDGE (Enhanced Data rates for GSM Evolution) cellular networks, EVDO (Evolution-Data Optimized) networks, and HSPA (High Speed Packet Access) networks, which have theoretical maximum download speeds of 0.38 megabits-per-second (Mbps), 3.1 Mbps, and 14.4 Mbps, respectively. EVDO and HSPA are known as 3G (third generation) cellular standards.

The iPhone 5 and later go further and also include support for the HSPA+ (Evolved High Speed Packet Access) and DC-HSDPA (Dual-Carrier High Speed Downlink Packet Access) networks, which offer theoretical maximum download speeds of 21 Mbps and 42 Mbps, respectively, as well as LTE (Long-Term Evolution), which tops out at an eyebrow-raising 150 Mbps. Note that although some marketing types call LTE a 4G (fourth generation) cellular technology, it in fact doesn't quite meet the standards for 4G (which is why some folks refer to LTE as "3.9G").

That's the good news. The bad news is that super-fast cellular downloads mean that you might burst through your data plan bandwidth limit at high-speed, as well. For example, if you have a 2GB monthly cap, and you managed to achieve 150 Mbps on an LTE network, you would bump up against your plan's ceiling after just one minute and 40 seconds! So, yes, by all means enjoy life in the fast lane with your new iPhone. Just remember to keep an eye on your data usage (tap Settings and then tap Cellular).

Working with Outgoing Calls

You can do much more with your iPhone than just make a call the old-fashioned way — by dialing the phone number. There are speedy shortcuts you can take, and even settings to alter the way your outgoing calls look on the receiver's phone.

Note   If you're getting low on minutes with your cellular plan, you might still be able to make a call without using up what little time you have left. That's because iOS supports *Wi-Fi calling*, which enables you to place a call using a Wi-Fi Internet connection instead of a cellular connection. Check with your cellular provider to see if it supports Wi-Fi calling.

Making calls quickly

The iPhone has a seemingly endless number of methods you can use to make a call. It's nice to have the variety, but in this have-your-people-call-my-people world, the big question is not how many ways can you make a call, but how *fast* can you make a call? Here are my favorite iPhone speed-calling techniques:

- **Favorites list.** This list acts as a kind of speed dial for the iPhone because you use it to store the phone numbers you call most often, and you have space to add your top 20 numbers. To call someone in your Favorites list, tap the Phone icon on the Home screen, tap Favorites, and then tap the number you want to call. I show you how to manage your Favorites later in this chapter.

- **Visual Voicemail.** If you're checking your voicemail messages (from the Home screen, tap Phone, and then tap Voicemail) and you want to return someone's call, tap the message and then tap Call Back.

- **Text message.** If someone includes a phone number in a text message, your iPhone handily converts it into a link. The number appears in blue text, much like a link on a web page, as shown in Figure 4.1. Tap the phone number to call it. You can also use a similar technique to call numbers embedded in web pages (see Chapter 5) and email messages (see Chapter 6).

4.1 Your iPhone is kind enough to convert a phone number in a text message into a link that you can tap to call.

Note
You can do a lot more than just call a number in a text message. Tap Contact in the upper right corner and then tap the blue Info icon (the circled, lowercase i) to see a menu of actions you can take with the phone number, including emailing the sender, initiating a FaceTime call, creating a new contact, and adding the number to an existing contact.

- **Recent numbers.** The Recent Calls list (from the Home screen, tap Phone and then tap Recents) shows your recent phone activity: calls you've made, calls you've received, and calls you've missed. Recent Calls is great because it enables you to quickly redial someone with whom you've had recent contact. To call the person using a different phone number, tap the Info icon (the arrow to the right of the name or number), and then tap the phone number you want to use to make the call. If you want to return a missed call, tap Missed and then tap the call.

- **Multitasking screen.** Your most recently called contacts also appear on your iPhone's multitasking screen, which you display by double-pressing the Home button. The Recents list at the top of the screen displays several icons for recently called contacts. Flick right to see the Favorites list, which has icons for your favorites. You tap an icon and then tap Phone to call that person.

Genius

If your Recent Calls list is populated with names or numbers that you know you won't ever call back, you should clear the list and start fresh. In the Recent screen, tap Edit, tap Clear, and then tap Clear All Recents.

Automatically dialing extensions or menu options

If you're calling a family member or friend at work, or if you're phoning a particular department or person in a company, chances are you have to dial an extension after the main number connects. Similarly, many businesses require you to negotiate a series of menus to get information or connect with a particular employee or section ("Press 1 for Sales; press 2 for Customer Service," and so on). This normally requires you to display the keyboard, listen for the prompts, enter the numbers, and repeat as necessary.

However, if you know the extension or phone menu sequence, you can program it into the number and have the Phone app do all the hard work for you. The Phone app can do either of the following:

- **Pause.** This option, which is represented by a comma (,) in the phone number, means that the Phone app dials the main number, waits for two seconds, then dials whatever extension or menu value that appears after the comma. You can add multiple commas to the number if you need a longer delay.

- **Wait.** This option, which is represented by a semicolon (;) in the phone number, means that the Phone app dials just the main number and also displays a button labeled **Dial "*extension*,"** where *extension* is whatever digits appear after the semicolon. When the phone system prompts you to enter the extension, just tap the Dial button.

You can set these up in two ways:

- **Contacts list.** When you're entering a phone number using the Contacts list, type the full number and then tap the +*# key that appears in the lower left corner of the on-screen keyboard. This temporarily adds two new keys: Pause and Wait. Tap Pause to add a comma, then tap the extension or menu value, and repeat as needed; tap Wait to add a semicolon, and then tap the extension.

- **Keypad.** Using the keypad in the Phone app, type the full number. To add a comma to tell the Phone app to pause, tap and hold the * key until a comma appears, then tap the extension or menu value; to add a semicolon to tell the Phone app to wait, tap and hold the # key until a semicolon appears, then tap the extension.

Voice dialing a call with Siri

Tapping a favorite number, a recent number, or a text message phone number link is a pretty easy method to launch a phone call, but there's an even easier way that doesn't require a single tap on your part. I speak, of course, of voice dialing, which is yet another hat worn by Siri, the voice-activated assistant. To voice dial, you tell Siri the name of the person you want to call (if she's in your Contacts list) or the number you want to call (for everyone else), and Siri does the rest. Here are the details:

1. **Say "Hey Siri" or tap and hold the Home button.** You can also press and hold the center button of the iPhone headset. The Siri screen appears.

2. **Say "Call" (or "Phone" or "Telephone" or "Dial") and then specify who or what:**

    - **If the person is in your Contacts list, say the person's first and last names.** If the contact is a business, say "*company,*" where *company* is the business name as given in your Contacts list. If you have multiple numbers for the contact, also say the label of that number (such as "mobile" or "home"). If you're not sure of the correct label, skip that part and Siri will let you know which labels are available.

    - **If the person is in your Contacts list and has a unique first name, say the person's first name.**

    - **If the person has a relationship with you that you've defined with Siri, say "*relationship,*" where *relationship* is the connection you've defined (such as brother or mother).**

    - **If you want to call one of your own numbers, say "Call *label,*" where *label* is the label of the number in your Contacts data that you want to call.**

    - **For anyone else, say the full phone number you want to dial.**

Genius

You can be fairly casual about the syntax you use when specifying a label. For example, you can say something like "Call Belinda Gray at home" or "Call my sister on her mobile phone."

3. **If the person has multiple numbers and you didn't specify a label, Siri displays a list of the available numbers, as shown in Figure 4.2.** You now need to say the label of the number you want to dial. Conveniently, Siri also responds verbally by listing the available labels for that person, so you don't have to guess which one to use.

Which phone number for Alex Blandman?

mobile

work

4.2 You see this screen if the person you're calling has multiple numbers and you don't specify a label.

That's it. For a contact, Siri responds with "Calling *name label*" (where *name* is the person's name and *label* is the label assigned to the phone number). For a phone number, Siri responds with "Calling *number*" (where *number* is the phone number you specified).

Configuring your iPhone not to show your caller ID

When you use your iPhone to call someone, and the called phone supports Caller ID, your number and often your name appear. If you'd rather hide your identity for some reason, you can configure your iPhone not to show your caller ID:

1. **On the Home screen, tap Settings.** The Settings app appears.

2. **Tap Phone.** The Phone screen appears.

3. **Tap Show My Caller ID.** The Show My Caller ID screen appears.

4. **Tap the Show My Caller ID switch to Off.** Your iPhone disables Caller ID.

Note

You might have good reasons to hide your caller ID when making a call, but just beware that many people automatically ignore incoming calls that don't specify the caller's name (the reasonable assumption being that someone who hides their caller ID is likely up to no good).

Placing Mac calls on your iPhone

The Handoff feature in iOS means that you can use your Mac to place a phone call using your iPhone. For this to work, your Mac must be running OS X Yosemite or later, your iPhone must be running iOS 8 or later, both machines must be signed in to the same iCloud account, and your iPhone must be within about 30 feet of your Mac. You have several ways to send a phone number from your Mac to your iPhone:

- In Safari, highlight a web page phone number, click the drop-down arrow that appears to the right of the number, and then click Call *"Number"* Using iPhone (where *Number* is the highlighted phone number).

- In Contacts, hover the mouse over a contact's phone number and then click the phone icon that appears to the right of the number.

- In FaceTime, click the phone icon that appears to the right of the contact and then click the phone number that appears under Call Using iPhone.

Note As I write this, only Macs that support Bluetooth 4.0 can use Handoff. To check, click the Apple icon, click About This Mac, click System Report, click Bluetooth, then read the LMP Version. If it says 0x6, then your Mac supports Bluetooth 4.0. Also, you need to turn on Handoff support for your Mac. Open System Preferences, click General, and then click to activate the Allow Handoff between this Mac and your iCloud devices check box.

Handling Incoming Calls

When a call comes in to your iPhone, you answer it, right? What could be simpler? You'd be surprised. Your iPhone gives you quite a few options for dealing with that call, aside from just answering it. After all, you don't want to talk to everyone all the time, do you?

Note If you have a Verizon or Sprint cellular plan, remember that these providers use the CDMA cellular protocol, which is a monotasking system. This means, for example, that if you're on the phone, you can't surf the web or perform any data-related activities. Similarly, if you're surfing the web, you can't send calls, and if a call comes in, your iPhone stops your web session to receive it. If you're on a non-CDMA network, such as AT&T, you can get simultaneous voice and data, but not using the LTE protocol. When you're on a call, your data connection falls back to HSPA+.

Silencing an incoming call

When you're in a situation where the ringing of a cell phone is inappropriate, bothersome, or just plain rude, you, of course, practice *celliquette* (that is, cell etiquette) and turn off your ringer. (On your iPhone, position the phone in portrait mode with the Home button at the bottom and then flick the Silent/Ring switch on the left side panel to the silent position.) However, we're merely human and we all forget to turn off our phone's ringer once in a while.

Your job in that situation is to grab your phone and answer it as quickly as possible. However, what if you're in a situation where answering the call is bad form? Or what if you'd prefer to delay answering the call until you can leave the room or get out of earshot? That's a stickier situation, for sure, but the iPhone designers have been there and they've come up with a simple solution: Press either the Sleep/Wake button on the phone's top panel (again, assuming you have the phone in portrait mode with the Home button at the bottom) or one of the Volume buttons on the left side panel. Either of these actions stops your iPhone from ringing (or vibrating). The ringing is still going on (your caller hears it on her end), so you've still got the usual four rings to answer the call should you decide to.

Answering a call on other devices

It has happened to all of us: You're in one room when you hear your iPhone ring in another room, and a mad dash ensues to answer the call before it goes to voicemail. However, if you happen to have your iPad or even your Mac nearby, that mad dash need not take place. That's because iOS supports a feature that enables you to answer incoming calls on your other devices, including iPads, iPhones, and even Macs. Follow these steps to ensure this feature is activated and to control which devices you can use to answer calls:

1. **On the Home screen, tap Settings to open the Settings app.**

2. **Tap Phone to display the Phone settings.**

3. **Tap Allow Calls on Other Devices.** Settings displays the Calls on Other Devices screen.

4. **Make sure the Allow Calls on Other Device switch is set to On.**

5. **In the list of devices, tap the switch to Off for any device that you don't want to receive calls.**

Sending an incoming call directly to voicemail

Sometimes you just don't want to talk to someone. Whether that person is your sister calling to complain, an acquaintance who never seems to have anything to say, or someone who calls while you're indisposed, you might prefer to ignore the call.

That's not a problem on your iPhone because it gives you several ways to decline a call:

- If the phone isn't locked, tap the red Decline button on the touchscreen.
- If you're using the EarPods, squeeze and hold the center button for two seconds.
- Press the Sleep/Wake button twice in quick succession.

Each of these methods sends the call directly to voicemail.

Note If you ignore a call, as with any phone, the caller will know that you've done so when voicemail kicks in before the normal four rings. If you don't want someone to know you're ignoring his or her call, press the Sleep/Wake button once to silence the ring. The caller still hears the standard four rings before the voicemail and will be none the wiser that you just didn't pick up your phone.

Replying with a message

In the previous section, you learned how to send an unwanted call directly to voicemail. That's great for calls you want to ignore, but there are plenty of situations where you can't answer the phone, but you also don't want to ignore the caller. For example, if you're expecting a call but get dragged into a meeting in the meantime, it would be rude to still answer the call when it comes in, but if you just send the call to voicemail your caller might wonder what's going on. Similarly, you might be a bit late for an appointment, and on your way there you see a call come in from the person you're meeting. Again, it might not be convenient to answer the call, but letting voicemail handle it might lead your caller to wonder if you're going to show up for the meeting.

iOS offers a feature that gives you an easy way to handle these sticky phone situations. It's called Respond with Text and it enables you to simultaneously decline a call *and* send the caller a prefab text message. That way, you avoid a voice conversation (which, depending on your current situation, might be rude or inconvenient) but you give the caller some feedback.

By default, Respond with Text comes with three ready-to-send messages:

Sorry, I can't talk right now.

I'm on my way.

Can I call you later?

There's also an option to send a custom message if none of these is quite right. Here's how to decline an incoming call and send the caller a text message:

1. **When the call comes in, tap Message, shown in Figure 4.3.** Your iPhone displays a button for each of the prefab text messages.

2. **Tap the reply you want to send.** If you want to send a different message, tap Custom, type your message, and then tap Send.

The caller sees User Busy in the Phone app and then receives a text message.

4.3 Tap Message to reply to the caller with a text message.

Note

You must have call display on your phone plan to see the Message button.

Genius

If you're not all that fond of the default replies, you can forge your own. Tap Settings, tap Phone, tap Respond with Text, and then use the three text boxes to type your own messages.

Setting a callback reminder

The Respond with Text feature is a handy trick to have up your iPhone sleeve, but it suffers from the same problem that plagues straight-up declining a call: If you want to talk to that person later, you have to *remember* to call back. In older versions of iOS, my solution was to use the Reminders app to nudge myself in an hour (or whenever) to make the return call. Now, however, I don't need to perform that extra step because the Phone app has a feature that lets you decline a call and automatically create a callback reminder. You can set up the reminder to fire in one hour or when you leave your current location.

Here's how to decline an incoming call and set a callback reminder:

1. **When the call comes in, tap Remind Me.** Your iPhone displays the callback reminder options.

2. **Tap the type of reminder you want to set:**

   - **In 1 hour.** Tap this option to set a time-based reminder.

   - **When I leave.** Tap this option to set a location-based reminder that triggers when you leave your current location.

Genius
Rather than declining all incoming calls, you might be in a situation where you want to decline all calls *except* for those from a particular person or group. A better way to handle this is to set up the Do Not Disturb feature to allow calls from just those people. For more details, see Chapter 2.

Turning off the call waiting feature

If you're already on a call and another one comes in, your iPhone springs into action and displays the person's name or number, as well as three options: Decline Incoming Call, Answer & Hold Current Call, and Answer & End Current Call. (See the section about handling multiple calls later in this chapter for more info on these options.) This is part of the call waiting feature on your iPhone, and it's great if you're expecting an important call or if you want to add the caller to a conference call that you've set up.

However, the rest of the time you might just find it annoying and intrusive (and anyone you put on hold or hang up on to take the new call probably finds it rude and insulting). In that case, you can turn off call waiting by following these steps:

1. **On the Home screen, tap Settings.** The Settings app appears.

2. **Tap Phone.** The Phone screen appears.

3. **Tap Call Waiting.** The Call Waiting screen appears.

4. **Tap the Call Waiting switch to Off.** Your iPhone disables call waiting.

Blocking incoming calls

Using your iPhone is a blast *until* you get your first call from a telemarketer, cold-calling salesperson, or someone similarly annoying. Landlines have had a call blocking feature for years, but until now that useful innovation was absent from the iPhone, despite being on just about everyone's wish list more or less from the day the iPhone was released. Fortunately, Apple eventually heeded our call, so to speak, and offered the welcome ability to block people from calling you. If you're getting unwanted calls from an old flame, an old schoolmate, or anyone else you used to know but no longer want to, you can follow these steps to block those calls:

1. **On the Home screen, tap Settings to open the Settings app.**

2. **Tap Phone to display the Phone settings.**

3. **Tap Blocked to open the Blocked screen.**

4. **Tap Add New.** Your Contacts list appears.

5. **Tap the person you want to block.** Your iPhone adds that person's phone numbers and email address to the Blocked list.

Note The blocking feature also applies to FaceTime calls and to text messages. So an alternative method for adding someone to the Blocked list is to open Settings, tap Messages, tap Blocked, tap Add New, and then tap the person in your Contacts list.

What about people *not* in your Contacts list? No problem. Open the Phone app, tap Recents, and then tap the blue Info icon to the right of any call placed by the person you want to block. In the Info screen, tap Block this Caller and then tap Block Contact when you're asked to confirm.

Forwarding calls to another number

What do you do about incoming calls if you can't use your iPhone for a while? For example, if you're going on a flight, you must either turn off your iPhone or put it in Airplane mode (as described in Chapter 3) so incoming calls won't go through. Similarly, if you have to return your iPhone to Apple for repairs or battery replacement, the phone won't be available if anyone tries to call you.

For these and other situations where your iPhone can't accept incoming calls, you can work around the problem by having your calls forwarded to another number, such as your work or home number. Here's how it's done:

1. **On the Home screen, tap Settings.** The Settings app appears.

2. **Tap Phone.** The Phone screen appears.

3. **Tap Call Forwarding.** The Call Forwarding screen appears.

4. **Tap the Call Forwarding switch to On.** Your iPhone displays the Forwarding To screen.

5. **Tap the phone number to use for the forwarded calls.**

6. **Tap Back to return to the Call Forwarding screen.** Figure 4.4 shows the Call Forwarding screen set up to forward calls. In the status bar at the top of the screen, note the little Phone icon with an arrow that appears to the left of the time to let you know that call forwarding is on.

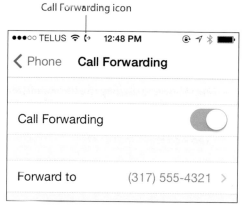

Call Forwarding icon

4.4 Activate call forwarding to have your iPhone calls forwarded to another number.

Juggling Multiple Calls and Conference Calls

We all juggle multiple tasks and duties these days, so it's not surprising that sometimes this involves juggling multiple phone calls:

- You might need to call two people on a related issue, and then switch back and forth between the callers as the negotiations (or whatever) progress.

● You might already be on a call and another call comes in from a person you need to speak to. So you put the initial person on hold, deal with the new caller, and then return to the first person.

● You might need to speak to two people at the same time on the same phone call — in other words, a conference call.

In the real world, juggling multiple calls and setting up conference calls often requires a special phone or a fancy phone system. In the iPhone world, however, these things are a snap. In fact, the way the iPhone juggles multiple calls really is something spectacular. Jumping back and forth between calls is simple, putting someone on hold to answer an incoming call is a piece of cake, and creating a conference call from incoming or outgoing calls is criminally easy.

When you're on an initial call, your iPhone displays the Call Options screen, as shown in Figure 4.5. To make another call, tap add call and then use the Phone app to place your second call.

4.5 When you're on a call, your iPhone displays these call options.

Genius

You may be wondering how you put a phone call on hold. For reasons that remain mysterious, your iPhone hides this useful feature. To see it, press and hold the mute button, shown in Figure 4.5. After several seconds, your iPhone replaces this icon with a hold icon and puts the caller on hold. To take the caller off hold, tap that icon.

Once the second call goes through, the Call Options screen changes: The top of the screen shows the first caller's name (or number) with HOLD beside it, and below that you see the name (or number) of the second caller and the duration of that call. Figure 4.6 shows the new screen layout. To switch to the person on hold, tap the swap button. iPhone puts the second caller on hold and returns you to the first caller. Congratulations! You now have two calls going at once.

If you're already on the phone and another call comes in, your iPhone displays the number (and the name if the caller is in your Contacts list), and gives you three ways to handle the call:

- **End & Accept.** Tap this option to drop the first call and answer the incoming call.

- **Send to Voicemail.** Tap this option to send the incoming call directly to voicemail.

4.6 The iPhone Call Options screen with two phone calls on the go.

- **Hold & Accept.** Tap this option to put the first call on hold and answer the incoming call. You're working with two calls again in this scenario, so you can tap swap to switch between the callers.

If you have two calls going, you might prefer that all three of you be able to talk to each other in a conference call. Easier done than said — just tap the merge calls option. iPhone combines everyone into a single conference call and displays Conference at the top of the Call Options screen. Tap the Info arrow and iPhone displays the participants' names (or numbers) in the Conference screen, as shown in Figure 4.7.

4.7 When you merge two phone calls, the participants' names or numbers appear in the Conference screen.

From here, there are a few methods you can use to manage your conference call:

- **To speak with one of the callers privately, tap the Private key below that person's name or number.** This places you in a one-on-one call with that person and places the other caller on hold.

- **To drop someone from the conference call, tap the End key below that person's name or number.** Your iPhone drops that caller and you resume a private call with the other party.

- **To add someone else to the conference call, tap Back to return to the Call Options screen.** Tap add call and then make the call. Once the call goes through, tap merge calls.

- **To add an incoming caller to the conference call, tap Hold & Accept.** Once you're connected, tap merge calls.

Clearly, juggling multiple calls on a phone has never been easier. The iPhone does a remarkable job of organizing calls and giving you an admirably easy process to swap, add, drop, or combine calls in conference.

Caution You can hold a conference call with up to five people at once by repeating the steps outlined for conference calls. However, remember that conference calls use up your minutes faster — two callers use them up twice as fast, three callers use them up three times as fast, and so on — so you may want to be judicious when using this feature.

Managing Your Favorites List

The Favorites list on your iPhone is great for making quick calls because you can often get someone on the horn in just three finger gestures (from the Home screen, tap Phone, tap Favorites, and then tap the number). Of course, this only works if the numbers you call most often appear on your Favorites list. Fortunately, your iPhone gives you a lot of different ways to populate the list. Here are the easiest methods to use:

- **In the Favorites list, tap + to open the All Contacts screen and then tap the person you want to add.** If that person has multiple phone numbers, tap the number you want to use as a favorite. When the iPhone asks how you want to call the person, tap Voice Call, FaceTime Audio, or FaceTime.

Note

This is a good place to remind you that the Favorites list isn't a list of people; it's a list of numbers. That's why the list shows both the person's name and the type of phone number (work, home, mobile, and so on).

● **In the Recent Calls list, tap the More Info icon to the right of the call from (or to) the person you want to add and then tap Add to Favorites.** If the person has multiple phone numbers, tap the number you want to use as the favorite, and then tap Voice Call, FaceTime Audio, or FaceTime. iPhone adds a star beside the phone number to remind you that it's a favorite.

● **In Visual Voicemail, tap the More Info icon beside a message, tap Add to Favorites, and then tap Voice Call, FaceTime Audio, or FaceTime.**

● **In the Contacts list, tap the person you want to add and then tap Add to Favorites.** If the person has multiple phone numbers, tap the number you want to use as the favorite, and then tap Voice Call, FaceTime Audio, or FaceTime. iPhone adds a star beside the phone number to remind you that it's a favorite.

You can add up to 20 numbers in the Favorites list, but the iPhone screen only shows 8 at a time. This means that if you want to call someone who doesn't appear in the initial screen, you need to scroll down to bring that number into view. Therefore, your Favorites list is most efficient when the people you call most often appear in the first eight numbers. Your iPhone adds each new number to the bottom of the Favorites list, so chances are that at least some of your favorite numbers aren't showing up in the top eight. Follow these steps to fix that:

1. **In the Favorites list, tap Edit.** Your iPhone displays Delete icons to the left of each favorite and Drag icons to the right, as shown in Figure 4.8.

Delete icons   Drag icons

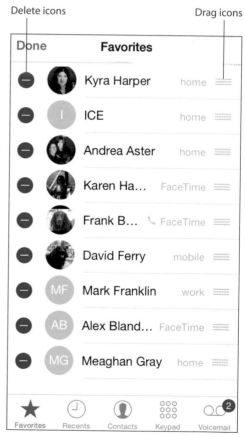

4.8 In Edit mode, the Favorites list shows Delete icons on the left and Drag icons on the right.

2. **If you want to get rid of a favorite, tap its Delete icon.**

3. **To move a favorite to a new location, tap and drag the Drag icon up or down until the favorite is where you want it, and then release the icon.**

4. **Tap Done.**

Converting a Phone Number into a Contact

Your iPhone is at its most efficient when the numbers you call are part of your Contacts list. Then, not only can you add contacts to the Favorites list for quick, speed-dial-like access, but you can also use the index (the letters A, B, C, and so on that run down the right side of the Contacts list). Then, it just takes a few finger flicks to rapidly find and tap the person with whom you want to chin-wag.

Genius

You can also convert a phone number on your Recent Calls list to a contact. On the Home screen, tap Phone, and then tap Recents to open the Recent Calls list. Locate the name or phone number you want to convert to a contact and then tap the blue More Info icon. Tap Create New Contact, fill in the other contact info, and then tap Done.

I talk about ways to add contacts in Chapter 10. For now, here's a quick way to add a contact right from the Phone app keypad:

1. **In the Home screen, tap Phone.** The Phone app appears.

2. **In the menu bar, tap Keypad.** The Keypad screen appears.

3. **Type the phone number of a person you want to add as a contact.**

4. **Tap Add to Contacts, the + that appears just to the left of the phone number, as shown in Figure 4.9.**

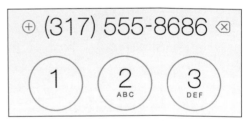

4.9 After you type a phone number using the keypad, tap Add to Contacts to create a contact for the number.

5. **Tap Create New Contact.** The New Contact screen appears.

6. **Fill in the other contact info as needed.**

7. **Tap Done.** Your iPhone adds the new contact and returns you to the Keypad screen.

8. **Tap Call to proceed with the phone call.**

Note

The phone number you're dialing might be an alternative number of an existing contact. For example, you may already have set up the contact with a home number, but now you're dialing that person's cell number. In that case, tap the Add Contact icon and then tap Add to Existing Contact. Use the Contacts list to tap the contact, choose the phone type (such as mobile), and then tap Done.

Video Calling with FaceTime

One of the most welcome features in the iPhone is a front-mounted camera, which means you can take pictures of yourself without guessing where the shutter button is! Fortunately, that's not all the front camera is good for. With the FaceTime app, you can use your iPhone to make video calls where you can actually see the other person face to face. It's an awesome feature, but to use it, the other person must be using an iPhone 4 or later, an iPad 2 or later, a fourth-generation (or later) iPod touch, or a Mac with a video camera and the FaceTime application installed.

Note that the front-mounted camera in the iPhone, iPad, and iPod touch, as well as the video camera on a Mac, are only required if you use FaceTime for video calling. You can also use FaceTime for audio-only calls.

Note

You can conduct FaceTime calls over a cellular connection, but you need to turn on this feature. Tap Settings, tap Cellular, and then tap the FaceTime switch to On. Note, as well, that some providers restrict cellular FaceTime calls to certain data plans.

The good news about FaceTime (besides how cool it is), is that it's a complete no-brainer to use. You don't have to activate any options, configure any settings, download any software, or connect to any servers.

Initiating a FaceTime call

To initiate a FaceTime call, you have a wide variety of choices:

- Call the other person normally, and once you're connected, tap the FaceTime icon.

- If the other person is in your Contacts list, open the contact and tap the FaceTime video camera icon for a video call, or the FaceTime phone icon for an audio call.

- In the Messages app, start a new conversation with the person — or open an existing one — scroll to the top of the window, and then tap FaceTime.

- Press and hold the Home button until you see the Siri app. Then, say "FaceTime *name label*" (where *name* is the name of the other person and *label* is the label associated with the phone number or the email address you want to use for the connection).

- If you've recently made a FaceTime call to someone, tap the Phone app's Recents icon, and then tap the FaceTime call (which the Phone app indicates with a FaceTime icon).

Note If the person has the same label applied to both a phone number and an email address, then you need to add either "phone" or "email" to the instruction. For example, "FaceTime Mom home email."

If another FaceTime user calls you, you see the message "*Name* would like FaceTime" (where *Name* is the caller's name if he is in your Contacts list). FaceTime also comes with Call Waiting support. If you're already on a voice or FaceTime call, you also get the option of either Declining the incoming call, or ending the current call and accepting the new call, as shown in Figure 4.10.

Tap Accept and your video call connects, just like that. You see your caller's (hopefully) smiling face in the full iPhone screen, and your own mug in a picture-in-picture (PIP) window.

The FaceTime calling screen includes three buttons in the menu bar (tap the screen if you don't see these buttons):

- **Switch cameras.** Tap this button to switch your video output to the rear camera (for example, to show your caller something in front of you).

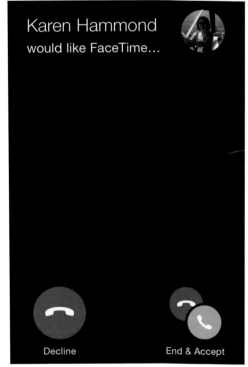

4.10 FaceTime supports Call Waiting, so you can decline or switch to an incoming call when you're already on a voice or video call.

- **End.** Tap this button (it's the one in the middle) to end the call.

- **Mute.** Tap this icon (it's the one on the left) to mute the sound from your end of the conversation (you can still hear sound from the other person's end).

Genius

> Your PIP window appears by default in the upper right corner. If you prefer a different position, tap and drag the PIP window to any corner of the screen.

Disabling FaceTime

There will certainly be times when you simply don't want a face-to-face conversation, no matter who's calling. Perhaps you're in a secret location or you just don't look your best that day. Whatever the reason, you can follow these steps to turn off FaceTime:

1. **In the Home screen, tap Settings.** The Settings app appears.

2. **Tap FaceTime.** The FaceTime screen appears.

3. **Tap the FaceTime switch to Off.**

Now, when people try to call you using FaceTime, they see a message saying that you're "not available for FaceTime."

How Can I Make the Most of iPhone Web Surfing?

One of the most popular modern pastimes is web surfing, and now you can surf even when you're out and about thanks to the large screen on your iPhone and support for speedy networks, such as LTE and Wi-Fi. You perform these surfin' safaris using, appropriately enough, the Safari web browser app, which is easy to use and intuitive. However, the Safari app offers quite a few options and features, many of which are hidden in obscure nooks and crannies of the iPhone interface. If you think your surfing activities could be faster, more efficient, more productive, or more secure, this chapter can help.

Touchscreen Tips for Websites

The touchscreen operates much the same way in Safari as it does in the other iPhone apps. You can use it to scroll pages, zoom in and out, tap links, fill in forms, enter addresses, and more. The screen is remarkably fluid in its motion, and its response to your touch is neither hyperactive nor sluggish. It actually makes surfing the web a pleasure, which isn't something you can say about most smartphones.

Here's a little collection of touchscreen tips that ought to make your web excursions even easier:

- **Double-tap.** A quick way to zoom in on a page that has various sections is to double-tap on the specific section — it could be an image, a paragraph, a table, or a column of text — that you want magnified. Your iPhone zooms the section to fill the width of the screen. Double-tap again to return the page to the regular view.

Note The double-tap-to-zoom trick works only on pages that have identifiable sections. If a page is just a wall of text, you can double-tap until the cows come home (that's a long time) and nothing much happens.

- **One tap to the top.** If you're reading a particularly long-winded web page and you're near the bottom, you may have quite a long way to scroll if you need to head back to the top to get at the address/search bar. Save the wear and tear on your flicking finger! Instead, tap the status bar at the top of the screen; Safari immediately transports you to the top of the page.

Genius If you're using an iPhone 6, 6 Plus, or 6s, you might find it hard to reach the top of the screen if you're surfing one-handed. Remember that you can lightly double-tap the Home button to drop the Safari screen down halfway and bring its top bar within easy reach.

- **Tap and hold to see where a link takes you.** You "click" a link in a web page by tapping it with your finger. In a regular web browser, you can see where a link takes you (that is, the URL) by hovering the mouse pointer over the link and checking out the link address in the status bar. That doesn't work on your iPhone, but you can still find out the address of a link before tapping it. Hold your finger on the link for a few seconds. Safari then displays a pop-up screen showing the link text and, more importantly, the URL, as shown in

Figure 5.1. If the link looks legit, either tap Open to surf there in the current browser page or tap Open in New Page to start a fresh page (see the section about opening and managing multiple browser tabs later in this chapter for more info). If you decide not to follow the link, tap Cancel.

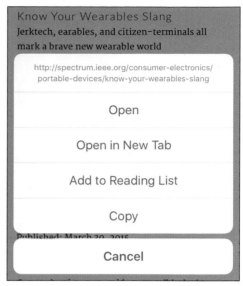

- ⦿ **Tap and hold to make a copy of a link address.** If you want to include a link address in another app, such as a note or an email message, you can copy it. Tap and hold your finger on the link for a few seconds and Safari displays the pop-up screen shown in Figure 5.1. Tap Copy to place the link address into memory, switch to the other app, tap the cursor, and then tap Paste.

5.1 Hold your finger on a link to see the URL and several link options.

- ⦿ **Quick access to common top-level domains.** A top-level domain (TLD) is the part of the domain name that comes after the last dot. For example, in wiley.com, the *.com* part is the TLD. You might think you have to type them the old-fashioned way. Nope! Tap and hold the period (.) key, and a pop-up appears with keys for .com, .net, .edu, and .org, and another for your current country TLD (such as .us for the United States). Just slide your finger over the one you want.

Browsing Tips for Faster Surfing

If you're like me, the biggest problem you have with the web is that it's just so darned huge. We spend great big chunks of our day visiting sites and still never seem to get to everything on that day's To Surf list. The iPhone helps lessen (but, alas, not eliminate) this problem by allowing you to surf wherever Wi-Fi can be found (or just wherever if you only have a cellular connection). Even so, the faster and more efficient your iPhone surfing sessions are, the more sites you see. The touchscreen tips I covered earlier can help, and in this section I take you through a few more useful tips for speedier surfing.

Opening and managing multiple browser tabs

When you're perusing web pages, what happens when you're on a page that you want to keep reading, but you also need to leap over to another page for something? On your computer's web browser, you probably open another tab, use that tab to open the other page, and then switch back to the first page when you finish. It's an essential web-browsing technique, but can it be done with the Safari browser on your iPhone?

The short answer: yes. The slightly longer answer: yes, although the "tabs" that Safari uses look (and act) more like separate browser windows. In any case, you can open a second tab and load a different page into it. Then, it's just a quick tap and flick to switch between them. You're not restricted to a meager two tabs either. Your iPhone lets you open up as many tabs as you need.

Note Some web page links are configured to automatically open the page in a new window, so you might see a new tab being created when you tap a link. Also, if you add a web clip to your Home screen (as described in Chapter 2), tapping the icon opens the web clip in a new Safari tab.

Here are the steps to follow to open and load multiple tabs:

1. **Tap the title bar that appears at the top of the Safari screen, or swipe down on the screen.** Safari reveals its menu bar.

2. **Tap the Tabs button in the menu bar (see Figure 5.2).** Safari displays a thumbnail version of the current tab.

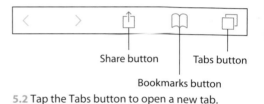

Share button Tabs button

Bookmarks button

5.2 Tap the Tabs button to open a new tab.

3. **Tap New Tab (the + button).** Safari opens a new tab and displays a list of recent sites you've visited.

4. **Load a website into the new tab.** You can do this by tapping a recent site, selecting a bookmark, entering an address, or whatever.

5. **Repeat Steps 1 to 4 to load as many tabs as you need.**

Once you have two or more tabs fired up, here are a couple of techniques you can use to impress your friends:

● **Switch to another tab.** Tap the title bar (or swipe down) and then tap the Tabs button to get to the thumbnail view (see Figure 5.3). Flick up or down to bring the page into view, and then tap the page.

● **When you no longer need a page.** Tap the title bar (or swipe down) and then tap the Tabs button, and flick up or down to bring the page into view. Then tap the X in the upper left corner (or tap and drag the page off the left edge of the screen). Safari trashes the page without a whimper of protest.

Working with iCloud tabs

Tabs are handy browsing tools because they let you keep multiple websites open and available while you surf other sites. That's fine as long as you use just a single device to surf the web, but how realistic is that? It's much more likely that you do some web surfing not only on your iPhone, but also on your Mac or Windows PC, your iPad, perhaps even your iPad touch. So what do you do if you're using your iPhone to surf and you remember a site that's open in a tab on one of your other devices?

If you have an iCloud account, you can use it to sync your open Safari tabs in multiple devices, and then access those tabs in your iPhone. For this to work, you must be using Safari 6 or later on OS X, Windows, or iOS, and you must configure iCloud on each of those devices to sync Safari data.

With that done, open Safari on your iPhone, tap the Tabs button in the menu bar, and then scroll down. Once you scroll below all your iPhone tabs, Safari displays a list of the open tabs on your other devices, as shown in Figure 5.4.

Opening a tab in the background

When you tap and hold a link and then tap Open in New Tab, Safari immediately switches to the new tab and loads the link while you wait. That's often the behavior you want because it lets you view the new web page as soon as it loads. However, you might find that most of the time you prefer to stay on the current web page and check out the new tab later. In those situations,

5.3 Tap the Tabs button to see thumbnail versions of your open tabs.

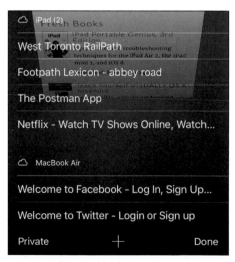

5.4 Tap the Tabs button and then scroll down to see a list of the Safari tabs that you have open in your other devices.

101

having to perform those extra taps to get back to the current tab gets old in a hurry. The solution is to configure Safari to always open new tabs in the background. Here's how:

1. **On the Home screen, tap Settings.** The Settings app slides in.
2. **Tap Safari.** Your iPhone displays the Safari screen.
3. **Tap Open Links.** Your iPhone displays the Open Links screen.
4. **Tap In Background.**

Viewing a page without distractions

Reading an article or essay online is no picnic. The problem is the sheer amount of distraction on almost any page: background colors or images that clash with the text; ads above, to the side of, and within the text; site features such as search boxes, feed links, and content lists; and those ubiquitous icons for sharing the article with your friends on Facebook, Twitter, Pinterest, and on and on. Figure 5.5 shows a typical example.

Fortunately, Safari helps to solve this problem by offering the Reader feature. Reader removes all those extraneous page distractions that just get in the way of your reading pleasure. So, instead of a cacophony of text, icons, and images, you see pure, simple, large-enough-to-be-easily-read text. How do you arrive at this blissful state? By tapping the title bar at the top of the Safari screen and then tapping the Reader button, which appears on the left side of the address bar, as pointed out in Figure 5.5. Safari instantly transforms the page, and you see something similar to the page shown in Figure 5.6 (which is the Reader version of the page shown in Figure 5.5).

Requesting a website's desktop version

Many websites recognize that you're surfing iPhone-style and display a "mobile" version of the site. This version is usually easier to read and navigate, but that ease almost always

Reader button

5.5 Today's web pages are all too often festooned with ads, icons, and other bric-a-brac.

comes at the cost of having access to fewer site features. If a site isn't displaying the feature you want, you can request the site's "desktop" version (that is, the full version that you'd see if you were using a desktop computer). Here's how:

1. **Swipe down on the screen to reveal the menu bar.**

2. **Tap the Share button (pointed out in Figure 5.2).**

3. **Scroll the bottom list of share actions to the right, then tap Request Desktop Site, as shown in Figure 5.7.**

Saving sites as bookmarks

Although you've seen that the Safari browser on your iPhone offers a few tricks to ease the pain of typing web page addresses, it's still slower and quite a bit more cumbersome than a full-size, physical keyboard (which lets even inexpert typists rattle off addresses lickety-split). All the more reason that you should embrace bookmarks with all your heart. After all, a bookmark lets you jump to a web page with precisely no typing — just a tap or three and you're there. Here are the steps to follow:

1. **On the iPhone, use Safari to navigate to the site you want to save.**

2. **Tap the web page title bar (or swipe down on the screen) and then tap the Share button in the menu bar.** This is the button with the arrow in the middle of the Safari menu bar (pointed out earlier in Figure 5.2).

3. **Tap Add Bookmark.** This opens the Add Bookmark screen.

4. **Tap in the top box and enter a name for the site that helps you remember it.** This name is what you see when you scroll through your bookmarks.

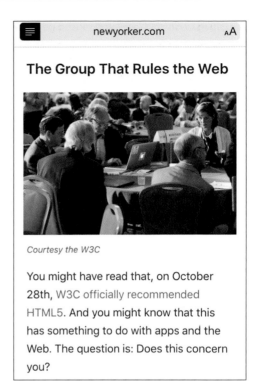

newyorker.com

The Group That Rules the Web

Courtesy the W3C

You might have read that, on October 28th, W3C officially recommended HTML5. And you might know that this has something to do with apps and the Web. The question is: Does this concern you?

5.6 The Reader version of a web page is a simple and easy-to-read text affair.

Print   Find on Page   Request Desktop Site   More

Cancel

5.7 To switch a site from mobile to desktop, tap Share, then tap Request Desktop Site.

5. **Tap Location.** This displays a list of your bookmark folders.

6. **Tap the folder you want to use to store the bookmark.** Safari returns you to the Add Bookmark screen.

7. **Tap Save.** Safari saves the bookmark.

Managing your bookmarks

Once you have a few bookmarks stashed away in the Bookmarks list, you may need to perform a few housekeeping chores from time to time, including changing a bookmark's name, address, or folder; reordering bookmarks or folders; or getting rid of bookmarks that have worn out their welcome.

Before you can do any of this, you need to get the Bookmarks list into Edit mode by following these steps:

1. **In Safari, tap the web page title bar (or swipe down on the screen) and then tap the Bookmarks button in the menu bar.** Safari opens the Bookmarks list.

2. **Tap the Bookmarks tab.**

3. **If the bookmark you want to mess with is located in a particular folder, tap to open that folder.** For example, if you've synced with Safari, then you should have a folder named Bookmarks Bar that includes all the bookmarks and folders that you've added to the Bookmarks Bar in your desktop version of Safari.

4. **Tap Edit.** Your iPhone switches the Bookmarks list to Edit mode. With Edit mode on the go, you're free to toil away at your bookmarks. Here are the techniques to master:

   - **Edit bookmark info.** Tap the bookmark to fire up the Edit Bookmark screen. From here, you can edit the bookmark name, address, or folder. Tap Done when you're ready to move on.

   - **Change the bookmark order.** Use the Drag icon on the right to tap and drag a book-mark to a new position in the list. Ideally, you should move your favorite bookmarks near the top of the list for easiest access.

   - **Add a bookmark folder.** Tap New Folder to launch the Edit Folder screen, then tap a folder title and select a location. Feel free to use bookmark folders at will because they're a great way to keep your bookmarks neat and tidy (if you're into that kind of thing).

   - **Delete a bookmark.** No use for a particular bookmark? No problem. Tap the Delete button — the minus (–) sign to the left of the bookmark — and then tap the Delete button that appears.

When the dust settles and your bookmark chores are done for the day, tap Done to get out of Edit mode, then tap Done to exit the Bookmarks screen.

Surfing links from your Twitter feed

If you've used your iPhone to connect to your Twitter account, as I describe in Chapter 2, Safari offers a bonus: the Shared Links list, which displays the recent links that have been shared by the people you follow on Twitter. Here's how you get there from here:

1. **In Safari, tap the web page title bar (or swipe down on the screen) to display the menu bar.**

2. **Tap the Bookmarks button in the menu bar.** Safari opens the Bookmarks list.

3. **Tap the Shared Links tab.** Safari displays your Twitter feed's most recent links, as shown in Figure 5.8.

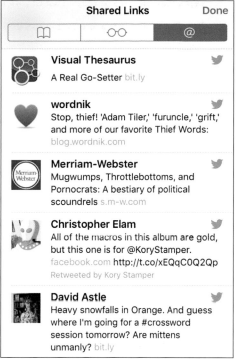

5.8 With your iPhone connected to your Twitter account, the Safari Shared Links list offers up recent links from the folks you follow.

Genius

The Shared Links list isn't just for Twitter links. If you have some favorite blogs, you can add their RSS (Real Simple Syndication) feeds to Shared Links. To do this, surf to a site that offers an RSS feed, open Shared Links, tap Subscriptions, tap Add Current Site, and then tap Done.

Saving a page to read later

In your web travels, you'll often come upon a page with fascinating content that you can't wait to read. Unfortunately, a quick look at the length of the article tells you that you're going to need more time than you currently have available. So what's a body to do? Quickly scan the article and move on with your life? No, when you come across good web content, you need to savor it. So, should you bookmark the article for future reference? That's not bad, but bookmarks are really for things you want to revisit often, not for pages that you might read only once.

The best solution is the Safari feature called the Reading List. As the name implies, this is a simple list of things to read. When you don't have time to read something now, add it to your Reading List and you can read it at your leisure.

There are a couple of techniques you can use to add a page to your Reading List:

- Use Safari to navigate to the page that you want to read later, tap the Share button, and then tap Add to Reading List.

- Tap and hold a link for the page that you want to read later and then tap Add to Reading List.

Note By default, Safari uses the cellular network to access your Reading List when there's no Wi-Fi in sight. To prevent this (for example, if you're nearing your plan's data cap), tap Settings, tap Safari, and then, in the Reading List section, tap the Use Cellular Data switch to Off.

When you're settled into your favorite easy chair and have the time (finally!) to read, open Safari, tap the Bookmarks button, and then tap the Reading List tab. Safari displays all the items you've added to the list and you just tap the article you want to read. To make the list a bit easier to manage, tap Show Unread to see just the pages you haven't yet perused.

Retracing your steps with the handy History list

Bookmarking a website is a good idea if that site contains interesting or fun content that you want to revisit in the future. However, sometimes you may not realize that a site had useful data until a day or two later. Similarly, you might like a site's stuff but decide against bookmarking it, only to regret that decision down the road. You could waste a big chunk of your day trying to track down the site. Unfortunately, you may have run into Murphy's Web Browsing Law: A cool site that you forget to bookmark is never found again.

Fortunately, your iPhone has your back. As you navigate the nooks and crannies of the web, iPhone keeps track of where you go, storing the name and address of each page in the History list. The limited memory on iPhone means that it can't store tons of sites, but it might have the one you're looking for. Here's how to use it:

1. **In Safari, tap the web page title bar (or swipe down on the screen) to display the menu bar, and then tap the Bookmarks button.** Safari opens the Bookmarks list.

2. **Tap the Bookmarks tab.**

3. **Tap History.** Safari opens the History screen, which shows the sites you've visited today at the top, followed by a list of previous surfing dates.

4. **If you visited the site you're looking for on a previous day, tap that day.** Safari displays a list of only the sites you visited on that day.

5. **Tap the site you want to revisit.** Safari loads it.

Filling in Online Forms

Many web pages include forms where you fill in some data and submit it, which sends the data off to some server for processing. Filling in these forms in your Safari browser is mostly straightforward:

● **Text box.** Tap inside the text box to display the touchscreen keyboard, tap out your text, and then tap Done.

● **Text area.** Tap inside the text area, and then use the keyboard to tap your text. Most text areas allow multiline entries, so you can tap Return to start a new line. When you finish, tap Done.

● **Check box.** Tap the check box to toggle the check mark on and off.

● **Radio button.** Tap the radio button to activate it.

● **Command button.** Tap the button to make it do its thing (usually submit the form).

Many online forms consist of a bunch of text boxes. If the idea of performing the tap-type-Done cycle over and over isn't appealing to you, fear not. The Safari browser on your iPhone offers an easier method:

1. **Tap inside the first text box.** The keyboard appears.

2. **Tap to type the text you want to submit.** Above the keyboard, notice the Previous and Next buttons, as shown in Figure 5.9.

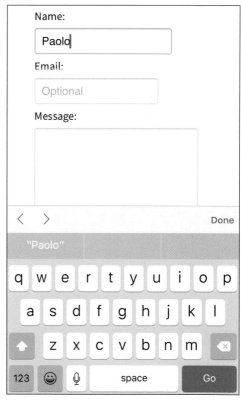

5.9 If the form contains multiple text boxes, you can use the Previous and Next buttons to navigate them.

3. **Tap Next to move to the next text box.** If you need to return to a text box, tap Previous instead.

4. **Repeat Steps 2 and 3 to fill in the text boxes.**

5. **Tap Done.** Safari returns you to the page.

I haven't yet talked about selection lists, and that's because the browser on your iPhone handles them in an interesting way. When you tap a list, Safari displays the list items in a picker, as shown in Figure 5.10. Tap the item you want to select. As with text boxes, if the form has multiple lists, you see the Previous and Next buttons, which you can tap to navigate from one list to another. After you make all your selections, tap Done to return to the page.

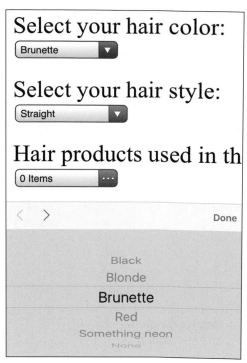

5.10 Tap a list to see its items in a separate box for easier selection.

Turning on AutoFill for faster form input

The Safari browser on your iPhone makes it relatively easy to fill in online forms, but it can still be slow going, particularly if you have to do a lot of typing. To help make forms less of a chore, Safari supports a welcome feature called AutoFill. Just as with the desktop version of Safari (or just about any other mainstream browser), AutoFill remembers the data you enter into forms and then enables you to fill in similar forms with a simple tap of a button. You can also configure AutoFill to remember usernames and passwords.

To take advantage of this nifty feature, you first have to turn it on by following these steps:

1. **In the Home screen, tap Settings.** Your iPhone opens the Settings app.

2. **Tap Safari.** The Safari screen appears.

3. **Tap AutoFill to open the AutoFill screen.**

4. **Tap the Use Contact Info switch to On.** This tells Safari to use your item in the Contacts app to grab data for a form. For example, if a form requires your name, Safari uses your contact name. Safari displays the All Contacts screen.

5. **Tap My Info and then tap your name in the All Contacts list.**

6. **If you want Safari to remember the usernames and passwords you use to log in to sites, tap the Names and Passwords switch to On.**

7. **If you want Safari to remember the credit card data you enter when making online purchases, tap the Credit Cards switch to On.**

Genius

You could add your credit card data by hand, but Safari enables you to enter the data automatically using the iPhone's camera. In the AutoFill screen, tap Saved Credit Cards, enter your passcode (you really should use a passcode or Touch ID if you're adding credit cards to your iPhone; see Chapter 2), then tap Add Credit Card. Tap Use Camera, position the credit card within the camera field, and then wait until the card info is recognized.

Now when you visit an online form and access any text field in the form, the AutoFill button becomes enabled. Tap AutoFill to fill in those portions of the form that correspond with your contact data, as shown in Figure 5.11. Notice that the fields Safari was able to automatically fill in appear with a colored background.

Saving website login passwords

If you enabled the Names & Passwords option in the AutoFill screen, each time you fill in a username and password to log in to a site, Safari displays the dialog shown in Figure 5.12. It asks if you want to remember the login data, and gives you three choices:

- **Save Password.** Tap this button to have Safari remember your username and password.

- **Never for This Website.** Tap this button to tell Safari not to remember the user-name and password, and to never again prompt you to save the login data.

First Name: Paul

Last Name: McFedries

Nickname: Author Boy

Nom de Plume: |

< > AutoFill   Done

5.11 Tap the AutoFill button to fill in form fields with your contact data.

Would you like to save this password?
You can view and remove saved passwords in Safari settings.

Save Password

Never for This Website

Unknown - Use precise location

Not Now

5.12 If you configured Safari to remember usernames and passwords, you see this dialog when you log in to a site.

⦿ **Not Now.** Tap this button to tell Safari not to remember the username and password this time, but to prompt you again next time you log in to this site.

Genius

If you tap Save Password, but then change your mind, you can remove the saved password from your iPhone. Tap Settings, tap Safari, tap Passwords, and then enter your passcode or Touch ID to see a list of the sites with saved passwords. Tap the site you want to fix, tap Edit, tap the red Delete icon that appears to the left of the site, and then tap Delete when Settings asks you to confirm.

Note

Your iPhone is cautious about this password stuff, so it doesn't offer to save all the passwords you enter. In particular, if the login form is part of a secure site, then your iPhone doesn't ask if you want to save the password. This means you won't be tempted to store the password for your online bank, corporate website, or any other site that requires secure access.

To use a saved password, surf to the site's login page and tap one of the login fields, such as the username or password field. Tap Passwords to see a list of saved passwords for the site (yes, you can have more than one saved password for a site), then tap the login you want to use. Safari fills in the login data, so all you have to do is tap Log In (or Sign In, or whatever).

Adding website passwords manually

For saving passwords on your iPhone, it's easiest just to fill in your username and password online and then let Safari save the logon data for you. However, if the site or your Internet connection is temporarily unavailable, you can still enter a website's password by hand. You might also want to add a second (or third) set of login data to an existing site, and that's usually easiest to do manually. Here's how:

1. **Tap Settings to display the Settings app.**

2. **Tap Safari.** The Safari screen appears.

3. **Tap Passwords.** Settings prompts you for your passcode or Touch ID.

4. **Enter your passcode or Touch ID.** The Passwords screen appears.

5. **Tap Add Password at the bottom of the screen.** The Add Password screen appears.

6. **Fill in the website's address, your username, and your password.** The password appears in regular text instead of the usual dots, so make sure no one's peeking over your shoulder as you do this.

7. **Tap Done.** Settings saves the login data for the site.

Getting More Out of Safari on Your iPhone

You've seen a lot of great Safari tips and techniques so far in this chapter, but I hope you're up for even more, because you've got a ways to go. In the rest of this chapter, you learn such useful techniques as maintaining your privacy, tweeting a web page, changing the default search engine, configuring the Safari security options, and searching a web page.

Maintaining your privacy by deleting the History list

The History list of sites you've recently surfed on your iPhone is a great feature when you need it, and it's an innocuous feature when you don't. However, there are times when the History list is just plain uncool. For example, if you visit a private corporate site, a financial site, or any other site you wouldn't want others to see, the History list might betray you.

And sometimes unsavory sites can end up in your History list by accident. For example, you might tap a legitimate-looking link in a web page or email message, only to end up in some dark, dank Net neighborhood. Of course, you high-tail it out of there right away with a quick tap of the Back button, but that nasty site is now lurking in your history.

Whether you've got sites on the History list that you wouldn't want anyone to see, or you just find the idea of your iPhone tracking your movements on the web to be a bit sinister, follow these steps to wipe out the History list:

1. **In Safari, tap the web page title bar (or swipe down on the screen) to display the menu bar, and then tap the Bookmarks button.** Safari opens the Bookmarks list.

2. **Tap the folder names that appear in the upper left corner of the screen until you get to the Bookmarks screen.**

3. **Tap History.** Safari opens the History screen.

4. **Tap Clear.** Safari asks how much of your history you want to clear.

5. **Tap a time period: The Last Hour, Today, Today and Yesterday, or All Time.** Safari deletes every site from the History list for that time period.

Deleting website data

As you wander around the web, Safari gathers and saves bits of information for each site. For example, it stores some site text and images so that it can display the page faster if you revisit the site in the near future. Similarly, if you activated AutoFill for names and passwords, Safari stores

111

Genius

One good thing about your website history is that Safari uses it (as well as your book-marks) to analyze each page you view and determine the most likely link you'll tap — the so-called *top hit* — and preloads that link. If you do tap that link, the page loads lickety-split. However, if you're not comfortable having Safari send your history and bookmarks to Apple, you can turn this feature off. Tap Settings, tap Safari, and then tap the Preload Top Hit switch to Off.

that data on your iPhone. Finally, most major sites store small text files called cookies on your iPhone that save information for things like site preferences and shopping carts.

Storing all this data on your iPhone is generally a good thing because it can speed up your surfing. However, it's not always a safe or private thing. For example, if you elect to have Safari save a site password, you might change your mind later on, particularly if you share your iPhone with other people. Similarly, cookies can sometimes be used to track your activities online, so they're not always benign.

Here are the steps to follow to delete data for individual websites:

1. **On the Home screen, tap Settings.** Your iPhone opens the Settings app.
2. **Tap Safari.** The Safari screen appears.
3. **Tap Advanced.** The Advanced screen appears.
4. **Tap Website Data.** Safari displays a list of the recent sites for which it has stored data, as well as the size of that data.
5. **If you don't see the site you want to remove, tap Show All Sites at the bottom of the list.**
6. **Tap Edit.**
7. **Tap the red Delete icon to the left of the site you want to clear.**
8. **Tap the Delete button that appears to the right of the site's data size value.** Safari removes the site's data.

Genius

Rather than deleting website data one site at a time, you might want to clean house by deleting *all* the website data currently stored by Safari. It's a drastic move, but it can come in handy if you're selling your phone or allowing someone else to use it for a while. In the Home screen, tap Settings, tap Safari, and then tap Clear History and Website Data. When your iPhone asks you to confirm, tap Clear History and Data.

Browsing privately

If you find yourself constantly deleting your browsing history or website data, you can save your-self a bit of time by configuring Safari to do this automatically. This is called *private browsing* and it means that Safari doesn't save any data as you browse. Specifically, it doesn't save the following:

- Sites aren't added to the history (although the Back and Forward buttons still work for navigating sites that you've visited in the current session).
- Web page text and images aren't saved.
- Search text isn't saved with the search box.
- AutoFill passwords aren't saved.

To activate private browsing, follow these steps:

1. **In Safari, tap the web page title bar (or swipe down on the screen) to display the menu bar.**

2. **Tap the Tabs button.**

3. **Tap Private in the lower left corner of the screen.** Safari creates a separate set of tabs for private browsing.

4. **Tap Add Tab (+).** Safari creates a new private tab.

Genius

Another way Safari might compromise your online privacy is by displaying sugges-tions as you enter search text into the address bar. If someone is looking over your shoulder or simply borrows your iPhone for a quick search, she might see these sug-gestions. To turn them off, open the Settings app, tap Safari, then tap both the Search Engine Suggestions switch and the Safari Suggestions switch to Off.

Tweeting a web page

If you have a Twitter account, there's a good chance that one of your favorite 140-characters-or-less pastimes is sharing interesting, useful, or funny websites with your followers. Using a client such as the official Twitter app or Tweetbot is fine for this, but it means you have to copy the site address, switch to the app, and then paste the address. For quick tweets, it's easier and faster just to stay in Safari, which lets you send a tweet directly from a web page. Here's what you do:

1. **Use Safari to navigate to the page that you want to tweet.**

2. **Tap the web page title bar (or swipe down on the screen) to display the menu bar, and then tap the Share button.** Alternatively, select the text you want to include in

your tweet, then tap Share in the pop-up menu that appears. Note, however, that this method doesn't include the page link in the tweet.

3. **Tap Twitter.** Safari displays the Twitter dialog.

4. **If you added more than one account to the Twitter settings, tap the username in the Account section and then tap the name of the account you want to use to send the tweet.**

5. **Type your tweet text in the large text box.** As you can see in Figure 5.13, the Tweet dialog displays a number in the lower left corner telling you how many characters you have left.

6. **If you want to include your present whereabouts as part of the tweet, tap Location.**

7. **Tap Post.** Your iPhone posts the tweet to your followers.

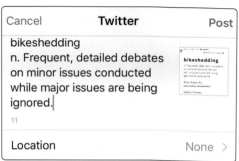

5.13 iOS lets you tweet about a website directly from Safari.

Sharing a link on Facebook

You learn in Chapter 2 that if you sign in to your Facebook account on your iPhone, you can use Siri to update your Facebook status. A timely, pithy, or funny status update is a time-honored (relatively speaking) Facebook tradition, but your friends would probably appreciate at least the occasional tidbit of non-narcissistic content. I speak, in this case, of sharing links to useful, interesting, funny, or even downright weird web pages.

Happily, link-sharing with your Facebook pals is now built directly into Safari, so there's no need to surf to the Facebook site or fire up the Facebook app to get the job done:

1. **Use Safari to display the web page you want to share.**

2. **Tap the web page title bar (or swipe down on the screen) to display the menu bar, and then tap the Share button.**

3. **Tap Facebook.** Safari displays the Facebook dialog.

4. **Use the large text box to type some text to accompany the link.**

5. **If you want to include your current location as part of the post, tap Location.**

6. **To select who will see the link, tap Audience and then tap a group in the list that appears.**

7. **Tap Post.** Your iPhone posts the link to your Facebook Timeline.

Changing the default search engine

Google is the default search engine on your iPhone. Almost everyone uses Google, of course, but if you have something against it, you can switch and use a different search engine. Here's how:

1. **In the Home screen, tap Settings.** Your iPhone opens the Settings app.

2. **Tap Safari.** The Safari screen appears.

3. **Tap Search Engine.** Your iPhone opens the Search Engine screen.

4. **Tap the search engine you want to use.** You have four choices: Google, Yahoo!, Bing, or DuckDuckGo.

Searching web page text

When you're perusing a page on the web, it's not unusual to be looking for specific information. In those situations, rather than reading through the entire page to find the info you seek, it would be a lot easier to search for the data. You can easily do this in the desktop version of Safari or any other computer browser, but, at first glance, the Safari app doesn't seem to have a Find feature anywhere. It's there all right, but you need to know where to look:

1. **Use the Safari app to navigate to the web page that contains the information you seek.**

2. **Tap the web page title bar (or swipe down on the screen) to display the menu bar, and then tap inside the address/search box at the top of the Safari window.**

3. **Tap the search text you want to use.** Safari displays the usual web page matches, but it also displays "On This Page (*X* matches)," where *X* is the number of times your search text appears on the web page.

4. **Flick the search results up to hide the keyboard.** The On This Page message now appears at the bottom of the results screen, as shown in Figure 5.14.

5. **Tap Find "*search*" (where *search* is the search text you entered).** Safari

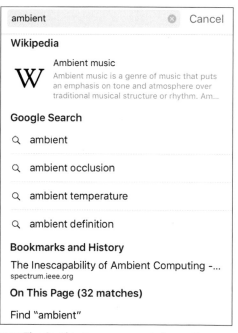

5.14 The On This Page message tells you the number of matches that appear on the current web page.

highlights the first instance of the search term, as shown in Figure 5.15.

6. **Tap the down-pointing arrow to cycle forward through the instances of the search term that appear on the page.** Note that you can also cycle backward through the results by tapping the up-pointing arrow. Also, when you tap the down-pointing arrow after the last result appears, Safari returns you to the first result.

7. **When you're finished with the search, tap Done.**

Searching the web with Siri voice commands

You can use Safari to type search queries either directly into the search box or by navigating to a search engine site. However, typing suddenly seems like such a quaint pastime thanks to the voice-recognition prowess of the Siri app. So why type a search query when you can just tell Siri what you're looking for?

5.15 Safari highlights the first instance of the search term that appears on the current web page.

Launch Siri by tapping and holding the Home button (or pressing and holding the Mic button of the iPhone headphones, or the equivalent button on a Bluetooth headset). Here are some general tips for web searching with Siri:

- **Searching the entire web.** Say "Search the web for *topic*," where *topic* is your search criteria.
- **Searching Wikipedia.** Say "Search Wikipedia for *topic*," where *topic* is the subject you want to look up.
- **Searching with a particular search engine.** Say "*Engine topic*," where *Engine* is the name of the search engine, such as Google or Bing, and *topic* is your search criteria.

Siri also understands commands related to searching for businesses and restaurants through its partnership with Yelp. To look for businesses and restaurants using Siri, the general syntax to use is the following (although, as usual with Siri, you don't have to be too rigid about this):

"Find (or Look for) *something somewhere*."

Here, the *something* part can be the name of a business (such as "Starbucks"), a type of business (such as "gas station"), a type of restaurant (such as "Thai restaurants"), or a generic product (such as "coffee"). The *somewhere* part can be something relative to your current location (such as "around here" or "near me" or "within walking distance") or a specific location (such as "in Indianapolis" or "in Broad Ripple"). Here are some examples:

- "Find a gas station within walking distance."
- "Look for pizza restaurants in Indianapolis."
- "Find coffee around here."
- "Look for a grocery store near me."

Note, too, that if you add a qualifier such as "good" or "best" before the *something* portion of the command, Siri returns the results organized by their Yelp rating.

Sharing a link via AirDrop

Here's an all-too-common scenario in this digital, mobile age: You're out with friends or colleagues, you look up something on your iPhone, and you find a page that one of your peeps wants to check out. How do you get the page address from your iPhone to her device? iOS uses AirDrop, a Bluetooth service that lets two nearby devices — specifically, an iPhone 5 or later, a fourth-generation iPad or later, an iPad mini, a fifth-generation iPod touch or later, or a Mac running OS X Yosemite or later — exchange a link wirelessly. Here's how it works:

1. **Use Safari to navigate to the web page you want to share.**

2. **Tap the web page title bar (or swipe down on the screen) to display the menu bar, and then tap the Share button.** The AirDrop section shows an icon for each nearby device, as shown in Figure 5.16.

5.16 When you tap Share, the AirDrop section shows an icon for each nearby AirDrop-friendly device.

3. **Tap the icon for the person with whom you want to share the link.** The other person sees a confirmation dialog. When she taps Accept (or Save and Open in OS X Yosemite or later), her version of Safari loads and displays the page. Pie-easy!

Email has been called the "killer app" of the Internet, and it certainly deserves that title. Yes, chat and instant messaging are popular; social networks such as Facebook, Twitter, and LinkedIn get a lot of press; and blogging sites appeal to a certain type of person. However, while not everyone uses these services, it's safe to say that almost everyone uses email. You probably use email all day, particularly when you're on the go with your iPhone in tow, so learning a few useful and efficient email techniques can make your day a bit easier and save you time for more important pursuits.

Managing Your iPhone Email Accounts

Your iPhone comes with the Mail app, which is a slimmed-down version of the Mail application that's the default email program on Mac machines. Mail on the iPhone may be smaller than its OS X cousin, but that doesn't mean it's a lightweight — far from it. It has a few features and settings that make it ideal for your traveling email show. First, however, you have to set up your iPhone with one or more email accounts.

Adding an account by hand

The Mail application on your iPhone is most useful when it's set up to use an email account that you also use on your computer. That way, when you're on the road or out on the town, you can check your messages and rest assured that you won't miss anything important (or even anything unimportant, for that matter). This is most easily done by syncing an existing email account between your computer and your iPhone, and I show you how that's done in Chapter 7.

Caution

For some accounts, you need to be careful that your iPhone doesn't delete incoming messages from the server before you have a chance to download them to your computer. I show you how to set this up later in this chapter (see "Managing multiple devices by leaving messages on the server").

However, you might also prefer to have an email account that's for iPhone only. For example, if you sign up for an iPhone newsletter, you might prefer to have those messages sent to only your iPhone. That's a darn good idea, but it means that you have to set up the account on the iPhone itself, which, as you'll soon see, requires a fair amount of tapping.

How you create an account on your iPhone with the sweat of your own brow depends on the type of account you have. First, there are the six email services that your iPhone recognizes:

- **iCloud.** This is the Apple web-based email service (that also comes with applications for calendars, contacts, and more).

- **Microsoft Exchange.** Your iPhone supports accounts on Exchange servers, which are common in large organizations like corporations or schools. Exchange uses a central server to store messages, and you usually work with your messages on the server, not your iPhone. However, one of the great features in the iPhone is support for Exchange ActiveSync, which automatically keeps your phone and your account on the server synchronized.

- **Google.** This is a web-based email service run by Google.

- **Yahoo!** This is a web-based email service run by Yahoo!.

- **AOL.** This is a web-based email service run by AOL.

- **Outlook.com.** This is a web-based email service run by Microsoft.

Genius

You might think you can avoid the often excessive tapping required to enter a new email account into your iPhone by creating the account in your computer's email program and then syncing with your iPhone. That works, but there's a hitch: You must leave the new account in your email program. If you delete it or disable it, iTunes also deletes the account from the iPhone.

Your iPhone knows how to connect to these services, so to set up any of these email accounts you only need to know the address and the account password.

Otherwise, your iPhone Mail app supports the following email account types:

- **POP (Post Office Protocol).** This is the most popular type of account. Its main characteristic for your purposes is that incoming messages are stored only temporarily on the provider's mail server. When you connect to the server, the messages are downloaded to your iPhone and removed from the server. In other words, your messages (including copies of messages you send) are stored locally on your iPhone. The advantage here is that you don't need to be online to read your email. Once it's downloaded to your iPhone, you can read it or delete it at your leisure.

- **IMAP (Internet Message Access Protocol).** This type of account is most often used with web-based email services. It's the opposite of POP (sort of) because all your incoming messages, as well as copies of messages you send, remain on the server. In this case, when Mail works with an IMAP account, it connects to the server and works with the messages on the server, not on your iPhone (although it looks like you're working with the messages locally). The advantage here is that you can access the messages from multiple devices and multiple locations, but you must be connected to the Internet to work with your messages.

Your network administrator or your email service provider can let you know what type of email account you have. Your administrator or provider can also give you the information you need to set up the account. This includes your email address, the username and password you use to check for new messages (and perhaps also the security information you need to specify to send messages), the host name of the incoming mail server (typically something like mail.*provider*.com, where *provider*.com is the domain name of the provider), and the host name of the outgoing mail server (typically either mail.*provider*.com or smtp.*provider*.com).

With your account information ready, follow these steps to forge a brand-new account:

1. **On the Home screen, tap Settings.** Your iPhone opens the Settings app.

2. **Tap Mail, Contacts, Calendars.** The Mail, Contacts, Calendars screen appears.

3. **Tap Add Account.** This opens the Add Account screen, as shown in Figure 6.1.

4. **You have two ways to proceed:**

   - **If you're adding an account for iCloud, Exchange, Google, Yahoo!, AOL, or Outlook.com, tap the corresponding logo.** In the account information screen that appears, enter your name, email address, password, and an account description. Tap Next, make sure the Mail switch is set to On, tap Save, and you're done!

   - **If you're adding another account type, tap Other and continue with Step 5.**

6.1 Use the Add Account screen to choose the type of email account you want to add.

5. **Tap Add Mail Account to open the New Account screen.**

6. **Use the Name, Email, and Description text boxes to enter the corresponding account information, and then tap Next.**

7. **Tap the type of account you're adding: IMAP or POP.**

8. **In the Incoming Mail Server section, use the Host Name text box to enter the host name of your provider's incoming mail server, as well as your username and password.**

9. **In the Outgoing Mail Server (SMTP) section, use the Host Name text box to enter the host name of your provider's outgoing (SMTP) mail server.** If your provider requires a username and password to send messages, enter those as well.

10. **Tap Save.** Your iPhone verifies the account info and then returns you to the Mail settings screen with the account added to the Accounts list.

Specifying the default account

If you've added two or more email accounts to your iPhone, Mail specifies one of them as the default account. This means that Mail uses this account when you send a new message, when you reply to a message, and when you forward a message. The default account is usually the first account you add to your iPhone. However, you can change this by following these steps:

1. **On the Home screen, tap Settings.** The Settings app appears.

2. **Tap Mail, Contacts, Calendars.** Your iPhone displays the Mail, Contacts, Calendars screen.

3. **Near the bottom of the Mail section, tap Default Account.** This opens the Default Account screen, which displays a list of your accounts. The current default account is shown with a check mark beside it.

4. **Tap the account you want to use as the default.** Your iPhone places a check mark beside the account.

Temporarily disabling an account

The Mail app checks for new messages at a regular interval. If you have several accounts configured in Mail, this incessant checking can put quite a strain on your iPhone battery. To ease up on the juice, you can disable an account temporarily to prevent Mail from checking it for new messages. Here's how:

1. **On the Home screen, tap Settings.** Your iPhone displays the Settings app.

2. **Tap Mail, Contacts, Calendars.** The Mail settings screen appears.

3. **Tap the account you want to disable.** Your iPhone displays the account's settings.

4. **Depending on the type of account, use one of the following techniques to temporarily disable the account:**

6.2 For an iCloud, Exchange, Google, Yahoo!, AOL, or Outlook.com account, tap the Mail switch to Off.

- **For an iCloud, Exchange, Google, Yahoo!, AOL, or Outlook.com account, tap the Mail switch to Off, as shown in Figure 6.2.** If the account syncs other types of data, such as contacts and calendars, you can also turn off those switches, if you want.

- **For a POP or IMAP account, tap the Account switch to Off.**

When you're ready to work with the account again, repeat these steps to turn the Mail switch or the Account switch back to On.

Deleting an account

If an email account has grown tiresome and boring (or you just don't use it anymore), you should delete it to save storage space, speed up sync times, and save battery power. Follow these steps:

1. **On the Home screen, tap Settings.** The Settings app appears.

2. **Tap Mail, Contacts, Calendars.** The Mail settings screen appears.

3. **Tap the account you want to delete.** This opens the account's settings.

4. **At the bottom of the screen, tap Delete Account.** Your iPhone asks you to confirm.

5. **Tap Delete Account.** Your iPhone returns you to the Mail settings screen, and the account no longer graces the Accounts list.

Switching to another account

When you open the Mail app, you usually see the Inbox folder of your default account. If you have multiple accounts set up on your iPhone and you want to see what's going on with a different account, follow these steps to make the switch:

1. **On the Home screen, tap Mail to open the Mail app.**

2. **Tap the Back button (the left-pointing arrow that appears in the top left corner of the screen but below the status bar).** The Mailboxes screen appears, as shown in Figure 6.3.

3. **Tap the account you want to work with:**

   • **If you want to see only the account's Inbox folder, tap the account name in the Inboxes section of the Mailboxes screen.**

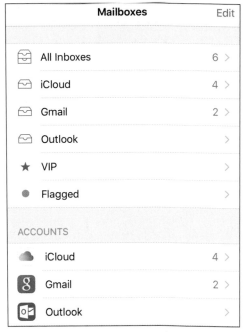

Mailboxes	Edit
✉ All Inboxes	6 >
✉ iCloud	4 >
✉ Gmail	2 >
✉ Outlook	>
★ VIP	>
● Flagged	>
ACCOUNTS	
☁ iCloud	4 >
8 Gmail	2 >
o Outlook	>

6.3 Use the Mailboxes screen to choose another email account.

- **If you want to see all the account's available folders, tap the account name in the Accounts section of the Mailboxes screen.** Mail displays a list of the account's folders, and you then tap the folder you want to work with.

Configuring Email Accounts

Setting up an email account on your iPhone is one thing, but making that account do useful things — or sometimes, anything at all — is quite another. The next few sections take you through a few useful settings that help you to get more out of email and to troubleshoot email problems.

Managing multiple devices by leaving messages on the server

In today's increasingly mobile world, it's not unusual to find you need to check the same email account from multiple devices. For example, you might want to check your business account not only using your work computer but also using your home computer, or using your iPhone while commuting or traveling.

If you need to check email on multiple devices, you can take advantage of how POP email messages are delivered over the Internet. When someone sends you a message, it doesn't come directly to your computer. Instead, it goes to the server that your Internet service provider (or your company) has set up to handle incoming messages. When you ask Apple Mail to check for new messages, it communicates with the POP server to see if any messages are waiting in your account. If so, Mail downloads those messages to your computer and then instructs the server to delete the copies of the messages stored on the server.

The trick, then, is to configure Mail so that it leaves copies of the messages on the POP server after you download them. That way, the messages are still available when you check messages using another device. Fortunately, the intuitive folks who designed the version of Mail on your iPhone must have understood this, because the program automatically sets up POP accounts to do just that. Specifically, after you download any messages from the POP server to your iPhone, Mail leaves the messages on the server.

Here's a good overall strategy that ensures you can download messages on all your devices, but prevents messages from piling up on the server:

- Let your main computer be the one that controls deleting the messages from the server. In OS X, the default setting in Mail is to delete messages from the server after one week, and that's fine.

● Set up all your other devices — particularly your iPhone — to not delete messages from the server.

It's a good idea to check your iPhone POP accounts to ensure they're not deleting messages from the server. To do that, or to use a different setting — such as deleting messages after a week or when you delete them from your Inbox — follow these steps:

1. **On the Home screen, tap Settings.** The Settings app appears.

2. **Tap Mail, Contacts, Calendars.** Your iPhone opens the Mail, Contacts, Calendars settings screen.

3. **Tap the POP account you want to configure.** The account's settings screen appears.

4. **Near the bottom of the screen, tap Advanced.** Your iPhone displays the Advanced screen.

5. **Tap Delete from Server.** The Delete from Server screen appears.

6. **Tap Never.** If you prefer that your iPhone delete messages from the server automatically, tap either Seven days or When removed from Inbox.

Fixing outgoing email problems by using a different server port

For security reasons, some Internet service providers (ISPs) insist that all their customers' outgoing mail must be routed through the ISP's Simple Mail Transport Protocol (SMTP) server. This usually isn't a big deal if you're using an email account maintained by the ISP, but it can lead to the following problems if you are using an account provided by a third party (such as your website host):

● Your ISP might block messages sent using the third-party account because it thinks you're trying to relay the message through the ISP's server (a technique often used by spammers).

● You might incur extra charges if your ISP allows only a certain amount of SMTP bandwidth per month or a certain number of sent messages, whereas the third-party account offers higher limits or no restrictions at all.

● You might have performance problems, with the ISP taking much longer to route messages than the third-party host.

● You might think you can solve the problem by specifying that the third-party host's outgoing mail is sent by default through port 25. When you use this port, the outgoing mail goes through the ISP's SMTP server.

To work around the problem, many third-party hosts offer access to their SMTP server via a port other than the standard port 25. For example, the iCloud SMTP server (smtp.icloud.com) also accepts connections on ports 465 and 587. Here's how to configure an email account to use a nonstandard SMTP port:

1. **On the Home screen, tap Settings.** You see the Settings app.

2. **Tap Mail, Contacts, Calendars.** The Mail, Contacts, Calendars settings screen appears.

3. **Tap the POP account you want to configure.** The account's settings screen appears.

4. **Near the bottom of the screen, tap SMTP.** Your iPhone displays the SMTP screen.

5. **In the Primary Server section, tap the server.** Your iPhone displays the server settings.

6. **In the Outgoing Mail Server section, tap Server Port and then type the port number.**

Configuring authentication for outgoing mail

Because spam is such a big problem these days, many ISPs now require SMTP authentication for outgoing mail, which means that you must log on to the SMTP server to confirm that you're the person sending the mail (as opposed to some spammer spoofing your address). If your ISP requires authentication on outgoing messages, you need to configure your email account to provide the proper credentials.

If you're not too sure about any of this, check with your ISP. If that doesn't work out, by far the most common type of authentication is to specify a username and password (this happens behind the scenes when you send messages). Follow these steps to configure your iPhone email account with this kind of authentication:

1. **On the Home screen, tap Settings.** Your iPhone displays the Settings app.

2. **Tap Mail, Contacts, Calendars.** The Mail settings screen appears.

3. **Tap the POP account you want to configure.** The account's settings screen appears.

4. **Near the bottom of the screen, tap SMTP.** Your iPhone displays the SMTP screen.

5. **In the Primary Server section, tap the server.** Your iPhone displays the server's settings screen.

6. **In the Outgoing Mail Server section, tap Authentication.** Your iPhone displays the Authentication screen.

7. **Tap Password.**

8. **Tap Back to return to the server settings screen.**

9. **In the Outgoing Mail Server section, type your account username in the User Name box and the account password in the Password box.**

10. **Tap Done.**

Configuring Email Messages

The rest of this chapter takes you through a few useful and timesaving techniques for handling email messages on your iPhone.

Creating email VIPs

Somebody once said that the world doesn't have an information overload problem; it has a filter problem. In other words, the tsunami of information that comes your way every day wouldn't be such a headache if you had the tools to separate the important from the trivial, the useful from pointless, the steak from the sizzle.

iOS Mail offers one such tool: the VIP list. This is a simple list of people that you designate as important. From an email perspective, "important" means people whose messages you want to read right away because they always contain information that's useful or interesting to you. To find messages from these people, you normally have to wade through the sea of messages in your various account inboxes (or the All Inboxes mailbox, which combines all your accounts). With the VIP list, however, Mail sets up a special VIP inbox that shows messages only from your VIPs, so they're easily located. Also, the VIP feature is part of the Notification Center, so you see a special banner alert whenever you receive a message from one of your VIPs. Take that, information overload!

Genius

If you just want to know when someone responds to a particular message you've sent, the VIP list isn't the best tool for that. Instead, when you're composing the message, tap the Subject line, tap the bell icon that appears on the right, and then tap Notify Me. This tells Mail to display a notification when you receive a reply to the message.

Follow these steps to set up your VIP list:

1. **On the Home screen, tap Mail to open the Mail app.**

2. **If you're currently viewing an inbox, return to the Mailboxes screen.**

3. **Tap VIP.** Mail displays the VIP List screen.

4. **Tap Add VIP.** Mail opens the All Contacts screen.

5. **Tap the contact you want to designate as a VIP.** Mail adds the contact to the VIP list.

6. Repeat Steps 4 and 5 until you've added all your VIPs. Figure 6.4 shows the VIP list with a few names added. Note that if you need to delete a VIP, you can tap Edit and then tap the red Delete icon beside the contact.

❮ Mailboxes	**VIP List**	Edit
Aldus Bembo		>
Alex Blandman		>
Carlos Hernandez		>
Christina Berglund		>
Victoria Ashworth		>
Add VIP…		
	VIP Alerts	

6.4 Use the new VIP list to filter your incoming mail by displaying messages from important people in the VIP mailbox.

Note

After you've added a VIP or three, tapping the VIP inbox displays recent messages from your important folks. To return to the VIP List screen, instead, tap the blue Info icon that appears to the right of the VIP inbox in the Mailboxes screen.

Emailing a link to a web page

The web is all about finding content that's interesting, educational, and, of course, fun. And if you stumble across a page that meets one or more of these criteria, then the only sensible thing to do is share your good fortune with someone else, right? So, how do you do that? Some pages are kind enough to include an Email This Page link (or something similar), but you can't count on having one of those around. Instead, the usual method is to copy the page address, switch to your email program, paste the address into the message, choose a recipient, and then send the message.

And, yes, with the copy-and-paste feature, you can do all that on your iPhone, but boy, that sure seems like a ton of work. So are you stuck using this unwieldy method? Not a chance (you probably knew that). Your iPhone includes a great little feature that enables you to plop the address of the current Safari page into an email message with just a couple of taps. You then ship out the message and you've made the world a better place.

Here's how it works:

1. **Use Safari to navigate to the page you want to share.**

2. **Tap the Share icon (the arrow) in the menu bar.** Safari displays a dialog with several options.

3. **Tap Mail.** This opens a new email message. As you can see in Figure 6.5, the new message already includes the page title as the Subject and the page address in the message body.

4. **Choose a recipient for the message.**

5. **Edit the message text as you see fit.**

6. **Tap Send.** Your iPhone fires off the message and returns you to Safari.

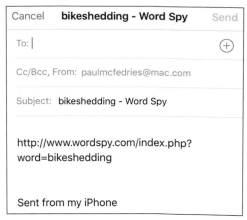

Cancel	**bikeshedding - Word Spy**	Send

To: | ⊕

Cc/Bcc, From: paulmcfedries@mac.com

Subject: bikeshedding - Word Spy

http://www.wordspy.com/index.php?
word=bikeshedding

Sent from my iPhone

6.5 When you tap the Mail Link to this Page option, your iPhone creates a new email message with the page title and address already inserted.

Creating iCloud message folders

In your email program on your computer, you've no doubt created a lot of folders to hold different types of messages that you want or need to save: projects, people, mailing list gems, and so on. This is a great way to reduce Inbox clutter and organize the email portion of your life.

Of course, these days the email portion of your life extends beyond your computer and probably includes a lot of time spent on your iPhone. Wouldn't it be great to have that same folder convenience and organization on your favorite phone? Happily, you can. If you have an iCloud account, any folders (technically, Apple calls them mailboxes) that you create on your iCloud account — either on your computer or on the iCloud site — are automatically mirrored on the iPhone Mail app.

Even better, you can create new iCloud message folders right from the comfort of your iPhone. Here's how:

1. **On the Home screen, tap Mail to open the Mail app.**

2. **Display the Mailboxes screen.**

3. **In the Accounts section, tap your iCloud account.** Mail displays the iCloud folders list.

4. **Tap Edit.** Mail opens the iCloud folders list for editing.

5. **Tap New Mailbox.**

6. **Type a name for the new folder.**

7. **Tap the Mailbox Location and then tap the folder in which you want to store your new folder.**

8. **Tap Save.** Mail adds the folder, and iCloud propagates the change to the cloud.

9. **Tap Done.**

Note

To move a message to your new folder, display the iCloud Inbox folder, tap the message, tap the Move icon (the folder), and then tap the new folder.

Attaching a file from iCloud Drive

If you've been using iCloud Drive to store documents in the cloud, you might need to share one of those documents with someone else over email. You'd normally log on to iCloud Drive to do this, but you can actually send an iCloud Drive file attachment directly from the comfort of your iPhone. Here's how it works:

1. **In Mail, start a new message, address it, and add a Subject.**

2. **Tap and hold an empty section of the message for a few seconds.**

3. **In the menu that appears, tap More (the right-pointing arrow).**

4. **If you don't see the Add Attachment command, tap More a second time.**

5. **Tap Add Attachment.** Mail opens the iCloud Drive screen.

6. **Open a folder, if needed, and then tap the file.** Mail attaches the file to your message.

Formatting email text

We're all used to rich text email messages by now, where formatting such as bold and italics is used to add pizzazz or emphasis to our e-musings. iOS Mail gives you a limited set of formatting options for text: bold, italics, and underline. It's not much, but it's a start, so here are the steps to follow to format text in the Mail app:

1. **In your email message, tap within the word or phrase you want to format.** The Mail app displays the cursor.

2. **Tap the cursor.** Mail displays a set of options.

3. **Tap Select.** Mail selects the word closest to the cursor.

4. **If needed, drag the selection handles to select the entire phrase you want to format.** Mail displays a set of options for the selected text.

5. **Tap the arrow on the right side of the options.** Mail displays more options.

6. **Tap the BIU button.** Mail displays the Bold, Italics, and Underline buttons, as shown in Figure 6.6.

7. **Tap the formatting you want to apply.** Mail leaves the formatting options on the screen, so feel free to apply multiple formats, if needed.

8. **Tap another part of the screen to hide the formatting options.**

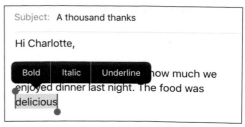

Subject: A thousand thanks

Hi Charlotte,

| Bold | Italic | Underline |

how much we enjoyed dinner last night. The food was delicious

6.6 You can format email text with bold, italics, or underline.

Genius

If you're composing a message on your computer and decide to work on it later, your mail program stores the message as a draft that you can reopen any time. The Mail app doesn't *appear* to have that option, but it does. In the message window, tap Cancel (unintuitive, I know!) and then tap Save Draft. When you're ready to resume editing, open the account in the Mailboxes screen, tap Drafts, and then tap your saved message.

Creating a custom iPhone signature

Email signatures can range from the simple — a signoff such as "Cheers," or "All the best," followed by the sender's name — to baroque masterpieces filled with contact information, snappy quotations, even text-based artwork! On your iPhone, the Mail app takes the simple route by adding the following signature to all your outgoing messages (new messages, replies, and forwards):

```
Sent from my iPhone
```

I like this signature because it's short, simple, and kind of cool (I, of course, *want* my recipients to know that I'm using my iPhone). If that default signature doesn't rock your world, you can create a custom one that does. Follow these steps:

1. **On the Home screen, tap Settings.** Your iPhone opens the Settings app.

2. **Tap Mail, Contacts, Calendars.** You see the Mail, Contacts, Calendars settings screen.

3. **Tap Signature.** The Signature screen appears.

4. **If you have multiple accounts and you prefer to create a unique signature for each one, tap Per Account.** If, instead, you leave the All Accounts item selected, Mail will use the same signature for all your accounts.

5. **Tap the default signature to open it for editing.** If you tapped Per Account in Step 4, tap the signature for the account you want to work with.

6. **Type the signature you want to use.** Mail saves your new signature as you type.

Continuing a Mac email message on your iPhone

I mentioned earlier that the Mail app is a scaled-down version of the OS X Mail application. If the Mail application has some features you want to use, you can now start your message on your iPhone and the use the Handoff feature to continue composing (complete with the same address-ees, Subject line, and body text) using your Mac. For this to work, your Mac must be running OS X Yosemite or later, your iPhone must be running iOS 8 or later, both machines must be signed in to the same iCloud account, and your iPhone must be within about 30 feet of your Mac. When your iPhone comes within that range, a Mail app icon appears to the left of the OS X Dock, and you click that icon to open the message in the Mail application.

Note

As I write this, only Macs that support Bluetooth 4.0 can use Handoff. To check, click the Apple icon, click About This Mac, click System Report, click Bluetooth, then read the LMP Version. If it says 0x6, then your Mac supports Bluetooth 4.0. Also, you need to turn on Handoff support for your Mac. Open System Preferences, click General, and then click to activate the Allow Handoff between this Mac and your iCloud devices check box.

Disabling remote images in messages

A lot of messages nowadays come not just as plain text but with fonts, colors, images, and other flourishes. This fancy formatting, called either rich text or HTML, makes for a more pleasant email experience, particularly when using images in messages, because who doesn't like a bit of eye candy to brighten his day?

Unfortunately, getting images into your email messages can sometimes be problematic:

- **A cellular connection might cause trouble.** For example, it might take a long time to load the images, or if your data plan has an upper limit, you might not want a bunch of email images taking a big bite out of that limit.

- **Not all email images are benign.** A *web bug* is an image that resides on a remote server and is added to an HTML-formatted email message by referencing an address on the remote server. When you open the message, Mail uses the address to download the image for display within the message. That sounds harmless enough, but if the message is junk email, it's likely that the address also contains either your email address or a code that points to your email address. So when the remote server gets a request to load the image, it knows not only that you've opened the message but also that your email address is legitimate. So, not surprisingly, spammers use web bugs all the time because, for them, valid email addresses are a form of gold.

Note

HTML, which stands for Hypertext Markup Language, is a set of codes that folks use to put together web pages.

The iPhone Mail app displays remote images by default. To disable remote images, follow these steps:

1. **On the Home screen, tap Settings.** Your iPhone opens the Settings app.

2. **Tap Mail, Contacts, Calendars.** You see the Mail, Contacts, Calendars settings screen.

3. **Tap the Load Remote Images switch to Off.** Mail saves the setting and no longer displays remote images in your email messages.

Preventing Mail from organizing messages by thread

In the Mail app, your messages get grouped by thread, which means the original message and all the replies you've received are grouped together in the account's Inbox folder. This is usually remarkably handy, because it means you don't have to scroll through a million messages to locate the reply you want to read.

Mail indicates a thread by displaying a double arrow (>>) instead of a single arrow (>) to the right of the first message in the thread, as shown in Figure 6.7. Tap the message to see a list of the messages in the thread, and then tap the message you want to read.

Organizing messages by thread is usually convenient, but not always. For example, sometimes you view your messages and scroll through them by tapping the Next (downward-pointing arrow) and Previous (upward-pointing arrow) buttons. When you come to a thread, Mail jumps into the thread and you then scroll through each message in the thread, which can be a real hassle if the thread contains a large number of replies.

If you find that threads are more hassle than they're worth, you can follow these steps to configure Mail to no longer organize messages by thread:

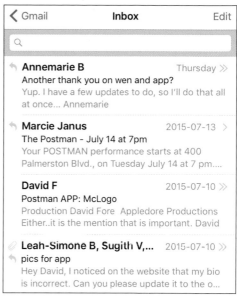

6.7 If you see a double arrow (>>) on the right side of a message, that tells you there are multiple messages in the thread.

1. **On the Home screen, tap Settings.** Your iPhone opens the Settings app.

2. **Tap Mail, Contacts, Calendars.** You see the Mail, Contacts, Calendars settings screen.

3. **Tap the Organize By Thread switch to Off.** Your iPhone saves the setting and no longer organizes your messages by thread.

Maintaining messages with gestures

If you have a long list of messages to process, Mail can help speed things up by enabling you to use gestures to perform basic message maintenance right from the account Inbox. Here's a summary:

● **To mark a message as read, swipe right on the message and then tap Read (see Figure 6.8).**

6.8 Swipe right on a message to mark it as read.

● **To flag a message, perform a short swipe left on the message and then tap Flag (see Figure 6.9).**

6.9 Swipe left on a message to flag it.

● **To see more message options, perform a short swipe left on the message, and then tap More.** The menu that appears includes the commands Reply, Forward, Flag, Mark as Read, Move to Junk, Move Message, and Notify Me.

● **To delete a message, either perform a short swipe left on the message and then tap Trash, or perform a long swipe left on the message until it disappears from the Inbox.**

Configuring Mail's swipe options

You saw in the previous section that Mail can make processing your messages a lot easier by letting you use swipe gestures to mark messages as read and flag messages. Even better, you have a bit of control over which tasks Mail presents when you swipe:

1. **On the Home screen, tap Settings.** Your iPhone opens the Settings app.

2. **Tap Mail, Contacts, Calendars.** You see the Mail, Contacts, Calendars settings screen.

3. **Tap Swipe Options to open the Swipe Options screen.**

4. **Tap Swipe Left, tap the action you want to see when you swipe left, then tap Swipe Options to return to the previous screen.**

5. **Tap Swipe Right, tap the action you want to see when you swipe right, then tap Swipe Options to return to the previous screen.**

Marking all messages as read

You saw in the previous section that you can use a swipe-right gesture to mark a message as read right from the Inbox. This is no big whoop for five or ten messages, but a very big whoop indeed for dozens or even hundreds of messages.

Happily, that annoyance needn't be added to your iOS gripe list because the Mail app also gives you a simple way to mark *everything* as read in one (more or less) fell swoop:

1. **In the Mail app, open the mailbox you want to manage.**

2. **Tap Edit.** Mail puts the mailbox into Edit mode.

3. **Tap Mark All.** Mail asks what you want marked.

4. **Tap Mark as Read.** Mail marks every message in the mailbox as having been read. Sweet!

Controlling email with Siri voice commands

You can use the Siri voice recognition app to check, compose, send, and reply to messages, all with simple voice commands. Tap and hold the Home button (or press and hold the Mic button of the iPhone headphones, or the equivalent button on a Bluetooth headset) until Siri appears.

To check for new email messages on your iCloud account, you need only say "Check email" (or just "Check mail"). You can also view a list of iCloud messages as follows:

- **Displaying unread messages.** Say "Show new email."

- **Displaying messages where the subject line contains a specified topic.** Say "Show email about *topic*," where *topic* is the topic you want to view.

- **Displaying messages from a particular person.** Say "Show email from *name*," where *name* is the name of the sender.

To start a new email message, Siri gives you a lot of options:

- **Creating a new message addressed to a particular person.** Say "Email *name*," where *name* is the name of the recipient. This name can be a name from your Contacts list or someone with a defined relationship, such as "Mom" or "my brother."

- **Creating a new message with a particular subject line.** Say "Email *name* about *subject*," where *name* defines the recipient, and *subject* is the subject line text.

- **Creating a new message with a particular body.** Say "Email *name* and say *text*," where *name* is the recipient and *text* is the message body text.

In each case, Siri creates the new message, displays it, and then asks if you want to send it. If you do, you can either say "Send" or tap the Send button.

If you have a message displayed, you can send back a response by saying "Reply." If you want to add some text to the response, say "Reply *text*," where *text* is your response.

You can also use Siri within Mail to dictate a message. When you tap inside the body of a new message, the keyboard that appears shows a Mic icon beside the spacebar. Tap the Mic icon and then start dictating. Here are some notes:

- For punctuation, you can say the name of the mark you need, such as "comma" (,), "semicolon" (;), "colon" (:), "period" or "full stop" (.), "question mark" (?), "exclamation point" (!), "dash" (–), or "at sign" (@).

- You can enclose text in parentheses by saying "open parenthesis," then the text, and then "close parenthesis."

- To surround text with quotation marks, say "open quote," then the text, then "close quote."

- To render a word in all uppercase letters, say "all caps" and then say the word.

- To start a new paragraph, say "new line."

- You can have some fun by saying "smiley face" for :-), "wink face" for ;-), and "frown face" for :-(.

- To spell out a word (such as "period" or "colon"), say "No caps on, no space on," spell the word, and then say "No space off, no caps off."

When you're finished, tap Done.

How Do I Synchronize My iPhone?

Your iPhone can function perfectly well on its own. After all, you can use it to create your own bookmarks, email accounts, contacts, and appointments; you can download music and other media from the iTunes Store; and you can take your own photos using its built-in cameras. If you want to use your iPhone as a stand-alone device, no one can stop you, but I'm not sure why you'd want to. With all the great iPhone synchronization features, you can also share tons of useful and fun content on your computer using your iPhone. This chapter shows you how to master syncing your iPhone and your Mac or Windows computer.

Connecting Your iPhone to Your Computer

When the iPhone was first released, it looked as though we might have finally arrived at that glorious day when computers and devices could just sort of *sense* each other's presence and begin a digital conversation without requiring something as inelegant as a *physical* connection. Ugh. However, even though the fancy-schmancy iPhone supported *three* wireless technologies — Wi-Fi, Bluetooth, and cellular — exchanging data between it and a Mac or PC required a wired connection.

Well, I'm happy to report that those days are behind us. Sort of. Yes, you can still use a cable to connect your iPhone and your computer, but iOS also supports *wireless* connections via Wi-Fi. The next couple of sections provide the details.

Connecting via USB

Although iOS supports Wi-Fi syncing, USB connections are still important for those times when you want to use iTunes to change your sync settings. To make an old-fashioned USB-style connection, you can proceed in a couple of ways:

- **USB cable.** Use the cable that came with your iPhone to attach the USB connector to a free USB port on your Mac or Windows PC. Then attach the other end of the cable to the 8-pin Lightning connector port on the bottom of the iPhone.

- **Dock.** Use the cable that came with your iPhone to attach the USB connector to a free USB port on your Mac or Windows PC and then attach the other end of the cable to the Lightning port on the back of the dock. Now insert your iPhone into the dock cradle.

The first time you connect your iPhone to your computer, iTunes displays a dialog telling you that you haven't chosen to have your iPhone trust this computer. Meanwhile, on your iPhone, you see a Trust This Computer? dialog. Tap Trust to proceed, and in iTunes click Continue.

Connecting via Wi-Fi

As long as your iPhone and your computer are connected to the same Wi-Fi network, the Wi-Fi connection happens automatically, but only if you prepare your iPhone. Specifically, you need to follow these steps:

1. **Connect your iPhone to your computer.**

2. **In iTunes, when your iPhone appears in the Devices list, click it.** In iTunes 12, the Devices list appears to the left of the My Music button, as shown in Figure 7.1.

3. **In the Summary tab, select the Sync with this iPhone over Wi-Fi check box.**

4. **Click Apply.** iTunes configures your iPhone to sync over Wi-Fi.

5. **Disconnect your iPhone.** Your iPhone remains in the iTunes Devices list without being physically connected to your computer.

After you do all that, you're ready to sync over Wi-Fi, as I describe a bit later in this chapter.

Devices list

7.1 After you connect your iPhone, it appears in the iTunes Devices list.

Synchronizing Your iPhone Automatically

Start with the look-ma-no-hands syncing scenario, where you don't have to pay the slightest attention: automatic syncing. If the amount of iPhone-friendly digital content you have on your Mac or Windows PC is less than the capacity of your iPhone, then you have no worries because you know it's all going to fit. All you have to do is turn on your iPhone and connect it to your computer.

That's it! iTunes opens automatically and begins syncing your iPhone (and, as an added bonus, it also begins charging the iPhone battery). Your iPhone displays the Sync icon in the menu bar (see Figure 7.2) while the sync runs, and, unlike in older versions of iOS, you can use your iPhone while the sync is running.

Sync icon

7.2 While your iPhone is in midsync, you see the Sync icon in the menu bar.

Bypassing the automatic sync

What do you do if you want to connect your iPhone to your computer, but you don't want it to sync? I'm not talking about switching to manual syncing full time (I get to that in a second). Instead, I'm talking about bypassing the sync one time only. For example, you might want to connect your iPhone to your computer just to charge it (assuming you either don't have the optional dock or don't have it with you). Or perhaps you just want to use iTunes to eyeball how much free space is left on your iPhone or check for software updates.

Caution You don't need to use iTunes to see how much free space is left on your iPhone. On the Home screen, tap Settings, tap General, and then tap About. In the About screen that slides in, the Available value tells you how many gigabytes (or megabytes) of free space you have to play with.

Whatever the reason, you can tell iTunes to hold off the syncing this time by using one of the following techniques:

- **Mac.** Connect the iPhone to the Mac and then quickly press and hold the Option and ⌘ keys.

- **Windows.** Connect the iPhone to the Windows PC and then quickly press and hold the Ctrl and Shift keys.

When you see that iTunes has added your iPhone to the Devices list, you can release the keys.

Troubleshooting automatic syncing

Okay, so you connect your iPhone to your computer and then nothing happens. iTunes doesn't wake from its digital slumber or, if iTunes is already running, it sees the iPhone but refuses to start syncing. What's up with that?

It could be a couple of things. First, connect your iPhone, switch to iTunes on your computer, and then click your iPhone in the Devices list. On the Summary tab (see Figure 7.3), make sure the Automatically sync when this iPhone is connected check box is selected.

7.3 Select the Automatically sync when this iPhone is connected check box.

If that check box was already selected, then you need to delve a bit deeper to solve the mystery. Follow these steps:

1. **Open the iTunes preferences:**

    - **Mac.** Choose iTunes ⇨ Preferences, or press ⌘+. (period).

    - **Windows.** Choose Edit ⇨ Preferences, or press Ctrl+. (period).

2. **Click the Devices tab.**

3. **Deselect the Prevent iPods, iPhones, and iPads from syncing automatically check box.**

4. **Click OK to put the new setting into effect and enable automatic syncing once again.**

Synchronizing Your iPhone via Wi-Fi

The capability to sync your iPhone with your computer without a wire in sight is one of the nicest iOS features. If you're sitting in your easy chair or relaxing on the front porch, who wants to get up, go to the computer, connect your iPhone, and then run a sync just to get, say, the latest podcasts? As long as your iPhone is plugged in and is connected to the same Wi-Fi network as your computer, you can run the sync by barely moving a muscle.

Follow these steps to sync with iTunes right where you are by using Wi-Fi:

1. **Make sure your computer is running and connected to the same Wi-Fi network as your iPhone.**

2. **On the iPhone Home screen, tap Settings.** The Settings app appears.

3. **Tap General.**

4. **Tap iTunes Wi-Fi Sync.**

5. **Tap Sync Now.** Your iPhone syncs with iTunes on your computer.

Synchronizing Your iPhone Manually

One fine day, you'll be minding your own business and performing what you believe to be a routine sync operation when a dialog will appear telling you that your iPhone "cannot be synced because there is not enough free space to hold all of the items." Groan! This most unwelcome dialog means just what it says: There's not enough free space on your iPhone to sync all the content from your computer. You have a couple of ways you can handle this:

- **Remove some of the content from your computer.** This is a good way to go if your iPhone is really close to having enough space. For example, the dialog may say that your computer wants to send 100MB of data, but your iPhone has only 98MB of free space. In this case, you can get rid of a few megabytes of stuff on your computer, and you're back in the sync business.

- **Synchronize your iPhone manually.** This means that you no longer sync everything on your computer. Instead, you handpick what playlists, podcasts, audiobooks, and so on are sent to your iPhone. It's a bit more work, but it's the way to go if there's a big difference between the amount of content on your computer and the amount of space left on your iPhone.

First, note that iTunes does *not* support syncing information such as contacts, calendars, email accounts, and bookmarks directly between iTunes and an iPhone. Instead, you must configure your Mac or PC to sync this data to your iCloud account, and then configure your iPhone to have this data synced from your iCloud account. See Chapter 13 for the details.

Syncing data manually

I'll get into a more detailed discussion of syncing music and photos shortly, but for now here are the general steps you'll follow to manually select which data to sync with your iPhone:

1. **In iTunes, click your iPhone in the Devices list.**

2. **Click the tab that corresponds to the type of data you want to sync.** For example, to set up syncing for podcasts, click the Podcasts tab.

3. **Select the Sync *Type* check box.** Here, *Type* is the type of data you selected in Step 2. For example, if you're syncing podcasts, then you select the Sync Podcasts check box.

4. **Choose how you want iTunes to select the items to sync:**

   - For some types of content (such as music, books, and tones), you select either All *Type* (where, again, *Type* is the type of content) or Selected *Type*. If you choose the latter, you then select the check box beside each item you want to include in the sync (for an example, see Figure 7.5 a bit later in this chapter).

   - For other types of content (such as podcasts, movies, and TV shows), you either select or deselect the Automatically Include check box. If you select this check box, you then use the accompanying list to choose how much to include (such as All or 5 Most Recent); if you deselect this check box, you then select the check box beside each item you want to include in the sync (as shown using podcasts as an example in Figure 7.4).

5. **Click Apply.** iTunes syncs your iPhone using the new settings.

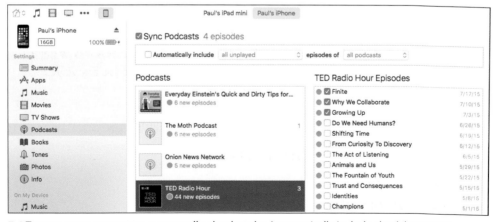

7.4 To sync some content types manually, deselect the Automatically Include check box and then select the items individually.

Syncing music and music videos

To get the most out of the Music app's music and video capabilities, you need to know all the ways you can synchronize these items. For example, if you use the Music app primarily as a music player and your iPhone has more disk capacity than you need for all your digital audio, feel free to throw all your music onto the player. On the other hand, your iPhone might not have much free space, or you might only want certain songs and videos on the player to make it easier to navigate. Not a problem! You can configure iTunes to sync only the songs that you select.

Genius Something I like about syncing playlists is that you can estimate in advance how much space your selected playlists will usurp on the iPhone. In iTunes, click the playlist and then examine the status bar, which tells you the number of songs in the playlist, its total duration, and — most significantly — its total size.

Before getting to the specific sync steps, you need to know that there are three ways to manually sync music and music videos:

- **Playlists.** With this method, you specify the playlists that you want iTunes to sync. Those playlists also appear on your iPhone Music app. This is by far the easiest way to manually sync music and music videos because you usually just have a few playlists to select. The downside is if you have large playlists and run out of space on your iPhone, the only way to fix the problem is to remove an entire playlist. Another bummer with this method is that you can only sync all or none of your music videos.

- **Check boxes.** With this method, you specify what songs and music videos are synced by selecting the little check boxes that appear beside every song and video in iTunes. This is precise syncing for sure, but because your iPhone can hold thousands of songs, it's also a lot of work.

- **Drag and drop.** With this method, you click and drag individual songs and music videos, and drop them on the iPhone icon in the iTunes Devices list. This is an easy way to get a bunch of tracks on your iPhone quickly. However, iTunes doesn't give you any way of tracking what files you've dragged and dropped.

Here are the steps to follow to sync music and music videos using playlists:

1. **In iTunes, click your iPhone in the Devices list.**
2. **Click the Music tab.**
3. **Select the Sync Music check box.**

4. **Select the Selected playlists, artists, albums, and genres option.**

5. **Select the check box beside each playlist, artist, album, and genre you want to sync, as shown in Figure 7.5.**

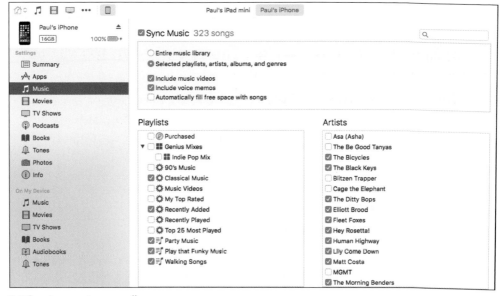

7.5 Syncing music manually.

6. **Select the Include music videos check box if you also want to add your music videos into the sync mix.**

7. **Select the Include voice memos check box if you also want to sync voice memos recorded on your iPhone.**

Genius

If you have a lot of music that has been ripped at a high bit rate (say, 256 Kbps or higher), those songs will take up a lot of space on your iPhone. To fix this, click the Summary tab and then select the Convert higher bit rate songs to *X* AAC check box, where *X* is the converted bit rate you want to use: 128, 192, or 256 Kbps.

8. **If you want iTunes to fill up any remaining free space on your iPhone with a selection of related music from your library, select the Automatically fill free space with songs check box.**

9. **Click Apply.** iTunes syncs your iPhone using the new settings.

Here are the steps to follow to sync using the check boxes that appear beside each track in your iTunes Music library:

1. **In iTunes, click your iPhone in the Devices list.**

2. **Click the Summary tab.**

3. **Select the Sync only checked songs and videos check box.**

4. **Click Apply.** If iTunes starts syncing your iPhone, click the Cancel button (X) in the iTunes status window to stop it.

5. **Either click Music in the Library list or click a playlist that contains the tracks you want to sync.** If a track's check box is selected, iTunes syncs it with your iPhone. If a track's check box is deselected, iTunes doesn't sync it with your iPhone. If the track is already on your iPhone, iTunes removes it.

6. **In the Devices list, click your iPhone.**

7. **Click the Summary tab.**

8. **Click Sync.** iTunes syncs just the selected tracks.

Genius

If you download a music video from the web and then import it into iTunes (by choosing File ⇨ Import), iTunes adds the video to its Movies library. To display it in the Music library instead, open the Movies library, right-click the music video, and then click Get Info. Click the Video tab and use the Kind list to choose Music Video. Click OK. iTunes moves the music video to the Music folder.

You can also use iTunes to drag tracks from the Music library (or any playlist) and drop them on your iPhone. There are two techniques you can use:

- **Select one or more tracks.** If all the tracks are together, Shift+click the first track, hold down Shift, and then click the last track. If the tracks are scattered all over the place, hold down ⌘ (or Ctrl in Windows) and click each track — right-click any selected track, click Add to Playlist, and then click your iPhone in the menu that appears.

- **Click the iTunes Playlists tab.** Notice that your iPhone appears in the Devices list. Either click and drag a playlist, or click a playlist and click and drag a track, and drop it on your iPhone, as shown in Figure 7.6.

7.6 In the Playlists tab, you can drag a song or playlist and drop it on your iPhone.

Syncing computer photos to your iPhone

No media collection on an iPhone is complete without a few choice photos to show off around the water cooler. One way to get those photos is to take them with the built-in digital cameras on your iPhone. However, if you have some good pics on your computer, you can use iTunes to send them to the iPhone. Note that Apple supports a number of image file types in addition to the most common TIFF and JPEG formats, including BMP, GIF, JPG2000 or JP2, PICT, PNG, PSD, and SGI.

Note

If you have another photo-editing application installed on your computer, chances are it will also appear in the Sync photos from list.

If you use your computer to process a lot of photos and you want to take copies of some (or all) of them with you on your iPhone, then follow these steps to sync them:

1. **In iTunes, click your iPhone in the Devices list.**

2. **Click the Photos tab.**

3. **Select the Sync Photos from check box.**

4. **Choose an option from the pop-up menu:**

   - **Photos (Mac only).** Choose this item to sync the photos, albums, and events you've set up in the Photos app.

   - **Choose folder.** Choose this command to sync the images contained in a folder you specify.

   - **Pictures (or My Pictures in some versions of Windows).** Choose this item to sync the images in the Pictures (or My Pictures) folder.

5. **Select the photos you want to sync.** The controls you see depend on what you chose in Step 4:

   - **If you chose Photos.** In this case, you get two further options: Select the All photos and albums option to sync your entire Photos library. Select the Selected Albums option, and then select the check box beside each item you want to sync.

   - **If you chose either Pictures or Choose folder.** In this case, select either the All photos option or the Selected folders option. If you select the latter, select the check box beside each subfolder you want to sync.

6. **Click Apply.** iTunes syncs the iPhone using your new photo settings.

Note iTunes doesn't sync exact copies of your photos to the iPhone. Instead, it creates what Apple calls TV-quality versions of each image. These are copies of the images that have been reduced in size to match the iPhone screen size. This not only makes the sync go faster, but it also means the photos take up much less room on your iPhone.

Syncing iPhone photos to your computer

If you create a Safari bookmark on your iPhone, that bookmark is transferred automatically via iCloud from the iPhone to the default web browser on your computer. That's a sweet deal, and it also applies to contacts and appointments. Unfortunately, it doesn't apply to media files that, with one exception, travel along a one-way street from your computer to your iPhone.

Ah, but then there's that one exception, and it's a good one. If you take any photos using the built-in cameras on your iPhone, the sync process reverses itself and enables you to send some (or all) of those images to your computer.

Note

Actually, there's a second exception to the one-way media syncing rule. If you use the iTunes app on your iPhone to purchase or download music, those files are transferred to your computer during the next sync. iTunes creates a Store category called Purchased on *iPhone* (where *iPhone* is the name of your iPhone). When the sync is complete, you can find your music there, as well as in the Music library.

The iPhone-to-computer sync process bypasses iTunes entirely. Instead, your computer deals directly with your iPhone and treats it just as though it was some garden-variety digital camera. How this works depends on whether your computer is a Mac or a Windows PC, so I use separate sets of steps.

To sync your iPhone camera photos to your Mac, follow these steps:

1. **Connect your iPhone to your Mac.** Photos opens, adds your iPhone to the Import tab, and displays the photos from the Camera Roll album for your iPhone, as shown in Figure 7.7.

7.7 When you connect your iPhone to your Mac, Photos shows up to handle the import of the photos.

2. **If you want Photos to delete the imported photos from your iPhone, click Settings (the gear icon) and then click Delete Items After Import.**

3. **If you want to import only some of the photos, click each one you want.**

4. **Start the import:**

● **If you're importing every photo, click Import All New Photos.** If you have one or more videos in your Camera Roll, this button will say Import All New Items, instead.

● **If you're importing only some of the photos, click Import *X* Selected (where *X* is the number of photos you've selected).**

Here's how things work if you're syncing with a Windows 10, Windows 8, or Windows 7 PC (these steps assume you've installed Windows Live Photo Gallery from the Windows Live Essentials site):

Genius

If you don't have Windows Live Photo Gallery installed, you can still access your iPhone photos in Windows 10, 8, or 7. In Windows 10, click File Explorer, and then click This PC. In Windows 8, click Desktop, click File Explorer, and then click Computer; in Windows 7, choose Start ⇨ Computer. Double-click your iPhone in the Portable Devices group. Open the Internal Storage folder, then the DCIM folder, and then the folder that appears (which will have a name such as 800AAAAA). Your iPhone photos appear and you can then copy them to your computer.

1. **Connect your iPhone to your Windows PC.**

2. **Open Windows Live Photo Gallery.**

3. **Choose Home ⇨ Import.** The Import Photos and Videos dialog box appears.

4. **Click the Icon for your iPhone, and then click Import.** Windows Live Photo Gallery connects to your iPhone to gather the photo information.

5. **Select the Import all new Items now option.** If you'd prefer to select the photos you want to import, select the Review, organize and group Items to import option. Then click Next, use the dialog box to choose the photos you want, and skip to Step 7.

6. **Type a tag for the photos.** A tag is a word or short phrase that identifies the photos.

7. **Click Import.** Windows Live Photo Gallery imports the photos.

Here's how things work if you're syncing with a Windows 10, 8.1, or 8 PC that doesn't have Windows Live Photo Gallery:

1. **Connect your iPhone to your Windows PC.** The AutoPlay notification appears.

2. **Click the notification and then click Import Photos and Videos.** The Photos app loads and displays the photos from your iPhone's Camera Roll. If you don't see the notification, open Photos, right-click the screen, click Import, and then click Apple iPhone.

3. **Click each photo you want to import.** You can also click Select All to import everything.

4. **Click Import.** Windows imports the photos and then opens the import folder.

Syncing photos via iCloud

Syncing photos from your computer isn't difficult, but it seems more than a little old-fashioned in this increasingly wireless age. Fortunately, if you have an iCloud account, you can place your feet firmly in the modern era by using the Photo Stream feature to sync photos without even looking at a USB cable. Photo Stream automatically syncs photos you take using your iPhone cameras to your iCloud account, which then downloads them to your computer, your iPad, or any other device associated with your account. Similarly, if you upload photos to iCloud using another device, those photos are synced automatically to your iPhone.

Follow these steps to activate Photo Stream on your iPhone:

1. **In the iPhone Home screen, tap Settings.** The Settings app appears.

2. **Tap Photos & Camera.**

3. **Tap the My Photo Stream switch to On.**

Genius

If you want to store your entire photo library in the cloud, thus making it available to all your iCloud-connected devices, tap the iCloud Photo Library switch to On.

Preventing your iPhone from sending photos to your computer

Each time you connect your iPhone to your computer, you see iPhoto (on your Mac), the AutoPlay dialog box (in Windows). This is certainly convenient if you actually want to send photos to your computer, but you might find that you do that only once in a blue moon. In that case, having to deal with iPhoto or a dialog box every time could cause even the most mild-mannered among us to start pulling hair out.

If you prefer to keep your hair, you can configure your computer not to pester you about getting photos from your iPhone.

Note Configuring your computer not to download photos from your iPhone means that in the future, you'll either need to reverse the setting to get photos or manually import them.

Here's how you set this up on your Mac:

1. **Click Spotlight, type image, and then click Image Capture.** The Image Capture application opens.

2. **In the Devices list, click your iPhone.**

3. **Click the Connecting this iPhone opens menu in the lower-left corner of the window, and then choose No application, as shown in Figure 7.8.**

4. **Choose Image Capture ⇨ Quit Image Capture.** Image Capture saves the new setting and then shuts down. The next time you connect your iPhone, iPhoto ignores it.

7.8 In the Image Capture Preferences window, choose No application to prevent iPhoto from starting when you connect your iPhone.

Follow these steps to convince Windows not to open the AutoPlay dialog box each time you connect your iPhone:

1. **Open the Default Programs window:**

   • **Windows 10.** In the taskbar's Search box, type **default** and then click Default Programs.

   • **Windows 8.** In the Start screen, type **default** and then click Default Programs.

   • **Windows 7 or Windows Vista.** Choose Start ⇨ Default Programs to open the Default Programs window.

2. **Click Change AutoPlay settings.** The AutoPlay dialog box appears.

3. **In the Devices section, open the Apple iPhone list and choose Take no action, as shown in Figure 7.9.**

4. **Click Save.** Windows saves the new setting. The next time you connect your iPhone, you won't be bothered by the AutoPlay dialog box.

7.9 In the Apple iPhone list, choose Take no action to prevent the AutoPlay dialog box from appearing when you connect your iPhone.

How Can I Get More Out of Audio Features on My iPhone?

Although the eye candy of the gorgeous screen garners the lion's share of kudos and huzzahs, your iPhone offers quite a bit of ear candy as well. With numerous audio accessories available, and with the built-in Music and iTunes apps, your iPhone packs a real audio punch. This chapter takes you on a tour of these audio features and shows you how to get the most out of them to maximize your listening pleasure.

Getting More Out of the Music App

Your iPhone is a full-fledged digital music player thanks to its built-in Music app, which you can fire up any time you want by tapping the Music icon in the Home screen's Dock. In the next few sections, you learn a few useful techniques that help you get more out of the Music app.

Navigating the Music app

The most recent incarnation of the Music app incorporate features of the Apple Music service which, after a free trial, will set you back $9.99 per month for an individual, or $14.99 per month for a family. If you're just interested in listening to the music on your phone, then you might find the configuration of the new app confusing (I know I did). Here are the basic steps to follow to navigate the app:

1. **In the iPhone Dock, tap Music to launch the app.**

2. **Tap My Music in the menu bar at the bottom of the screen.** This shows you the music that's on your iPhone.

3. **Tap the Category list, which appears about a third of the way down the screen and has Artists selected by default.** You see a list of all the categories you can use, as shown in Figure 8.1.

4. **Tap the category you want to use.**

5. **To play, create, or edit playlists, tap Playlists in the menu bar.** See "Working with Playlists," later in this chapter.

6. **To listen to online radio stations curated by Apple, tap Radio in the menu bar and then sign in with your Apple ID, if prompted.**

7. **To follow bands, singers, and other music artists, tap Connect in the menu bar and then sign in with your Apple ID, if prompted.**

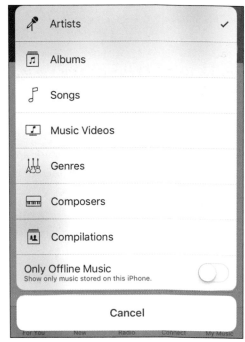

8.1 The categories available in the My Music section of the Music app.

Controlling music with Siri voice commands

If you're using your iPhone in a hands-free environment, you can still control your music by using the handy Siri app, which recognizes a number of music-related voice commands. To get started, tap and hold the Home button (or press and hold the mic button of the iPhone headset, or the equivalent button on a Bluetooth headset) until the Siri screen appears.

The most basic music voice commands mimic the on-screen controls you see when you play a song. That is, while a song is playing, you can speak any of the following commands to control the playback:

- "Pause."
- "Play."
- "Next track (or next song)."
- "Previous track (or previous song)."

In each case, your iPhone repeats the command back to you so you know whether it heard you correctly. You can also get more sophisticated by speaking commands that use roughly the following format:

Verb object subject.

Here, *verb* is the action you want the Music app to take, which will most often be play; *object* is the type of item you want to work with, such as a song, album, or playlist; and *subject* is the particular item you want included in the action, such as the name of a song, album, playlist, or artist. Here are a few examples:

- "Play songs by the Submarines."
- "Play album *Blue Horse.*"
- "Play some blues."
- "Play playlist My Top Rated."

Again, Siri confirms the command by saying it back to you (for example, "Playing songs by the Submarines").

Here are a few more voice commands to play with:

- **"Shuffle."** Activates the Music app's Shuffle mode.

- **"Shuffle *playlist*."** Plays the specified playlist in Shuffle mode.

- **"Skip."** Skips to the next track.

- **"What song is this?"** Tells you the name of the current song and artist. Siri responds, "Naming that tune," and then identifies the song, as shown in Figure 8.2.

This sounds like 'The Golden Age' by The Asteroids Galaxy Tour.

The Golden Age
by The Asteroids Galaxy Tour ▶

ⓢ SHAZAM

8.2 Ask Siri "What song is this?" and most of the time you get the name of the song, the artist, and the album.

Genius

The "What song is this?" command works with songs external to your iPhone, such as tunes you're hearing on the radio or in a coffee shop. Siri has the Shazam music-recognition engine built in, so it can recognize almost any recorded music and even provides you with a link to purchase the song.

Answering an incoming call while listening to music on the headset

If you're listening to music on your iPhone and a call comes in, you obviously don't want the caller to be subjected to Tame Impala at top volume. Fortunately, your iPhone smartphone is smart enough to know this, and it automatically pauses the music. If you have your iPhone headset on when the call arrives, use the following techniques to deal with it:

- **Answer the call.** Press and release the headset mic button (it's the plastic button on one of the headset cords).

- **Decline the call (send it directly to voicemail).** Press and hold the mic button for about two seconds, and then release. If you hear a couple of beeps, you successfully declined the call.

- **End the call.** Press and release the mic button.

Using AirPlay to stream iPhone audio

If you have an Apple TV that supports AirPlay, you can use AirPlay to stream audio from your iPhone to your TV or other audio device. Here's how it works:

1. **Make sure your Apple TV is turned on.**

2. **On your iPhone, start the audio you want to stream.**

3. **Swipe up from the bottom of the screen to open the Control Center, and then tap AirPlay.** The Music app displays a menu of output choices, as shown in Figure 8.3.

4. **Tap the name of your Apple TV device.** Your iPhone streams the video to that device and, hence, to your TV or receiver.

8.3 Tap the AirPlay button in the Control Center to stream the audio to your Apple TV.

Getting More Out of the iTunes Store App

If you have a fast Wi-Fi connection going (an LTE or 3G cellular connection will do in a pinch), you can use your iPhone to purchase music directly from the iTunes Store. To get there, tap the iTunes Store icon in the Home screen.

Creating a custom iTunes Store menu bar

Just like the Music app, the iTunes Store also presents you with a series of browse buttons, each one of which represents a section or feature of the mobile version of the iTunes Store. For example, tapping the Search browse button enables you to search for artists, albums, songs, and more.

You see four browse buttons in the default menu bar: Music, Movies, TV Shows, and Search. A fifth button called More displays a list of five more browse buttons. Here's a summary of all nine:

- **Music.** Enables you to browse and purchase music on the iTunes Store using the Genres, Featured, and Charts tabs.

- **Movies.** Enables you to browse movie content on the iTunes Store and then buy or rent movies to watch on your iPhone.

- **TV Shows.** Enables you to browse TV series content on the iTunes Store and then buy episodes to watch on your iPhone.

- **Search.** Enables you to search the iTunes Store.

- **Tones.** Enables you to browse ringtones on the iTunes Store using the New Releases, Top Tens, and Genres tabs.

- **Genius.** Displays Genius-generated lists of music, movies, and TV shows based on your current content in these categories.

- **Purchased.** Displays a list of songs that you have purchased from the iTunes Store.

- **Downloads.** Lists the current downloads in progress. This button appears only while content is downloading from the iTunes Store.

If there's a browse button on the More list that you use all the time, you can move it to the menu bar for easier access. Here's how:

1. **On the Home screen, tap iTunes to open the iTunes app.**

2. **Tap More in the menu bar.**

3. **Tap Edit.** Your iPhone displays the Configure screen, which lists all the browse buttons.

4. **Drag a browse button that you want to add to the menu bar and drop it on whatever existing menu bar browse button you want it to replace.** For example, if you want to replace the TV Shows browse button with Purchased, drag the Purchased button and drop it on TV Shows. Your iPhone replaces the old browse button with the new one.

5. **Repeat Step 4 to add any of your other preferred browse buttons to the menu bar.**

6. **Tap Done to save the new menu bar configuration.**

Redeeming an iTunes gift card

If you've been lucky enough to receive an iTunes gift card or gift certificate for your birthday or some other special occasion (or just for the heck of it), you'd normally use the iTunes Store on your computer to redeem it. However, if you're not at your computer and the gift card is burning a hole in your pocket, don't fret: You can redeem the gift card right on your iPhone. Here's how:

1. **Sign in to the iTunes Store on your iPhone.** You do this by tapping Settings, tapping iTunes & App Store, tapping Sign In, typing your iTunes Store username and password, and then tapping Sign In.

2. **On the Home screen, tap iTunes Store.** The iTunes Store screen appears.

3. **Tap any content-related browse button in the menu bar, such as Music, Movies, or TV Shows.**

4. **Scroll to the bottom of the screen and then tap Redeem.** You might need to type your iTunes password at this point. iTunes displays the Redeem screen.

5. **To use the iPhone camera to enter the redeem code, tap Use Camera, and then align the white box on-screen with the box containing the redeem code.** Otherwise, tap You Can Also Enter Your Code Manually and then type the code from the gift card or gift certificate.

6. **Tap Redeem.** iTunes redeems the gift card and adds the amount to your iTunes Store credit.

Genius

To view your current iTunes Store credit amount, tap any content-related browse button in the menu bar, scroll down to the bottom of the screen, tap your Apple ID, and then tap View Apple ID.

Creating a Custom Ringtone

Your iPhone comes stocked with a few dozen predefined ringtones. Although some of them are amazingly annoying, you ought to be able to find one you can live with. If you can't, or if you crave something unique, you can create a custom ringtone and use that.

In earlier versions of iTunes, the easiest way to cobble together a custom ringtone was to convert a song you purchased through the iTunes Store. Unfortunately, that feature was removed in iTunes 10. You can always purchase ringtones in the iTunes Store, but there are still a couple of techniques you can use to create a custom (and free!) ringtone, as the next couple of sections show.

Using iTunes to create a custom ringtone

The old Create Ringtone command may be gone from iTunes, but that application still comes with features that enable you to create a custom ringtone. Here's how it works:

1. **In iTunes, play the track you want to use.** While the track is playing, watch the playback time and note the start time and end time of the portion of the track you want to use as your ringtone.

2. **Choose File ⇨ Get Info, or press ⌘+I.** The track's Info dialog appears.

3. **Click the Options tab.**

Note

Ringtones can be a maximum of 40 seconds long, so select a portion of the track that is no longer than 40 seconds.

4. **Use the Start Time and Stop Time text boxes to type the starting and ending points for your ringtone snippet (see Figure 8.4), and then click OK.**

5. **With the track still selected, choose File ⇨ Create New Version ⇨ Create AAC Version.** iTunes creates a version of the track that includes only the snippet you specified in Step 4.

6. **Click the new version of the track, then choose File ⇨ Show in Finder, or press Shift+⌘+R.** A new Finder window appears with the short version of the track selected.

7. **Press Return to open the filename for editing, change the extension from m4a to m4r, and then press Return.** The m4r extension designates the file as a ringtone. OS X asks you to confirm the extension change.

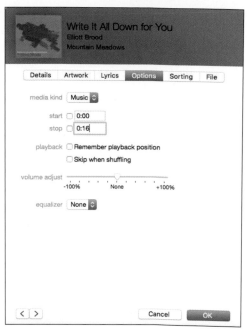

8.4 Use the Options tab to set the start and end points of the ringtone snippet.

8. **Click Use .m4r.** OS X converts the file to a ringtone.

9. **In iTunes, make sure the short version of the track is selected, and then choose Edit ⇨ Delete.** iTunes asks you to confirm.

10. **Click Delete Song.** iTunes asks if you want to move the file to the Trash.

11. **Click Keep File.**

12. **Return to the Finder window that contains the ringtone, and then double-click the file.** iTunes plays the ringtone, but more importantly, it adds the file to the Tones section of the library.

Using GarageBand to create a custom ringtone

The technique I showed you in the previous section is easy, for sure, but it's a bit convoluted. So let's look at a second, more straightforward method that uses GarageBand, the Apple application for making homebrew music.

Genius

There's no reason you have to use commercial music for your ringtone. GarageBand makes it easy to create your own music from scratch. For example, choose File ⇨ New, click Magic GarageBand, click a music genre, and then click Choose. GarageBand creates a whole song for you, and you can even add your own instruments! (Click Audition, and then click Create Project when you're done.)

First, here are the steps to follow to create a ringtone out of any song in your iTunes library:

1. **Click the GarageBand icon in the Dock to launch the program, click Ringtone, click Choose.** GarageBand starts a new project for you.

2. **Switch to iTunes, click the song you want to use for your ringtone, and then choose File ⇨ Show in Finder, or press Shift+⌘+R.** OS X displays the song's file in a Finder window.

3. **Click and drag the file and drop it inside GarageBand.** Note that you need to drop the song inside the box that includes the message "Drag Apple loops here." The program creates a new track for the song.

Note

If the song is protected by digital rights management (DRM), you won't be able to import it into GarageBand.

4. **If needed, drag the song to the left so that the beginning of the song lines up on the left edge of the box.**

5. **Click and drag the Cycle Range to the approximate area of the song you want to use for the ringtone.** The Cycle Range, pointed out in Figure 8.5, defines the portion of the song that you would use for a ringtone. If you don't see the Cycle Range tool, click the Cycle Range button pointed out in Figure 8.5.

6. **Click and drag the left edge of the Cycle Range to define the starting point of the ringtone.** By default, the left edge of the Cycle Range starts at 0:00.

7. **Click and drag the right edge of the Cycle Range to define the ending point of the ringtone.** By default, the right edge of the Cycle Range starts at 0:20.

8. **Click Play to play back the ringtone.**

9. **If your start and end points aren't quite right, repeat Steps 6 to 8 until your ringtone is set.**

10. **Choose Share ⇨ Send Ringtone to iTunes.** GarageBand converts the track to a ring-tone, and then adds it to the Tones category in iTunes.

Cycle Range tool   Cycle Range button

8.5 Use the Cycle Range to define what part of the song you want to use for the ringtone.

Note The maximum length for a GarageBand ringtone is 40 seconds.

Syncing ringtones

The next time you sync your iPhone through iTunes, follow these steps to include one or more custom ringtones in the sync:

1. **Click your iPhone in the iTunes Devices list.**

2. **Click the Tones tab.**

3. **Select the Sync Tones check box.**

4. **Select the Selected tones option.**

5. **Select the check box beside each custom ringtone you want to use on your iPhone.**

6. **Click Apply.**

To use the custom ringtone on your iPhone, tap Settings in the Home screen, tap Sounds, and tap Ringtone. Your ringtones appear at the top of the Ringtone list. Tap a custom ringtone to use the snippet as your ringtone.

Note

You can also use the Sounds screen to apply a custom ringtone to other sound events, such as incoming text messages, voicemails, and email messages.

Working with Playlists

Although you can purchase and download songs directly from the iTunes Store on your iPhone, I'm going to assume that the vast majority of your music library is cooped up on your Mac or PC, and that you're going to want to transfer that music to your iPhone. Or perhaps I should say that you're going to want to transfer *some* of that music to the iPhone. Most of us now have multigigabyte music collections and, depending on the storage capacity of your iPhone and the amount of other content you've stuffed into it (particularly videos and movies), it's likely that you want to copy only a subset of your music library.

If that's the case, iTunes gives you three choices when it comes to selecting what tunes to transfer: artist, genre, and playlists. The first two are self-explanatory, but it's the last of these three where you can take control of syncing music to your iPhone.

A *playlist* is a collection of songs that are related in some way, and using your iTunes library, you can create customized playlists that include only the songs that you want to hear. For example, you might want to create a playlist of upbeat or festive songs to play during a party or celebration. Similarly, you might want to create a playlist of your current favorite songs.

Playlists are the perfect way to control music syncing for the iPhone, so before you start transferring tunes, consider creating a playlist or three in iTunes.

Creating a favorite tunes playlist for your iPhone

Your iTunes library includes a Rating field that enables you to supply a rating for your tracks: one star for songs you don't like so much, up to five stars for your favorite tunes. You click the song you want to rate, and then click a dot in the Rating column (click the first dot for a one-star rating, the second dot for a two-star rating, and so on). Rating songs is useful because it enables you to organize your music. For example, the Playlists section features a My Top Rated playlist that includes all your four- and five-star-rated tunes, ordered by the Rating value.

Rating tracks comes in particularly handy when deciding what music to use to populate your iPhone. If you have tens of gigabytes of tunes, only some of them will fit on your iPhone. How do you choose? One possibility would be to rate your songs, and then just sync the My Top Rated playlist to your iPhone.

The problem with the My Top Rated playlist is that it includes only your four- and five-star-rated tunes. You can fit thousands of tracks on your iPhone, but it's unlikely that you've got thousands of songs rated at four stars or better. To fill out your playlist, you should also include songs rated at three stars, a rating that should include a lot of good, solid tunes.

To set this up, you have two choices:

- **Modify the My Top Rated playlist.** In iTunes, click Playlists, right-click the My Top Rated playlist, and then click Edit Smart Playlist. In the Smart Playlist dialog, click the second star, and then click OK.

- **Create a new playlist.** This is the way to go if you want to leave My Top Rated as your best music. In iTunes, choose File ➪ New ➪ Smart Playlist to open the Smart Playlist dialog. Choose Rating in the Field list, choose Is Greater Than in the Operator list, and then click the second star. Figure 8.6 shows the configured dialog. Click OK, type a title for the playlist (such as Favorite Tunes), and then press Return (or Enter).

8.6 Use the Smart Playlist dialog to create a playlist that contains your tracks rated at three stars or more.

The next time you sync your iPhone, be sure to include either the My Top Rated playlist or the Smart Playlist you created.

Creating a playlist on your iPhone

The playlists on your iPhone are those you've synced via iTunes, and those playlists are either generated automatically by iTunes or they're ones you've cobbled together yourself. However, when you're out in the world and listening to music, you might come up with an idea for a different collection of songs. It might be girl groups, boy bands, or songs with animals in the title.

Whatever your inspiration, don't do it the hard way by picking out and listening to each song one at a time. Instead, you can use your iPhone to create a playlist on the fly.

To create a playlist using the Music app, follow these steps:

1. **Open the Music app.**

2. **Tap the Playlists browse button.** If you're signed in to Apple Music, tap the My Music browse button, instead, and then tap the Playlists tab. This displays your playlists.

3. **Tap New.** The Music app displays the New Playlist screen.

4. **Type the name of your playlist.** You can also type an optional description of the playlist.

5. **Tap Add Songs to open the Add Music screen.**

6. **Tap Songs (or whatever category you prefer) and then tap each song you want to add to your list.**

7. **When you've added all the songs you want, tap Done.** The Music app displays the playlist.

8. **Tap Done.** The Music app returns to the Playlists screen.

Your playlist isn't set in stone by any means. You can get rid of songs, change the song order, and add more songs. Follow these steps:

1. **In the Music app, tap the Playlists browse button to see your playlists.**

2. **Tap your playlist.** The Music app displays the playlist settings and music.

3. **Tap Edit.** This changes the list to the editable version, as shown in Figure 8.7.

4. **To remove a song, tap the red Minus (–) button to the left of the song.** Then, tap the Delete button that appears. If you change your mind, tap the red minus button again to cancel the deletion.

5. **To move a song within the playlist, slide the song's Drag button (it's on the right) up or down to the position you prefer.**

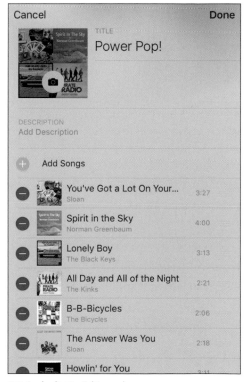

8.7 A playlist in Edit mode.

171

Note If your playlist is a bit of a mess, or if your mood suddenly changes, don't delete all the tracks one by one. Instead, open the playlist and then tap Clear. When your iPhone asks you to confirm, tap Clear Playlist.

6. **To add more tracks, tap Add Songs, tap a category, and then tap each song you want to add.**

7. **When you finish editing, tap Done.** This sets the playlist.

Customizing Your Audio Settings

Audiophiles in the crowd don't get much to fiddle with in the iPhone, but there are a few audio settings to play with. Here's how to get at them:

1. **Press the Home button to get to the Home screen.**

2. **Tap the Settings icon.** The Settings app opens.

3. **Tap the Music icon.** Your iPhone displays the Music settings screen.

You get nine settings to try:

- **Show Apple Music.** This switch toggles the Music app's Apple Music features on and off.

- **Use Cellular Data.** If you tap this setting to On, Music will play iCloud tracks and download music even when you're using a cellular connection. If you'd rather not have your music eating up your data plan, leave this switch Off.

- **Sort Albums.** Tap this setting and then tap a sort order for the Albums browse button: By Artist or By Title.

- **Genius.** If you tap this switch to On, you enable the Genius feature, which you can use to listen to music that's similar to a particular song. To set this up, display the album that contains the song, tap the song's More button (the three dots to the right of the song), and then tap Create Genius Playlist.

- **iCloud Music Library.** When this setting is On, Music shows not only the albums and songs that you've purchased on or synced to your iPhone, but also those tunes that are associated with your iCloud account that currently reside in the cloud. These albums and songs display a cloud icon with a downward pointing arrow, and you tap that icon to download the music to your iPhone. If you want to see only the music that is physically on your iPhone, tap this setting to Off.

- **iTunes Match.** If you have an iCloud account and you've shelled out the extra $24.99 per year for the iTunes Match service, tap this switch to On to activate iTunes Match on your iPhone. This means that any songs that you own that aren't available via the iTunes Store will be automatically synced to your iPhone as soon as you upload those songs to iCloud.

- **EQ.** This setting controls the built-in equalizer in your iPhone, which is actually a long list of preset frequency levels that affect the audio output. Each preset is designed for a specific type of audio: vocals, talk radio, classical music, rock, hip-hop, and a lot more. To set the equalizer, tap EQ and then tap the preset you want to use (or tap None to turn off the equalizer).

- **Volume Limit.** You use this setting to prevent the iPhone volume from being turned up too high and damaging your (or someone else's) hearing. You know, of course, that pumping up the volume while you have your EarPods on is an audio no-no, right? I thought so. However, I also know that when a great tune comes on, it's often a little too tempting to go for 11 on the volume scale. If you can't resist the temptation, use Volume Limit to limit the damage. Tap Volume Limit and then drag the Volume slider to the maximum allowed volume.

- **Sound Check.** Every track is recorded at different audio levels, so invariably you get some tracks that are louder than others. With the Sound Check feature, you can set your iPhone to play all your songs at the same level. This feature affects only the baseline level of the music and doesn't change any of the other levels, so you still get the highs and lows. If you use it, you don't need to worry about having to quickly turn down the volume when a really loud song comes on. To turn on Sound Check, in the Music settings page, tap the Sound Check switch to On.

Genius

If you're setting up an iPhone for a younger person, you should set the Volume Limit. However, what prevents the young whippersnapper from setting a higher limit? To prevent this, open Settings, tap General, tap Restrictions, and then tap Enable Restrictions. In the Set Passcode screen, tap out a four-digit code, and then tap the code again to confirm. Tap Volume Limit (it's near the bottom of the screen) and then tap Don't Allow Changes. This disables the Volume slider in the Volume Limit screen.

Your iPhone is a perk-filled device, to be sure, and one of the best of those perks is that the iPhone moonlights as a digital media player. Not only do you have the music, podcasts, and audiobooks that I talk about briefly in Chapter 8, but you also have movies, TV shows, videos, photos, and even YouTube right there in the palm of your hand. So when you're tired of calling, researching, emailing, scheduling, and other serious iPhone pursuits, you can kick back with a photo slide show or a video to relax. However, your iPhone is capable of more than just playing and viewing media. It's actually loaded with cool features that enable you to create and manipulate photos and videos, and use those files to enhance other parts of your digital life. This chapter is your guide to these features.

Getting More Out of iPhone Photos

Your iPhone comes with a couple of built-in digital cameras that you can use to take pictures while you're running around town. Taking a picture is straightforward. First, on the Home screen, tap Camera. (Alternatively, from any screen, swipe up from the bottom to display the Control Center, then tap the Camera icon.) If this is the first time you've opened the Camera app, it asks if it can use your current location. This is an excellent idea because it tags your photos with your present whereabouts, so be sure to tap OK. When the Camera app appears, make sure the Mode switch (pointed out later in Figure 9.1) is on Photo (or Square, to take a square shot). Now line up your shot and tap either the Shutter button (which, again, I point out in Figure 9.1) or the Volume Up switch, which appears on the top edge of the iPhone when you hold it in the landscape position with the Home button on the left. To view your photo, tap the Camera Roll button, which appears in the lower left corner of the Camera app screen (see Figure 9.1).

Genius When your iPhone is locked, you can get to the Camera app in seconds flat by pressing the Home button and then sliding up on the Camera icon that appears in the bottom right corner of the Lock screen.

While using the cameras may be simple, what you can do with photos on your iPhone is pretty cool. You can email photos to friends, take a photo and assign it to a contact, or make a slide show with music in the background. The large screen on your iPhone makes it the perfect portable photo album. No more whipping out wallet shots of your kids. Now you can show people your iPhone photo album!

To get to your photos, tap the Photos icon in your iPhone Home screen to display the Albums screen, which lists your photo albums. Tap an album to see its pictures, and then tap the picture you want to check out.

Understanding the iPhone camera features

Before getting to the Photos app, I should take a second here to talk about the coolest camera features found in the iPhone:

- **Rear and front-facing cameras.** The iPhone 6s and 6s Plus come with two cameras: an 12-megapixel iSight camera on the back for regular shots, and a 5-megapixel FaceTime HD camera on the front for taking self-portraits. In the Camera app, tap the Switch Camera button (pointed out in Figure 9.1) to switch between the front and rear cameras.

- **Live Photos.** The iPhone 6s and 6s Plus automatically enable this feature, which takes a series of still images for 1.5 seconds before and after you press the Shutter button. The result is a special animated JPEG image that, when pressed using 3D Touch, displays these images sequentially, resulting in what appears to be a 3-second video clip. To turn off this feature, tap the Live Photos button (pointed out in Figure 9.1).

● **Autofocus.** The iPhone cameras automatically focus on whatever subject is in the middle of the frame.

Genius Autofocus is a handy feature, except when you've got the perfect shot lined up and Autofocus kicks in and wrecks the focus or exposure (or both!). To prevent this, compose your shot and then tap and hold on the person or object you want to focus on for about three seconds (or until the focus rectangle pulses). When you release your finger, you see AE/AF Lock (short for AutoExposure/AutoFocus) at the top of the screen. Your current focus and exposure settings are now locked. Fire away!

● **Tap to set the focus and exposure.** If the subject you want to focus on is not in the middle of the frame, you can tap the subject and the iPhone automatically moves the focus to that object. It also automatically adjusts the white balance and exposure.

● **5X digital zoom.** You can zoom using the iPhone back camera. Pinch two fingers together on the screen to display the zoom slider, shown in Figure 9.1. Then tap and drag the slider right to zoom in, or left to zoom out.

● **Auto image stabilization.** The iPhone 5s and later actually takes multiple shots at the same time and combines them automatically to produce a sharp, stable image. The iPhone 6s iSight camera also features optical image stabilization, which uses the iPhone gyroscope and motion chip to precisely adjust the lens to compensate for hand shake.

● **Burst mode.** When you hold down the Shutter button in the iPhone 5s and later the Camera app takes photos at a rate of ten per second.

● **Geotagging.** The iPhone can use its built-in GPS sensor to add location data to each photo, a process called *geotagging*. This means you can organize your photos by location, which is great for vacation snaps and other trip-related photos.

Genius When you first launch the Camera app, it asks whether it can use your current location. In the case of the Camera app, if you allow this it means the app only accesses your location while you're using the app. You can control this — that is, you can toggle geotagging on and off — by launching the Settings app, tapping Privacy, tapping Location Services, tapping Camera, and then tapping either Never or While Using the App.

● **LED flash.** The iPhone has a built-in LED flash that sits right beside the rear camera, so you can take pictures at night or in extremely low-light conditions. The LED flash is in

Auto mode by default, which means it flashes automatically when the ambient light is low. To control this in the Camera app, tap the Flash button (pointed out in Figure 9.1), and then tap On (to use the flash with every shot), Off (to never use the flash), or Auto.

HDR button

Switch Camera button

Flash button

Time Delay button

Camera Roll button

Filter button

Zoom slider   Shutter button   Mode switch

9.1 Tap the screen and then drag the slider to zoom in and out.

Taking a panoramic photo

One of the biggest challenges all photographers face is capturing very wide shots, particularly landscapes. If you have a high-end digital SLR camera, you can swap out your regular lens for a wide-angle lens, but that's not an option with the iPhone. In the past, the only alternative was to take a series of side-by-side shots and then use an app such as AutoStitch or Photosynth to combine those photos into a single panoramic shot. The results were usually decent, but not always great.

That should change since the Photos app comes with its own Panorama feature. Panorama beats out other panoramic photo apps because it uses the built-in three-axis gyroscope to precisely align the images as you shoot them, even if the iPhone shakes or your pan isn't perfectly straight. The result is a seamless panoramic view of up to 240 degrees (up to a maximum image resolution of 63 megapixels).

Follow these steps to take a panoramic photo:

1. **On the Home screen, tap Camera.** The Camera app appears.

2. **Use the Mode switch to select Pano.** Camera displays the Panorama tool, shown in Figure 9.2.

3. **Position the iPhone so that the camera is pointing at the leftmost part of the panoramic scene you want to capture.** If you'd prefer to pan from right to left, instead, tap the arrow to reverse the direction.

4. **Tap the Shutter button to begin the shot.**

5. **Pan the iPhone, keeping the following pointers in mind:**

   - Pan the iPhone steadily and continuously.

   - Don't pan too fast. If you see "Slow down" on the screen, it means you're panning too quickly.

   - Don't pan in the opposite direction or Camera will end the shot.

9.2 Use the Mode switch to select Pano to see the Panorama tool.

   - Try to keep the arrow centered on the horizontal line.

   - If the arrow falls below the line, either raise the iPhone or tilt the top of the iPhone toward you.

   - If the arrow moves above the line, either lower the iPhone or tilt the top of the iPhone away from you.

6. **When your panorama is complete, tap Done.** Camera also stops the shot automatically if you pan a full 240 degrees. Camera stitches together the shots and saves the panorama to the Camera Roll.

Taking High Dynamic Range photos

Your iPhone usually takes a pretty decent picture, but it works best when the ambient light isn't too extreme — that is, not too dark or too light. In particular, your iPhone has trouble taking good photos in places where the light conditions cause a wide variation in tone. The best example is an outdoor scene on a bright, sunny day, where some parts of your subject are bathed in sunlight and others are mired in shade. This large contrast between bright and dark elements is called a *High Dynamic Range (HDR)*, and your iPhone — indeed, *any* digital camera — won't do well in these scenarios. Depending on where you focus the shot, you usually end up with either the sunlit elements overexposed and washed out or the shaded elements underexposed and murky. Either way, you lose crucial details and the photo just doesn't look right.

Fortunately, your iPhone comes with a feature called HDR that can often compensate for these problems and actually produce beautiful, detailed photos of high-contrast scenes. The HDR feature works by taking not one, not two, but *three* photos of the scene: one underexposed to capture the high-contrast areas of the scene, one overexposed to capture the low-contrast areas, and one with normal exposure. The iPhone then blends all three shots into a finished photo that — theoretically, at least — combines the best parts of each shot. No, I'm sorry to say that it doesn't work perfectly every time, but I think you'll be pleasantly surprised at how often it *does* work.

Before you get started with HDR, you need to make a decision. As I mentioned earlier, HDR takes three photos: underexposed, overexposed, and normal. By default, HDR saves the composite version that combines all three exposures, as well as the normal exposure photo. Keeping the normal exposure shot is a good idea because that photo is sometimes better than the composite version. If you don't want to clutter your iPhone Camera Roll with extra pictures — or if later you find that the normal exposure shot is rarely (or never) superior to the composite version — then you can configure HDR not to save the normal exposure.

Genius

In the Camera Roll, how do you know which photo is the HDR version and which is the normal exposure? Display the photo and tap the screen. If the photo is the HDR version, you see HDR in the upper left corner of the screen.

Note

Because the HDR feature has to take three consecutive shots, it takes a few seconds for the operation to complete. Therefore, try to keep the iPhone as steady as possible while the Saving HDR message appears on the screen.

Follow these steps:

1. **On your iPhone Home screen, tap Settings.** The Settings app appears.

2. **Tap Photos & Camera.** The Photos screen appears.

3. **In the HDR section, tap the Keep Normal Photo switch to Off.**

To take an HDR shot, open the Camera app, tap the HDR button, tap On, and then take your shot. Figure 9.3 shows a High Dynamic Range scene shot with normal exposure, and Figure 9.4 shows the HDR version of the same scene.

Taking a time-delayed photo

The term *selfie* (that is, a photo that you take of yourself, possibly with a friend or two included) was named Oxford Dictionaries' Word of the Year for 2013, which I'm sure isn't even remotely shocking news to you. You only have to look around at any event or occasion to realize that each of us has become our favorite photo subject. To make selfies even easier to shoot, just switch to the iPhone's front camera, which seems nearly tailor-made for taking selfies.

I say "nearly" because the front camera method for taking selfies does come with a couple of drawbacks:

- The front camera is low resolution compared to the rear camera, and it doesn't support flash.

- All shots must be taken more or less at arm's length, which gives every such photo a characteristic "This is me taking a selfie" look.

9.3 A High Dynamic Range scene captured with normal exposure.

9.4 The HDR version of the same scene shown in Figure 9.3.

181

Creative selfie-takers have worked around these limitations by using mirrors and other tricks, but iOS offers a simpler alternative: time-delay. This feature tells the Camera to wait for several seconds after you tap the Shutter button before taking the photo. This means your photo-taking steps change as follows:

1. **Use Switch Camera to select the camera you want to use.**

2. **Tap the Time Delay button (see Figure 9.1) and then tap the number of seconds you want to use for the delay: 3 seconds or 10 seconds.**

3. **Position the iPhone (on, say, a desk or chair) so that it's pointing toward the scene you want to shoot.**

4. **Tap Shutter.**

5. **Scurry into the frame before the shot is taken.**

Note that the Camera app takes not one photo, but a burst of 11 photos. To choose what photo you want to keep, tap Camera Roll, tap the photo burst, tap Select, tap the photo you want to keep, tap Done, and then tap Keep Only 1 Favorite.

Genius

Burst mode isn't only available when you're taking time-delayed photos. You can snap a burst of photos any time you want by tapping and holding the Shutter button.

Taking time-lapse photos

If you want to document a scene that's changing, the two standard-issue techniques are to take a new photo every so often, or switch to video mode and shoot the entire scene. These techniques work well enough, but it's a pain to have to remember to take individual shots, and for a scene that's changing slowly, a video might be overkill.

In many such cases a better solution is to use the new Time Lapse mode, which creates a video of a scene by automatically taking a picture every second or so. This saves you the hassle of taking individual shots as well as the storage space required for a full-blown video.

To take time-lapse photos, set the Mode switch to Time Lapse and then tap the Shutter button.

Preventing blurry iPhone photos

The iPhone camera hardware is gradually getting better and the iPhone generally takes pretty good shots. However, probably the biggest problem most people have with iPhone photos is blurry images, which are caused by not holding the phone steady while taking the shot.

The iPhone 6 and 6s do does offer optical image stabilization, but still there are a few things you can do to minimize or hopefully eliminate blurred shots:

- Widen your stance to stabilize your body.

- Lean your shoulder (at least) or your entire side (at best) against any nearby object, such as a wall, doorframe, or car.

- Place your free arm across your torso with your forearm parallel to the ground, then rest the elbow of your "shooting" arm (that is, the one holding the iPhone) on the free arm, which should help steady your shooting arm.

- Hold your breath while taking the shot.

- Remember that your iPhone takes the shot when you *release* the Shutter button, not when you *press* it. Therefore, keep your subject composed and yourself steadied as best you can until you lift your finger off the Shutter button.

Caution   You might be tempted to press and hold the Shutter button and release it only when you're steady. Unfortunately, that technique no longer works because pressing and holding the Shutter button initiates burst mode.

- After you release the Shutter button, keep the phone steady until the photo thumbnail appears in the lower left corner of the screen. If you move while the iPhone is finalizing the photo, you'll blur the shot.

Keep some or all of these pointers in mind while shooting with your iPhone, and you'll soon find that blurry iPhone photos are a thing of the past.

Marking a photo as a favorite

If you take a lot of photos with your iPhone (and I know you do), you'll probably like most of them, but a few will be real gems. That's great, but the problem is you must scroll through a ton of not-so-gemlike images to view your favorites. I know you don't have time for that, so what's the solution? Tell your iPhone which of your photos are your favorite ones. The Photos app maintains an album named Favorites that stores these keepers, so you can access your greatest hits with just a few taps.

To mark a photo as a favorite, display it in the Camera Roll and then tap the Favorite button (the heart icon).

Scrolling, rotating, zooming, and panning photos

You can do quite a lot with your photos after they are in your iPhone, and it isn't your normal photo browsing experience. You aren't just a passive viewer because you actually have some control over what you see and how the pictures are presented.

You can use the following techniques to navigate and manipulate your photos:

- **Scroll.** You move forward or backward through your photos by flicking. Flick from the right to left to view the next photo; flick left to right to view the previous shot. Alternatively, tap the screen, and then tap the Previous and Next buttons to navigate your photos.

- **Rotate.** When a landscape shot shows up on your iPhone, it gets letterboxed at the top (that is, you see black space above and below the image). To get a better view, rotate the screen into the landscape position and the photo rotates right along with it, filling the entire screen. When you come upon a photo with a portrait orientation, rotate the iPhone back to the upright position for best viewing.

- **Zoom.** Zooming magnifies the shot that's on the screen. There are two methods to do this:

  - **Double-tap the area of the photo on which you want to zoom in.** The iPhone doubles the size of the portion you tapped. Double-tap again to return the photo to its original size.

  - **Spread and pinch.** To zoom in, spread two fingers apart over the area you want magnified. To zoom back out, pinch two fingers together.

  - **Pan.** After you zoom in on the photo, you may find that the iPhone didn't zoom in exactly where you wanted or you may just want to see another part of the photo. Drag your finger across the screen to move the photo along with your finger — an action known as *panning*.

Note You can scroll to another photo if you're zoomed in, but it takes a lot more work to get there because the iPhone thinks you're trying to pan. For faster scrolling, return the photo to its normal size by double-tapping the screen, and then scroll.

Adding an existing photo to a contact

You can assign a photo from one of your albums to any of your contacts. This is one of my favorite iPhone features because when the person calls you, her smiling mug appears on your screen. Now that's caller ID! There are two ways to assign a photo to a contact: straight from a photo album or via the Contacts app.

First, here's how you assign a photo from a photo album:

1. **Tap Photos in the Home screen.** The Photos screen appears.

2. **Tap the photo album that has the image you want to use.**

3. **Tap the photo you want to use.** Your iPhone opens the photo.

4. **Tap the image to reveal the controls.**

5. **Tap the Activities button.** This is the icon with the arrow on the left side of the menu bar. (If you don't see the menu bar, tap the screen.) Photos displays a list of activities you can perform.

6. **Tap Assign to Contact.** A list of all your contacts appears.

7. **Tap the contact you want to associate with the photo.** The Move and Scale screen appears.

8. **Drag the image so that it's positioned on the screen the way you want.**

9. **Pinch or spread your fingers over the image to set the zoom level you want.**

10. **Tap Choose.** iPhone assigns the photo to the contact and returns you to your photo album.

Enhancing a photo

Don't worry if you have a photo that's too bright in some spots or if the color is washed out in others — the Photos app comes with an Enhance tool that can automatically adjust the color and brightness. Here's how to use it:

1. **In the Photos app, open the photo you want to fix.**

2. **Tap the photo to display the controls.**

3. **Tap Edit.** The Photos app displays its editing tools.

4. **Tap Enhance (the magic wand icon in the upper right corner).** The Photos app adjusts the color and brightness.

5. **Tap Done.** The Photos app saves your changes.

Cropping and straightening

If you have a photo containing elements that you do not want or need to see, you can often cut them out. This is called *cropping* and you can use the Photos app to do it. When you crop a photo, you specify a rectangular area of the image that you want to keep. The Photos app then discards everything outside of the rectangle. Cropping is a useful skill because it can help you give focus to the true subject of a photo. Cropping is also useful for removing extraneous elements that appear on or near the edges of a photo.

Genius

If your iPhone photos are consistently askew, turn on the Camera grid, which adds lines that divide the Camera screen into nine rectangles (that is, a 3 × 3 grid). Open the Settings app, tap Photos & Camera, and then tap the Grid switch to On. The grid is also useful for composing pictures using the Rule of Thirds, where you place your subject on one of the grid lines instead of in the middle of the screen.

As you probably know from hard-won experience, getting an iPhone camera perfectly level when you take a shot is very difficult. It requires a lot of practice and a steady hand. Despite your best efforts, you might still end up with a photo that is not quite level. To fix this problem, you can also use the Photos app to rotate the photo clockwise or counterclockwise so that the subject appears straight.

Follow these steps to crop and straighten a photo:

1. **In the Photos app, open the photo that you want to edit.**

2. **Tap the photo to display the controls.**

3. **Tap Edit.** The Photos app displays its editing tools.

4. **Tap Crop (the button to the right of Cancel).** The Photos app displays a grid for cropping and straightening, as shown in Figure 9.5.

5. **Tap and drag a corner of the grid to set the area you want to keep.**

6. **To straighten the photo, tap and drag the Straightening tool (the arc with the degree markings) left or right until the image is level.**

7. **Tap Done.** The Photos app applies the changes to the photo.

Rotate   Aspect

9.5 Tap Crop to display the cropping and straightening tools.

Genius

The fastest way to crop some photos is to tell the Photos app the dimensions you want to use for the resulting photo. Tap Aspect (pointed out in Figure 9.5), and then tap either a specific shape (Original or Square) or a specific ratio, such as 5:7 or 4:5. You then drag the photo (not the grid!) so the portion you want to keep is within the grid.

Note

The Crop feature also enables you to rotate a photo 90 degrees, say, from portrait to landscape. To do this, tap the Rotate icon (see Figure 9.5) until the photo is in the orientation you want.

Applying a filter

The stunning popularity of the Instagram app and similar apps such as Hipstamatic has created a mania for applying filters to photos. A *filter* is a special effect applied to a photo's colors to give it a different feel. The Camera app comes with a Filters icon (see Figure 9.1), as does the Photos app in Edit mode. When you tap Filter, you see nine effects that you can apply to your photo, including Mono (which gives you a black-and-white photo) and Instant (which makes the photo look as though it was taken by an old Polaroid film camera). Here's how to apply a filter to a photo using the Photos app:

1. **Open the photo you want to edit.**

2. **Tap the photo to display the controls.**

3. **Tap Edit.** The Photos app displays its editing tools.

4. **Tap Filters.** This is the button in the middle of the menu bar. Photos displays thumbnail versions of the photo that demonstrate each effect.

5. **Tap the effect you want to use.**

6. **Tap Save.** The Photos app applies the filter to the photo.

Sending a photo via email

More often than you'd think, it really comes in handy to be able to email photos from your iPhone. This is particularly true if it's a photo you've just taken with one of the iPhone cameras, because then you can share the photo pronto, without having to trudge back to your computer. You also have the option of emailing an existing photo in one of your iPhone photo albums.

187

Here are the steps to follow to email a photo:

1. **If necessary, use the Camera app to take the photo you want to send, then tap the Camera Roll button to open the Camera Roll photo album.** Otherwise, open Photos and then display the photo album that has the image you want to send.

2. **Tap the photo.** Your iPhone opens the photo.

3. **Tap the Activities button.** Your iPhone displays a list of activities you can perform.

4. **Tap Mail.** The New Message screen appears and displays the photo in the body of the message.

5. **Choose your message recipient and enter a Subject line.**

6. **Tap Send.** If the photo is large, your iPhone asks whether you want to scale the image to a smaller size.

7. **If you want to send the photo as is, tap Actual Size.** Otherwise, tap either Small or Medium to create a scaled-down version of the photo. Your iPhone sends the message and returns you to the photo.

Note

To send a photo via email, you must have a default email account set up on your iPhone. See Chapter 6 for information about setting up a default email account.

Texting a photo

The new Messages app sends text messages outside of your cellular provider's messaging system. This means that you can use the Messages app to send unlimited (yes, that's right: *unlimited*) text messages via Wi-Fi or cellular to other people using iOS devices, including iPads, iPod touches, other iPhones, as well as Macs running OS X Mountain Lion or later. You can also send a photo in a text message. Here are the steps to follow:

1. **If necessary, use the Camera app to take the photo you want to send, then tap the Camera Roll button to open the Camera Roll photo album.** Otherwise, open Photos and then display the photo album that has the image you want to send.

2. **Tap the photo.** Your iPhone opens the photo.

3. **Tap the Activities button.** Your iPhone displays a list of activities you can perform.

4. **Tap Message.** The New Message screen appears and displays the photo in the body of the message.

5. **Select a message recipient.**

6. **Type your message text.**

7. **Tap Send.** Your iPhone sends the message with the photo attached.

Sending and receiving a photo via AirDrop

Sharing a photo via email or text message works well, but it has a slightly primitive feel to it. After all, your iPhone is the ultimate wireless device, so surely there must be some way to send a photo directly from one device to another? Happily, the answer to that question is a resounding "Yes!" A feature called AirDrop is a Bluetooth service that lets two nearby devices — specifically, an iPhone 5 or later, a fourth-generation iPad or later, an iPad mini, or a fifth-generation iPod touch or later — exchange photos directly. Here are the steps to follow:

1. **Use the Photos app to open the photo you want to share.**

2. **Tap the Activities button.** The AirDrop section shows an icon for each nearby device.

3. **Tap the icon for the person with whom you want to share the photo.** The other person sees a dialog asking for permission to accept the photo. When she taps Accept, her version of the Photos app loads and displays the photo.

Posting a photo to Facebook

If you set up your Facebook account on your iPhone (I cover this in Chapter 2), you can post a photo for your friends to see. Here's how it works:

1. **In the Photos app, open the photo you want to post.**

2. **Tap the Activities button.**

3. **Tap Facebook.** The Photos app displays the Facebook dialog.

4. **Type your post text in the large text box, as shown in Figure 9.6.**

5. **To change the Facebook album where the photo will appear, tap Album, and then tap the album you want to use.**

6. **If you want to include your present whereabouts as part of the post, tap Location.**

9.6 Type some text to accompany your Facebook photo.

7. **Tap Post.** Your iPhone posts the photo to your Facebook Timeline.

Tweeting a photo

If you set up your Twitter account (or accounts) on your iPhone (again, see Chapter 2), you can use it to tweet a sweet photo to your followers. Here's how it works:

1. **In the Photos app, open the photo you want to tweet.**

2. **Tap the Activities button.**

3. **Tap Twitter.** The Photos app displays the Twitter dialog.

4. **If you added more than one account to the iPhone Twitter settings, tap Account and then tap the name of the account you want to use to send the tweet.**

5. **Type your tweet text in the large text box.**

6. **If you want to include your present whereabouts as part of the tweet, tap Location.**

7. **Tap Post.** Your iPhone posts the photo as a tweet.

Controlling photo sharing options

In the previous few sections, you learned how to share a photo via email, text message, Facebook, and Twitter. These and several other sharing options — including Flickr and iCloud — appear in the Activities screen. If you don't use some of these services, you can remove them from the Activities screen to reduce clutter. Similarly, if there are services you use most often, you can change the order so that those frequently used services appear on the left side of the Activities screen. Follow these steps:

1. **In the Photos app, open any photo.**

2. **Tap the Activities button.**

3. **Flick left on the sharing services to display the rest of the options.**

4. **Tap More.** The Activities screen appears, as shown in Figure 9.7.

5. **To remove a service from the Activities screen, tap its switch to Off.**

6. **To change the order of the services, tap and drag the icons that appear to the right of each service.**

7. **Tap Done.** Your iPhone puts the new settings into effect.

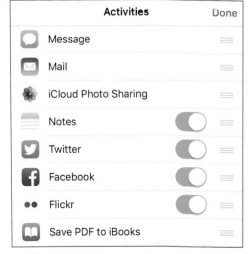

9.7 Use this Activities screen to specify which services you use with the Photos app and what order you prefer them.

Saving a photo from a text message

If someone sends you a nice photo in a text message, you might want to save it to your iPhone so you can check it out whenever you want, assign it to a contact, sync it to your computer, and so on. Follow these steps to save a photo from a text message:

1. **On the Home screen, tap Messages.** The Messages screen appears.

2. **Tap the conversation that contains the photo message.** The Messages app opens the conversation screen.

3. **Tap the photo.** Your iPhone opens the photo for viewing.

4. **Tap the Activities button.** The Activities options appear.

5. **Tap Save Image.** Your iPhone saves the image to the Camera Roll.

Genius

You can also open the text message, tap and hold the photo, then tap Save in the Edit menu that appears.

Activating your iCloud Photo Library

If you have an iCloud account, the My Photo Stream feature is turned on automatically. This feature ensures that your latest iPhone photos are not only stored in iCloud but are also sent to your other iCloud devices, such as your iPad and your iPod touch. My Photo Stream is a wonderful feature, but it could be better. For example, the copies of the photos that get stored in iCloud and your other devices are scaled-down versions of the originals. Also, My Photo Stream shares only your most recent 1,000 photos with your other devices.

To overcome these problems, iOS offers the iCloud Photo Library. This service not only stores full-resolution versions of each photo on iCloud, but it also syncs those same versions to your iCloud devices. Not only that, but iCloud Photo Library stores *all* your photos, not just your most recent ones. Or, I should say, it stores all your photos up to the size of your iCloud Photo Library storage capacity. You get 5GB of storage free with your iCloud account, and you can purchase more storage as you need it (in the U.S., the current prices are 50GB of storage for $0.99 a month, up to 1TB for $9.99 a month).

Follow these steps to turn on the iCloud Photo Library for your iPhone:

1. **Tap Settings to open the Settings app.**

2. **Tap Photos & Camera to open the Photos & Camera screen.**

3. **Tap the iCloud Photo Library switch to On.** Settings lets you know that it will activate the iCloud Photo Library as well as disable My Photo Stream.

4. **Tap OK.** Your iPhone activates the iCloud Photo Library and begins syncing your photos.

Playing a slide show with background music

Here's a little bonus that the iPhone throws your way. Yes, you can wow them back home by running a slide show, but you can positively make their jaws hit the floor when you add a music soundtrack to the show! They'll be cheering in the aisles.

Here's how you do it:

1. **Tap the Photos icon.** The Photos app appears.

2. **Open the photo album you want to use.**

3. **Tap the first photo you want to see in the slide show.**

4. **Tap the Activities button and then tap Slideshow.** The Photos app begins the slide show.

5. **Tap Options.** The Photos app displays the Slideshow Options screen.

6. **Tap Music.**

7. **Tap the preset theme music you want to play.** If you prefer to use your own music, tap iTunes Music, tap a category (such as Songs), and then tap the song you want to play.

8. **While you have the Slideshow Options screen displayed, you can also tap Theme and choose a display theme (such as the always popular Ken Burns effect), toggle the Repeat switch On or Off, and use the slider to set the speed of the show.**

9. **Tap Done.** Photos continues the slide show with your new music and options in effect.

Creating a photo album

Normally you'd use your computer to organize your photos into albums prior to syncing them to your iPhone. However, if you have been taking a lot of pictures on your iPhone and your computer is nowhere in sight, you don't have to wait to organize your pics. The Photos app enables you to create your own photo albums right on your iPhone. These albums aren't transferred to your computer when you sync, but they're handy if you need to organize your photos quickly. Here's what you do:

1. **In the Photos app, tap Albums.** The Albums screen appears. If you see an album, instead, tap Albums in the upper left corner.

2. **Tap the Add (+) button.** The Photos app prompts you for an album name.

3. **Type the name and then tap Save.** Photos displays the Moments collection, which organizes your photos by date and location.

4. **Tap each image that you want to include in your new album.** A check mark appears next to each photo you select.

5. **Tap Done.** The Photos app creates the new album, adds it to the Albums screen, and populates it with the photos you selected.

Note

To remove a custom album you no longer need, tap Albums, tap Edit, tap the red Delete icon to the left of the custom album, tap the Delete button that appears, and then tap Delete Album when Photos asks you to confirm.

Deleting a photo

If you mess up a photo using one of the iPhone cameras, you should delete it before people think you have shoddy camera skills (because we all know it was the phone's fault, right?).

You might think that deleting a photo would be a straightforward proposition. Nope, not even close. That's because your iPhone differentiates between two types of photos:

- Photos that you add to the iPhone via syncing with iTunes.
- Photos that you create directly on the iPhone by using the cameras; taking a screenshot; saving a photo from an email, text message, or web page; and so on.

Synced photos *can't* be deleted directly via the iPhone, but photos you create on the iPhone *can* be deleted. Clear as mud, I know.

To delete a photo, follow these steps:

1. **Tap Photos in the Home screen.**

2. **Tap the photo album that has the image you want to blow away.**

3. **Tap the doomed photo.** Your iPhone opens it.

Genius

What happens if you have duplicate synced photos on your iPhone if you can't delete the copies? The way you fix that is to connect the iPhone to your computer, click the iPhone in iTunes, click the Photos tab, deselect Sync Photos, and then click Apply. This removes all the synced photos from the iPhone. You then reselect Sync Photos and click Apply. You should end up with no duplicates on the iPhone.

4. **Tap the Trash icon.** The Trash icon is on the right side of the menu bar. (If you don't see the menu bar, tap the screen.) Your iPhone asks you to confirm the deletion.

5. **Tap Delete Photo.** Your iPhone tosses the photo into the trash, wipes its hands, and displays the previous photo in the album.

Getting More Out of iPhone Videos

The iPhone is a visual medium (it uses a touchscreen, after all). The large screen makes it a perfect portable media device. The Videos app organizes and plays back videos that you import from your computer. Your commute (okay, your nondriving commute) doesn't have to be boring any more. Just put on your headphones and start an episode of your favorite show.

Playing iPhone videos on your TV

You can carry a bunch of videos with you on your iPhone, so why shouldn't you be able to play them on a TV if you want? That's a good question; you can indeed connect your phone to your TV. You have to buy another cable, but that's the only investment you have to make to watch iPhone videos right on your TV.

For the iPhone 5 or later you have two choices:

- **Apple Lightning Digital AV Adapter.** This $49 cable has a Lightning connector on one end to attach your iPhone, and an HDMI connector at the other end to attach an HDMI cable that in turn connects to your TV's HDMI input port.

- **Apple Lightning to VGA Adapter.** This $49 cable has a Lightning connector on one end, and a VGA connector on the other to attach a VGA cable that connects to your TV's VGA input port.

To connect your iPhone 4s or earlier to your TV, you have two choices:

- **Apple 30-pin Digital AV Adapter.** This $45 cable has a 30-pin connector on one end that connects to the iPhone or an Apple Universal Dock. The other end has another 30-pin connector so you can connect your iPhone to a power outlet and an HDMI port that enables you to make a connection to the corresponding HDMI input on your HDTV.

- **Apple Composite AV cable.** This $45 cable plugs into the iPhone or Apple Universal Dock connector on one end and the composite inputs on your TV at the other.

The cable you choose depends on the type of TV you have. Older sets have composite inputs, more recent TVs have component inputs, and the latest sets have at least one HDMI port.

194

After connecting your cables, set your TV to the input and play your videos as you normally would.

Streaming iPhone video to Apple TV

If you have an Apple TV that supports AirPlay, you can use AirPlay to stream a video from your iPhone to your TV. Here's how it works:

1. **Make sure your Apple TV is turned on.**

2. **On your iPhone, start the video you want to stream.**

3. **Swipe up from the bottom of the screen to display the Control Center.**

4. **Tap AirPlay.** Your iPhone displays a menu of output choices.

5. **Tap the name of your Apple TV device.** Your iPhone streams the video to that device, and hence to your TV.

Mirroring the iPhone screen on your TV

You can set up a *mirrored* display, which means that what you see on your iPhone is also displayed on your TV in HD. One way to do this is to use the Apple Lightning Digital AV Adapter or the Apple 30-pin Digital AV Adapter to connect your iPhone to your TV's HDMI port. However, iOS also offers wireless AirPlay mirroring through Apple TV. As long as you have a second-generation Apple TV (and it has been updated with the latest software), you can use AirPlay mirroring to send not only videos to your TV but also photos, slide shows, websites, apps, games, and anything else you can display on your iPhone.

Follow these steps to start mirroring the iPhone screen on your TV:

1. **Turn on your Apple TV device.**

2. **On your iPhone, swipe up from the bottom of the screen to display the Control Center.**

3. **Tap the AirPlay button.** Your iPhone displays the AirPlay screen, which offers a menu of output choices.

4. **Tap the name of your Apple TV device.**

5. **Tap the Mirroring switch to On, as shown in Figure 9.8.** Your iPhone streams the screen to your Apple TV.

6. **Tap Done.**

9.8 To display your iPhone screen on your Apple TV, select your Apple TV as the AirPlay device and then tap the Mirroring switch to On.

Watching videos from a shared iTunes library

If you have iTunes Home Sharing activated on your computer, you can use your iPhone to tap in to that library and play its video content. I show you how to activate iTunes Home Sharing in Chapter 8. Assuming that's done, your next task is to configure your iPhone Videos app with the same Home Sharing Apple ID and password. (If you already did this using the Music settings, as I describe in Chapter 8, then you can skip the steps that follow.) Follow these steps:

1. **On your iPhone Home screen, tap Settings.** The Settings app appears.

2. **Tap Videos to open the Videos screen.**

3. **In the Home Sharing section, use the Apple ID and Password boxes to type the same account information that you used to set up Home Sharing in iTunes.**

Make sure you have iTunes running on the Macs or PCs where you have set up Home Sharing, open the Videos app on your iPhone, and then tap Shared. The Videos app displays icons for the available shared libraries. Tap the library you want to access, and the Videos app displays that library's video content instead of your iPhone videos.

Converting a video file to iPhone format

Your iPhone is happy to play video, but only certain formats are compatible with it. Here's the list:

● **H.264 video.** Up to 1080p, 30 frames per second, High Profile level 4.1 with AAC-LC audio up to 160 Kbps, 48 kHz, stereo audio in M4V, MP4, and MOV file formats.

● **MPEG-4 video.** Up to 2.5 Mbps, 640 × 480 pixels, 30 frames per second. Simple Profile with AAC-LC audio up to 160 Kbps, 48 kHz, stereo audio in M4V, MP4, and MOV file formats.

● **Motion JPEG video.** Up to 35 Mbps, 1280 × 720 pixels, 30 frames per second, audio in u-law PCM stereo audio using the AVI file format.

If you have a video file that doesn't match any of these formats, you might think you're out of luck. Nope. You can use iTunes to convert that video to an MPEG-4 file that's iPhone friendly. Here's how:

1. **If the video file isn't already in iTunes, choose File ➪ Add to Library, or press ⌘+O.** The Add To Library dialog appears. If the file is already in iTunes, skip to Step 3.

2. **Locate and choose your video file, and then click Open.** iTunes copies the file into the library, which may take a while depending on the size of the video file. Usually, iTunes adds the video to the Movies section of the library.

3. **In iTunes, click your movie.**

4. **Choose File ➪ Create New Version ➪ Create iPod or iPhone Version.** iTunes begins converting the video to the MPEG-4 format. This might take some time for even a relatively small video. When the conversion is complete, a copy of the original video appears in the iTunes library.

Genius   Because the converted video has the same name as the original, you should probably rename one of them so you can tell them apart when you sync your iPhone. If you're not sure which file is which, right-click one of the videos and then click Get Info. In the File tab, read the Kind value. The iPhone-friendly file has a Kind setting of MPEG-4 video file.

Recording video with an iPhone camera

Any smartphone worthy of the name should do all the things you need it to do during the course of your busy life, and one of the things you probably want to do is record events, happenings, moments, or just whatever's going on. Sure, a picture is worth the proverbial thousand words, but at 30 frames per second, a video is worth a lot more than that.

Caution   The high-definition (HD) video recording capabilities of the iPhone are so welcome that you might start shooting everything in sight. Be my guest! However, just be aware that your iPhone churns through disk space at the rapid rate of 17 Mbps when shooting 1080p video, which means each minute of video carves out nearly 130MB of disk real estate.

Your iPhone 5 or later is very smart, indeed, and it comes with a rear iSight video camera that supports 4K (3840 x 2160) recording at 30 frames per second, 1080p HD recording at 30 frames per second (up to 60 frames per second on the iPhone and 6s) and a video stabilization feature that helps to reduce shaky shots. The iPhone 5s and later also come with a Slo-Mo video setting that captures video at 120 frames per second (up to 240 frames per second on the iPhone and 6s) for slow-motion fun. (The front FaceTime HD camera supports 720p HD recording at 30 frames per second.) And, this being an iPhone and all, it's no surprise that recording a video is almost criminally easy. Here's what you do:

1. **On the Home screen, tap Camera.** The Camera screen appears.

2. **Flick the Mode switch to Video (or Slo-Mo on the iPhone 5s and later).**

3. **Tap the screen to focus the video, if necessary.**

4. **Tap the Flash icon, and then tap On, Off, or Auto.**

5. **Tap the Switch Camera icon if you want to use the front camera rather than the rear camera.**

6. **Tap the Record button.** Your iPhone starts recording video and displays the total recording time in the upper right corner of the screen.

7. **If you want to take a still photo while you're recording the video, tap the Shutter icon in the lower left corner of the screen.**

8. **When you're done, tap the Record button again to stop the recording.** Your iPhone saves the video to the Camera Roll.

Setting the recording format for video and slo-mo

As mentioned in the previous section, the iPhone 6 and later can take all things video up a notch by recording at 60 frames per second (fps). This produces super-smooth video motion, especially when filming fast-moving objects. The downside is that, at a bitrate of about 27 Mbps, each minute of 60 fps video eats up about 200MB of disk space.

If you're filming people or objects that are going really fast, you might want to slow things *way* down and record them in slow motion. In that case, your iPhone drops the resolution down to 720p, but ups the frame rate to 120 fps. It's a beautiful effect, but it consumes disk space at a rate of 31 Mbps, or about 230MB per minute. Lots of free space to burn, you say? Well, in that case you can crank up (or is it down) the slo-mo to 720p at 240 fps, which can capture even the fastest motion smoothly. The disk cost, in case you're wondering, is 42 Mbps, or about 315MB per minute.

Here are the steps to follow to select a recording format for regular and slo-mo video:

1. **On the Home screen, tap Settings.** The Settings app loads.

2. **Tap Photos & Camera.**

3. **To set the video format, tap Record Video, tap the format — 1080p HD at 30 fps or 1080p HD at 60 fps — and then tap Photos & Camera to return.**

4. **To set the slo-mo format, tap Record Slo-mo, tap the format — 720p HD at 120 fps or 720p HD at 240 fps — and then tap Photos & Camera to return.**

Editing recorded video

Okay, being able to record video at the tap of a button is pretty cool, but your iPhone tops that by also letting you perform basic editing chores right on the phone. (Insert sound of jaw hitting floor here.) It's nothing fancy — basically, you can trim video from the beginning and end of the file — but it sure beats having to first sync the video to your computer and then fire up iMovie or some other video-editing software.

Here's how to edit a video right on your iPhone:

1. **Open the Camera Roll album:**

   - **Camera app.** Tap the Camera Roll button in the lower left corner of the screen.

   - **Photos app.** Display the Albums screen and then tap Camera Roll. You can also tap the Videos album for a more direct route to your recorded videos.

2. **Tap the video you want to edit.** The Photos app displays the video and a timeline of the video along the bottom of the screen.

3. **Tap and drag the left edge of the timeline to set the starting point of the video.**

4. **Tap and drag the right edge of the timeline to set the ending point of the video.** The trimmed timeline appears surrounded by orange, as shown in Figure 9.9.

5. **Tap Play to ensure you've set the start and end points correctly.** If not, repeat Steps 3 and 4 to adjust the timeline as needed.

9.9 Use the video timeline to set the start and end points of the video footage you want to keep.

Note

Video thumbnails show a video camera icon in the lower left corner and the duration of the video in the lower right corner.

199

6. **Tap Done.** Your iPhone asks whether you want to trim the original or save the trimmed version as a new clip.

7. **Tap either Trim Original or Save as New Clip.** Your iPhone trims the video and then saves your work.

Genius

If you need more precision when trimming the timeline, tap and hold either the start trim control or the end trim control. Your iPhone expands the timeline to show more frames, which enables you to make more precise edits.

Sending a video via email

If you want to share your newly shot and edited video with someone, you can email it by following these steps:

1. **Open the Camera Roll album:**

   - **Camera app.** Tap the Camera Roll button in the lower left corner of the screen.

   - **Photos app.** Display the Albums screen and then tap Camera Roll.

2. **Tap the video you want to send.**

3. **Tap the Activities button in the lower left corner.** The Activities options appear.

4. **Tap Mail.** Your iPhone creates a new email message that includes your video as an MPEG-4 video file attachment.

5. **Fill in the rest of your message and send it.**

Note

If your video is too long to send via email, your iPhone lets you know and asks if you want to send a shorter version. If so, tap OK, use the trim control to shorten the clip, and then tap Email.

Uploading recorded video to YouTube

Of course, you want to be able to instantly record something because you can then upload that video to YouTube and share it with the world. Your iPhone is happy to help here, too, as shown by the following steps:

1. **Open the Camera Roll album:**

   - **Camera app.** Tap the Camera Roll button in the lower left corner of the screen.

   - **Photos app.** Display the Albums screen and then tap Camera Roll or Videos.

2. **Tap the video you want to share.**

3. **Tap the Activities button in the lower left corner.**

4. **Tap YouTube.** Your iPhone compresses the video and prompts you to log in to your YouTube account.

5. **Enter your YouTube username and password, and then tap Sign In.** The Publish Video screen appears.

6. **Tap a title, description, and tags for your video, and then choose a category.**

7. **If you want to upload an HD version of the video, tap HD.** HD versions of iPhone videos are more than three times larger than standard-definition versions, so uploading them takes longer.

8. **Tap Publish.** Your iPhone publishes the video to your YouTube account. This may take several minutes, depending on the size of the video. When the video is published, you see a dialog with a few options.

9. **Tap one of the following options:**

   - **View on YouTube.** Tap this option to cue up the video on YouTube.

   - **Tell a Friend.** Tap this option to send an email message that includes a link to the video on YouTube.

   - **Close.** Tap this option to return to the video.

Editing Video with iMovie for iPhone

Earlier I showed you the built-in editing feature that comes with the iPhone, which essentially boils down to being able to trim video clips. That's pretty handy, but proper video editing requires features such as adding transitions and titles, changing the theme, and adding a music track. "Ah," you might be saying to yourself, "all I have to do is sync my videos to my computer, and then use video-editing software, such as iMovie on the Mac, to do all that."

Well, yes, you can certainly do that, but what if your computer is nowhere in sight? If it's just you, your iPhone, and some cool-but-not-ready-for-primetime video, you can go well beyond the native iPhone video-editing capabilities by purchasing the iMovie for iPhone app, which is available from the App Store for $4.99. With iMovie for iPhone, you can perform many of the same tasks that you can using the full-fledged iMovie application, such as importing live or recorded videos and photos, trimming clips, adding transitions, applying a Ken Burns effect to a photo, adding titles and music tracks, applying themes, and much more.

Creating a new iMovie project

Assuming you've already purchased and installed the iMovie for iPhone app, to get started with it (which, for efficiency's sake, I just call iMovie from here on), tap the iMovie icon. In the opening screen, follow these steps to create a fresh iMovie project:

1. **Tap the Projects tab.**

2. **Tap the Add (+) button.** iMovie asks if you want to create a movie or trailer.

3. **Tap Movie.** iMovie prompts you to select a theme.

4. **Tap the theme you want to use.** You can change the theme anytime you want (see "Changing the project theme," later in this chapter).

5. **Tap Create.** iMovie saves your new project and adds it to the Projects list.

At this point, iMovie prompts you to insert or record media. I show you how this works later in this chapter.

Opening a project for editing

For the rest of this chapter, you'll be working within a specific project, so go ahead and use the Projects list to tap the one with which you want to work. You end up in the iMovie project-editing environment. Figure 9.10 shows an example of the editing environment for a project that already has clips and other media imported.

There are three main elements in the iMovie editing environment:

- **Timeline.** This is the strip along the bottom of the screen. It displays your video clips, photos, transitions, and music track.

- **Playback window.** This is the larger pane that takes up most of the top half of the window. It shows your video when you play it and when you scroll through the timeline.

- **Toolbars.** These appear to the left and right of (or, in portrait mode, above and below) the playback window. There are eight buttons (see Figure 9.10): *Back,* which returns you to the previous screen; *Record Audio,* which enables you to record a voiceover track for the video; *Camera,* which you use to import videos or photos shot with an iPhone camera; *Add Media,* which you use to import existing videos, photos, and music; *Help,* which displays descriptive labels and instructions for the current screen; *Settings,* which lets you set various project options; *Undo,* which reverses your most recent action; and *Play,* which plays your movie.

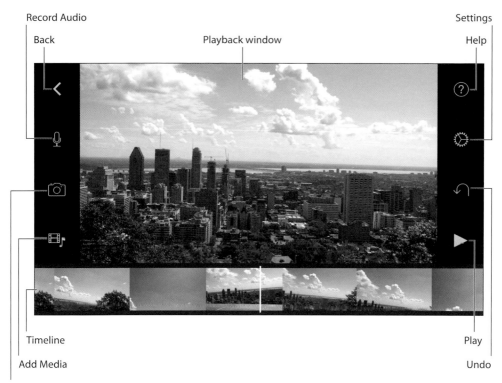

Record Audio

Settings

Back

Playback window

Help

Timeline

Play

Add Media

Undo

Camera

9.10 You see a screen similar to this when you open a video for editing in iMovie.

Importing media into your project

With your new project on the go, your first task is to import media into it. With iMovie, you can import four kinds of media: recorded video, existing video, photos, and music (which I cover later in this chapter).

Importing a video from an iPhone camera

You can record whatever is happening around you and import it directly into your iMovie project using one of the built-in iPhone cameras. Here's how you do it:

1. **Open your iMovie project.**

2. **Scroll through the timeline to the location where you want the video to appear.**

3. **Tap the Camera icon and then tap Allow if iMovie requests your current location.**
   Your iPhone switches to the Camera app, which activates the Video mode switch.

4. **Tap the Switch Camera icon to choose a different camera, if necessary.**

5. **Tap the screen to focus the video, if necessary.**

6. **Tap the red Record button.** Your iPhone starts recording video and displays the total recording time in the upper right corner of the screen.

7. **When you're done, tap the Record button again to stop recording.** iMovie displays a preview of the recorded video.

8. **If the video looks good, tap Use Video to add it to the timeline.** Otherwise, tap Retake and then reshoot the video.

Importing existing video

If you've already recorded your video or synced one from your computer, you can add it to your project timeline. Here are the steps to follow:

1. **Open your iMovie project.**

2. **Scroll through the timeline to the location where you want the video to appear.**

3. **Tap the Add Media icon.** iMovie displays the importing screen.

4. **Tap Video.**

5. **Tap a category, such as All of Recently Added**. iMovie displays thumbnails of the videos in the category you selected.

6. **Scroll through the videos until you find the one you want to import.**

7. **Double-tap the video.** iMovie adds it to the timeline.

Importing a photo from the camera

You can take a still image and import it directly into your iMovie project using one of the built-in cameras on your iPhone. Here's how you do it:

1. **Open your iMovie project.**

2. **Scroll through the timeline to the location where you want the video to appear.**

3. **Tap the Camera icon.** Your iPhone switches to the camera.

4. **Flick the Mode switch from Video to Photo.**

5. **Tap the screen to focus the photo, if necessary.**

6. **Tap the Shutter button.** Your iPhone takes the photo and displays a preview of the result.

7. **If the photo looks good, tap Use Photo to add it to the timeline.** Otherwise, tap Retake and then reshoot the photo.

Importing an existing photo

You can also import a photo to your project, which iMovie automatically animates by applying a 5-second-long Ken Burns effect (which is a pan-and-zoom effect popularized by filmmaker Ken Burns). Follow these steps to add a photo to your project:

1. **Open your iMovie project.**

2. **Scroll through the timeline to the location where you want the photo to appear.**

3. **Tap the Import icon.** iMovie displays the importing screen.

4. **Tap Photos.** iMovie displays the Photos screen.

5. **Tap the album that contains the photo you want to import.** iMovie displays thumbnails of the album's photos.

6. **Tap the photo.** iMovie adds the photo to the timeline.

Working with video clips

iMovie gives you a surprisingly complete collection of video-editing tools that enable you to move and trim clips, change transitions, work with a photo's Ken Burns effect, and add clip titles.

Moving a clip

If a clip doesn't appear where you want it, follow these steps to move it to the position you prefer:

1. **Tap and hold the middle of the clip you want to move.**

2. **Drag the clip left or right through the timeline.**

3. **Drop the clip when you reach the location you want.** iMovie moves the clip.

Trimming a clip

If an imported video clip includes footage at the beginning or end (or both) that you don't want to include in your movie, you can trim those unwanted scenes. Here are the steps to follow:

1. **Tap the clip you want to trim.** iMovie displays the trim controls, as shown in Figure 9.11.

2. **Tap and drag the left trim control to set the starting point of the clip.**

3. **Tap and drag the right trim control to set the ending point of the clip.**

4. **Tap the playback window.** iMovie saves your changes.

Genius

For more precise trimming, spread your fingers on the clip to expand it in the timeline. If you go too far, pinch the clip to shrink it.

9.11 Tap a clip to display the trimming tools.

Changing the transition between two clips

iMovie makes transitions a no-brainer because it adds them automatically between any two clips when you add videos or photos to the timeline. It also defines different transitions for each theme applied to a project. (I show you how to change themes a bit later.) If you don't like the theme transitions, you can switch to one of the built-in transitions (such as Dissolve, where the end of one clip dissolves into the beginning of the next), or you can turn off the transition altogether. You can also vary the length of the transition.

Here are the steps to follow:

1. **Tap the transition you want to change.** iMovie displays the Transition Settings window, shown in Figure 9.12.

2. **Tap the transition you want: Theme, a built-in effect (Dissolve, Slide, Wipe, or Fade), or None.**

3. **Tap the length of the transition in seconds: 0.5s, 1.0s, or 1.5s.**

4. **Tap the playback window.** iMovie saves the transition settings.

Adjusting a photo's Ken Burns effect

I mentioned earlier that when you import a photo, iMovie automatically applies a Ken Burns effect, which pans and zooms the photo. You can control the panning and zooming by following these steps:

9.12 Double-tap the transition to open the Transition Settings window.

1. **Tap the photo you want to edit.** iMovie selects the photo and displays the Ken Burns effect tools, as shown in Figure 9.13.

2. **Set the start of the pan by dragging the photo to the starting position you prefer.**

3. **Set the opening zoom level by pinching or spreading on the photo.**

4. **Tap Start.**

5. **Set the end of the pan by dragging the photo to the ending position you prefer.**

6. **Set the closing zoom level by pinching or spreading on the photo.**

7. **If you want to return to the start settings, tap End and repeat Steps 2 and 3.**

8. **Tap Done.** iMovie saves the settings.

Adding a title to a clip

You can get your movie off to a proper start by adding a title to your opening clip. iMovie offers a number of title styles that you can choose from, and it automatically adds the video location (picked up from the geolocation data supplied by the iPhone cameras) as the subtitle.

Follow these steps to add a title to any clip:

1. **Tap the clip with which you want to work.** iMovie displays the clip tools.

2. **Tap Title Style (the T icon).** iMovie opens the Title Style screen.

3. **Tap the title position you want: Center or Lower.**

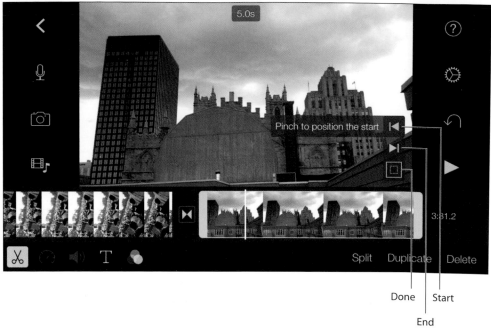

9.13 Tap the photo to display the Ken Burns effect tools.

4. **Tap the title style you want.**

5. **Tap inside the Title Text Here text box.** iMovie displays the Edit Title screen.

6. **Type the title and tap Done to return to the Title Style screen.**

7. **Tap the playback screen.** iMovie adds the title to the clip.

Removing a clip

If you add a clip accidentally or decide a clip is no longer needed, you can use either of the following techniques to remove it from your project:

- Double-tap the clip to display the clip menu bar, and then tap Delete.
- Tap and drag the clip up and off the timeline. When you release the clip, iMovie deletes it.

Working with your project

Your iMovie project is coming along nicely, with its trimmed clips, transitions, Ken Burns effects, and titles. What else can iMovie do? Three things, actually: add music, change the theme, and export your project to a movie file.

Adding a music track

What would a video be without a music track playing in the background? Boring, that's what! Fortunately, iMovie lets you add either a song from your iTunes library or an audio track from the project's current theme. Here's how it works:

1. **Tap the Add Media icon.** iMovie displays the Import screen.

2. **Tap Audio.** iMovie displays the Audio screen.

3. **Tap the music category you want to use.** To use an audio track from the project's theme, tap Theme Music; otherwise, tap an iTunes music category, such as Playlists, Albums, or Artists.

4. **Navigate the music until you locate the track you want to add.** For example, if you selected the Artists category, you'd need to select an artist and then an album.

5. **Double-tap the track.** iMovie adds the track to the bottom of the timeline, as shown in Figure 9.14.

9.14 After you select a song or audio track, iMovie displays the track as a green strip at the bottom of the timeline.

Changing the project theme

The secret to easy iMovie-making is the project theme. As you've seen, the project theme enables you to automatically apply clip transitions, title styles, and music tracks to give your movie a cohesive and consistent feel. iMovie ships with five built-in themes, so you can pick the one that best complements your movie subject.

Follow these steps to change the project theme:

1. **Open your iMovie project.**

2. **Tap the Settings icon.** iMovie displays the Project Settings screen, as shown in Figure 9.15.

9.15 In the Project Settings screen, tap a theme.

3. **Tap the theme you want to use.**

4. **If you want to apply a filter to the project, tap an item in the Project Filter section.**

5. **If you want to use the music tracks that come with the theme, tap the Theme Music switch to On.**

6. **To control how the movie fades in and out, tap either or both of the Fade In From Black and Fade Out to Black switches to On.**

7. **Tap Done.** iMovie saves your settings and updates the project with the new theme.

Naming your project

Your movie just isn't complete without a snappy title, so follow these steps to name your project:

1. **If you have your project open in the editing environment, tap Back to return to the project's main screen.**

2. **Tap the project's existing title.** iMovie opens the title for editing.

3. **Type the movie title.**

4. **Tap Done.**

Exporting your project

With your clips imported and trimmed, your transitions and titles in place, your music added and your theme applied, your movie is finally ready for prime time. Although you can play the movie within the editing environment (by tapping the Play button), you won't really be able to show it off until you export it to a movie file. iMovie gives you four choices: HD - 1080p, HD - 720p, Large - 540p, or Medium - 360p.

Follow these steps to export your project to your iPhone's photo library:

1. **If you have your project open in the editing environment, tap Back to return to the project's main screen.**

2. **Tap the Actions icon (the rectangle with the upward-pointing arrow).** iMovie displays a list of actions you can perform.

3. **Tap Save Video.** iMovie asks you to select an export size, as shown in Figure 9.16.

4. **Tap the size you want.** iMovie exports the project to a movie file, which it then stores in the Videos album within the Photos app.

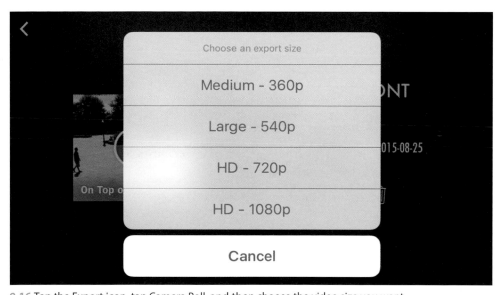

9.16 Tap the Export icon, tap Camera Roll, and then choose the video size you want.

211

Can I Use My iPhone to Manage Contacts and Appointments?

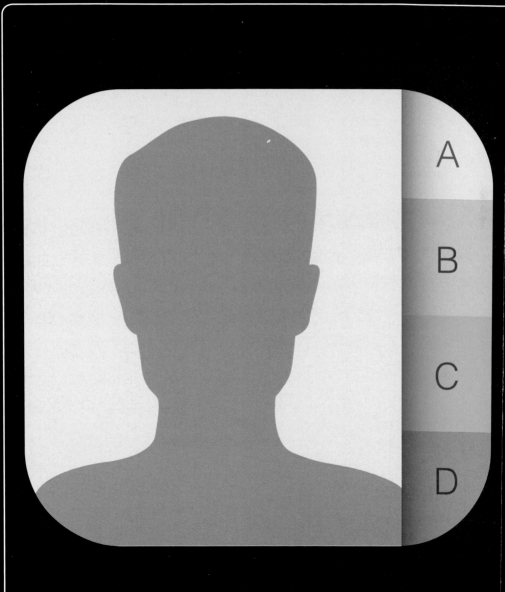

The iPhone has never just been about the technology. Yes, it looks stylish, has enough bells and whistles to cause deafness, and it just works. iPhone users don't know or care about things like antennae, flash drives, memory chips, and whatever else Apple somehow managed to cram into that tiny case. These things don't matter because iPhone has always been about helping you get things done and making your life better, more creative, and more efficient. And, as you'll see in this chapter, your iPhone can also go a long way toward making your life — particularly your contacts and your calendar — more organized.

Managing Your Contacts

One of the paradoxes of modern life is that as contact information becomes more important, you store less and less of it in the easiest database system of all — your memory. Instead of memorizing phone numbers like you used to, you now store your contact info electronically. When you think about it, this isn't exactly surprising. It's not just a landline phone number that you have to remember for each person anymore but also a cell number, email and website addresses, a Twitter username, a physical address, and more. That's a lot to remember, so it makes sense to go the electronic route. And for the iPhone, *electronic* means the Contacts app, which seems basic enough but is actually loaded with useful features that can help you get organized and get the most out of the contact management side of your life.

Creating a new contact

I show you how to sync your computer's contacts program (such as Contacts on Mac or Windows or the Outlook Contacts folder) in Chapter 7. That's by far the easiest way to populate your iPhone Contacts app with a crowd of people, but it might not include everyone in your posse. If someone's missing and you're not around your computer, you can add that person directly to your iPhone Contacts.

Begin by creating a contact with just the basic info: first name, last name, and company name. In subsequent sections, I show you how to add data such as phone numbers and email addresses. Here are the steps to follow:

1. **In the Home screen, tap the Contacts icon.** Note that, in a bit of a head scratcher, Apple has secreted the Contacts app on the second Home screen inside the Extras folder. Your iPhone opens the All Contacts screen. If you're in the Phone app, you can also tap the Contacts button.

2. **Tap the New Contact (+) button at the top right corner of the screen.** The New Contact screen appears, as shown in Figure 10.1.

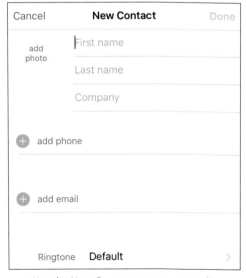

10.1 Use the New Contact screen to type the person's name and company name.

3. **Tap the First box and then type the person's first name.** If you're jotting down the contact data for a company or some other inanimate object, skip to Step 5.

4. **Tap the Last box and then type the person's surname.**

5. **If you want to note where the person works (or if you're adding a business to your Contacts app), tap the Company box and type the company name.**

6. **Tap Done.** Contacts saves the new contact and returns you to the All Contacts screen.

Editing an existing contact

Now that your new contact is off to a flying start, you can go ahead and fill in details, such as phone numbers, addresses (email, web, and real world), and anything else you can think of (or have the patience to enter into your iPhone; it can be a lot of tapping!). The next few sections take you through the steps for each type of data. When you're done, be sure to tap Done to preserve all your hard work.

Here are the steps required to open an existing contact for editing:

1. **Open Contacts and tap the contact you want to edit.**

2. **Tap Edit.** Contacts displays the contact's data.

3. **Make your changes, as described in the next few sections.**

4. **Tap Done.** Contacts saves your work and returns you to the All Contacts screen.

Note

See Chapter 9 to get the scoop on sprucing up your contact with a photo.

Assigning phone numbers to a contact

Your iPhone is, of course, a phone, so it's only right and natural to use it to call your contact. Sure, but which number? Work? Home? Cell? Fortunately, there's no need to choose just one, because your iPhone is happy to store all these numbers, plus a few more if need be.

Here are the steps to follow to add one or more phone numbers for a contact:

1. **With the contact's data open for editing, tap Add Phone.** Contacts creates a new phone field and displays a numeric keypad.

2. **Type the phone number with the area code first.** Contacts helpfully adds extra stuff like parentheses around the area code and the dash.

3. **Examine the label box to see if the default label (home) is the one you want.** If it is, skip to Step 5; if it's not, tap the label box to open the Label screen, shown in Figure 10.2.

4. **Tap the label that best applies to the phone number you're adding (Contacts automatically sends you back to the contact's data screen after you tap), such as mobile, iPhone, home, or work.**

5. **Repeat Steps 1 to 4 to add any other numbers you want to store for this contact.** Note that each time you add a number, Contacts creates a new Add Phone field below the current field, and you tap that field to add a new number.

Cancel	**Label**	Edit
home		✓
work		
iPhone		
mobile		
main		
home fax		
work fax		
pager		
other		
Add Custom Label		

10.2 Tap the label you want to use for a contact's phone number.

Assigning email addresses to a contact

It makes sense that you might want to add a phone number or three for a contact, but would you ever need to enter multiple email addresses? Well, sure you would! Most people have at least a couple of addresses — usually for home and work — and some type-A emailers have a dozen or more. Life is too short to enter that many email addresses, but you need at least the important ones if you want to use your iPhone Mail app to send a note to your contacts.

Follow these steps to add one or more email addresses for a contact:

1. **With the contact's data open for editing, tap Add Email.** Contacts creates a new email field and displays the keyboard.

2. **Type the person's email address.**

3. **Check out the label box to see if the default label (home) is the one you want.** If it is, skip to Step 5; if it's not, tap the label box to open the Label screen.

4. **Tap the label that best applies to the email address you're inserting (Contacts automatically sends you back to the contact's data screen after you tap), such as home or work.**

5. **Repeat Steps 1 to 4 to add other email addresses for this contact, as you see fit.** Note that each time you add an email address, Contacts creates a new Add Email field below the current one. You tap inside that new field to add a new email address.

Assigning web addresses to a contact

Who on earth doesn't have a website these days? It could be a humble home page, a blog, a Facebook page, a home business site, or someone's corporate website. Some busy web beavers may even have all five! Whatever web home a person has, it's a good idea to toss the address into her contact data because then you can simply tap it and your iPhone (assuming it can see the Internet from here) immediately fires up Safari and takes you to the site. Does your pal have multiple websites? No sweat: Your iPhone is happy to take you to all of them.

Genius

To save some wear and tear on your tapping finger, don't bother adding the http:// stuff at the beginning of the address. Your iPhone adds those characters automatically anytime you type an address to visit a site. Same with the www prefix. So if the full address is http://www.wordspy.com, you need only type wordspy.com.

You can add one or more web addresses for a contact by making your way through these steps:

1. **With the contact's data open for editing, tap Add URL.** Contacts creates a new URL field and displays the keyboard. Note the . (period) and .com keys in the on-screen keyboard, which come in very handy.

2. **Type the person's web address.**

3. **Examine the label box to see if the default label is the one you want.** If it is, skip to Step 5; if it's not, tap the label box to open the Label screen.

4. **Tap the label that best applies to the web address you're inserting (Contacts automatically sends you back to the contact's data screen after you tap), such as homepage or work.**

5. **Repeat Steps 1 to 4 to add other web addresses for this contact.** Note that each time you add a web address, Contacts creates a new Add URL field below the current one and you tap inside that field to add a new URL.

Assigning social network data to a contact

These days, many of us are far more likely to contact friends, family, and colleagues via social networks, such as Twitter, Facebook, and LinkedIn, than we are through more traditional methods like email. The Contacts app reflects this new reality by enabling you to save social network data for each contact, including data for Twitter, Facebook, LinkedIn, and Flickr. Here are the steps to follow to add one or more social network details to a contact:

Cancel	Done
Twitter	✓
Facebook	
Flickr	
LinkedIn	
Myspace	
Sina Weibo	
Add Custom Service	

10.3 Tap Twitter to see the social networks supported by the Contacts app.

1. **With the contact's data open for editing, tap Add Social Profile.** Contacts creates a new Social Profile field.

2. **If you want to use a different social network, tap the Twitter label to see a list of social networks, as shown in Figure 10.3.**

3. **Tap the label that suits the social network data you're entering, such as Facebook or Flickr.** The Contacts app adds the new label.

4. **Tap inside the field and then tap the person's username for the chosen social network.**

5. **If necessary, repeat Steps 1 to 4 to add more social networks as needed.**

Assigning physical addresses to a contact

With all this talk about cell numbers, email addresses, and web addresses, it's easy to forget that people actually live and work somewhere. You may have plenty of contact information in which the location of that somewhere doesn't much matter. But, if you ever need to get from here to there, taking the time to insert a contact's physical address really pays off. Why? Because you need only tap the address and your iPhone displays a map that shows you the precise location. From there you can get directions, see a satellite map of the area, and more. (I talk about all this great map stuff in Chapter 11.)

Tapping out a full address is a bit of work, but as the following steps show, it's not exactly root-canalishly painful:

1. **With the contact's data open for editing, tap Add Address.** Contacts displays the address fields.

2. **Tap the first Street field and then type the person's street address.**

3. **If necessary, tap the second Street field, and type even more of the person's street address.**

4. **Tap the City field and type the person's city.**

5. **Tap the State field and type the person's state.** Depending on what you later select for the country, this field might have a different name, such as Province.

6. **Tap the ZIP field and type the ZIP code.** Again, depending on what you later select for the country, this field might have a different name, such as Postal Code.

7. **Tap the Country field to open the Country screen, and then tap the contact's country.**

8. **Examine the label box to see if the default label is the one you want.** If it is, skip to Step 10; if it's not, tap the label box to open the Label screen.

9. **Tap the label that best applies to the physical address you're inserting (Contacts automatically sends you back to the contact's data screen after you tap), such as home or work.**

10. **Repeat Steps 1 to 9 to add other addresses for this contact.**

Creating a custom label

When you fill out contact data, your iPhone insists that you apply a label to each tidbit, such as home, work, and mobile. If none of the predefined labels fits, you can always just slap on the generic *other* label. However, this seems so, well, dull. If you've got a phone number or address that you can't shoehorn into any of the prefab labels, get creative and make one up. Here's how:

1. **With the contact's data open for editing, tap the label beside the field you want to work in.** The Label screen appears.

2. **Tap Add Custom Label.** Scroll to the bottom of the screen to see this command. The Custom Label screen appears.

3. **Type the custom label.**

4. **Tap Done.** Contacts returns you to the screen for the field you were editing and applies the new label.

Conveniently, you can apply your custom label to any type of contact data. For example, if you create a label named college, you can apply that label to a phone number, email address, web address, or physical address.

Adding extra fields to a contact

The New Contact screen (which appears when you add a contact) and the data screen (which appears when you edit an existing contact) display only the fields you need for basic contact info. Besides the fields you've looked at so far, you can also click the following items to add more fields to a contact's data:

- **Add Birthday.** Tap this item to add the contact's day, month, and year of birth.

- **Add Date.** Tap this item to add any other date, such as an anniversary.

- **Add Related Name.** Tap this item to specify another contact who is related to the contact you're editing. For example, if you also have the contact's brother in your Contacts list, tap Add Related Name, tap More Info (the *i* icon), tap the brother, tap the field label (the default is *mother*), and then tap the relationship type.

- **Add Instant Message.** Tap this item to add the contact's instant messaging data for a service such as Skype, Google Talk, or AIM.

- **Notes.** Use this field to add general observations or contact data that doesn't fit into any other field.

Despite these additional fields, the contact data screen still lacks quite a few common fields. For example, you might need to specify a contact's prefix (such as Dr. or Professor), suffix (such as Jr., Sr., or III), or job title. Thankfully, your iPhone is merely hiding these and other useful fields. There are nine hidden fields that you can add to any contact, as shown in Figure 10.4. The iPhone is only too happy to let you add as many of these extra fields as you want. Here are the steps involved:

1. **With the contact's data open for editing, tap Add Field.** The Add Field screen appears, as shown in Figure 10.4.

2. **Tap the field that you want to add.** Your iPhone adds the field to the contact's data.

Cancel	Add Field
Prefix	
Phonetic first name	
Pronunciation first name	
Middle name	
Phonetic middle name	
Phonetic last name	
Pronunciation last name	
Maiden name	
Suffix	
Nickname	
Job title	
Department	

10.4 The Add Field screen shows the hidden fields that you can add to any contact.

3. **Type the field data.**

4. **Tap Done.** Your iPhone saves the new info.

Creating a new contact from an electronic business card

Entering a person's contact data by hand is a tedious bit of business at the best of times, so it helps if you can find a faster way to do it. If you can cajole a contact into sending his contact data electronically, then you can add it with just a couple of taps. What do I mean when I talk about sending contact data electronically? Long ago, the world's contact-management gurus came up with a standard file format for contact data — the vCard. It's a kind of digital business card that exists as a separate file. People can pass this data along by attaching their (or someone else's) card to an email message.

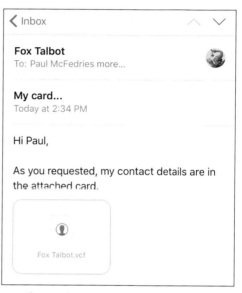

If you get a message with contact data, you see an icon for the VCF file, as shown in Figure 10.5.

10.5 If your iPhone receives an email message with an attached vCard, an icon for the file appears in the message body.

To get this data into your Contacts app, follow these steps:

1. **In the Home screen, tap Mail to open the Mail app.**

2. **Tap the message that contains the vCard attachment.**

3. **Tap the icon for the vCard file.** Mail opens the vCard.

4. **Tap Create New Contact.** If the person is already in your Contacts app, but the vCard contains new data, tap Update Contact "*Name*," where *Name* is the name of the existing contact. If you want to add this data to a different contact, tap Add to Existing Contact and then tap the contact.

5. **If you're creating a new contact, tap Done.** If you're updating a contact or adding data to an existing contact, tap Update, instead.

221

Sending and receiving a contact via AirDrop

Sharing your contact data using a vCard has worked well for many years, but sharing data via attachments is beginning to feel decidedly old-fashioned. Fortunately, these days of exchanging virtual business cards may soon be over thanks to an iOS feature called AirDrop, which is a Bluetooth service that lets two nearby devices — specifically, an iPhone 5 or later, a fourth-generation iPad or later, an iPad mini, a fifth-generation iPod touch or later, or a Mac running OS X Yosemite or later — swap contacts directly. Here are the steps to follow:

1. **Use the Contacts app to open the contact you want to share.**

2. **Tap Share Contact.** The AirDrop section shows an icon for each nearby device.

3. **Tap the icon for the person with whom you want to share the contact.** The other person sees a dialog asking for permission to accept the contact. When she taps Accept, her version of the Contacts app loads and displays the contact.

Working with Facebook contacts

If you've signed in to your Facebook account on your iPhone, as I describe back in Chapter 2, iOS automatically updates Contacts with all your Facebook friends. This means that all the profile data that each person shares with friends is automatically available via Contacts. This often includes info such as the person's profile picture, occupation, company name, email address, location, and birthday, but it can also include the following fields:

- **Mobile.** Tap this field to call the friend's cell phone.
- **URL.** Tap this field to visit the friend's website.
- **Facebook.** Tap this field to view the friend's Facebook profile page.
- **Facebook Message.** Tap this field to send an instant message to the friend.

Note   Although you can add new data to a Facebook contact, you can't edit any data that comes via Facebook. (When you tap Edit to display the Info screen, you see that each Facebook-generated field appears with a Facebook logo beside it and that the field isn't editable.)

Managing contacts with Siri voice commands

The Siri voice recognition app enables you to locate and query your contacts using simple voice commands. To get started, tap and hold the Home button (or press and hold the Mic button of the iPhone headphones, or the equivalent button on a Bluetooth headset) until Siri appears.

To display one or more contacts, use the following techniques within Siri:

- **Displaying a specific contact.** Say "Show (or Display or Find) *first last*," where *first* and *last* are the person's first and last names as given in the Contacts list; you can also just say the person's name. If the contact is a business, say "Show (or Display or Find) *company*," where *company* is the business name as given in your Contacts list; you can also just say the company name.

- **Displaying a contact who has a relationship with you.** Say "Show (or Display or Find) *relationship*," where *relationship* is the connection you've defined (such as sister or father).

- **Displaying a contact with a unique first name.** Say "Show (or Display or Find) *first*," where *first* is the person's first name as given in your Contacts list.

- **Displaying multiple contacts who have some information in common.** Say "Find people *criteria*," where *criteria* defines the common data. Examples: "Find people named Stevens" or "Find people who live in New York."

To query your contacts, you use the following general syntax:

Question contact info?

Here, *question* can be "What is" (for general data), "When is" for dates, or "Who is" (for people); *contact* specifies the name (or relationship) of the contact; and *info* specifies the type of data you want to retrieve (such as "birthday" or "home phone number"). Here are some examples:

- "What is Alex Blandman's mobile phone number?"
- "When is my sister's anniversary?"
- "What is David Cutrere's address?"
- "Who is Kyra's husband?"

Tracking Your Events

When you meet someone and ask, "How are you?" the most common reply these days is a short one: "Busy!" We're all as busy as can be these days, and that places-to-go, people-to-see feeling is everywhere. All the more reason to keep your affairs in order, and that includes your appointments. Your iPhone comes with a Calendar app that you can use to create items called *events*, which represent your appointments, vacations, trips, meetings, and anything else that can be scheduled. Calendar acts as a kind of electronic personal assistant, leaving your brain free to concentrate on more important things.

Adding an event to your calendar

I show you how to sync your computer's calendar application (such as Calendar on the Mac, or the Outlook Calendar folder) in Chapter 7, and that's the easiest way to fill your iPhone with your events. However, something always comes up when you're running around, so you need to know how to add an event directly to your iPhone Calendar.

Here are the steps to follow:

1. **In the Home screen, tap the Calendar icon.** The Calendar app appears.

2. **Using the week calendar near the top of the screen, scroll to the date on which the event occurs, then tap to select it.** If the event happens sometime in the future, tap the current month in the upper left corner of the screen, scroll to the date, and then tap it.

3. **Tap the + button at the top right corner of the screen.** The New Event screen appears, as shown in Figure 10.6.

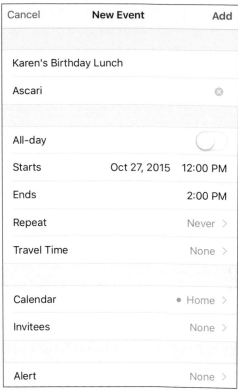

Cancel	New Event	Add
Karen's Birthday Lunch		
Ascari		⊗
All-day		⬯
Starts	Oct 27, 2015	12:00 PM
Ends		2:00 PM
Repeat		Never >
Travel Time		None >
Calendar		• Home >
Invitees		None >
Alert		None >

10.6 Use the New Event screen to create your event.

4. **The cursor starts off in the Title box, so enter a title for the event.**

5. **Tap the Location box, type the location of the event, and then either tap the location if it appears in the search results, or tap Done.**

6. **Tap Starts and then use the scroll wheels to set the date and time that your event begins.**

7. **Tap Ends and then use the scroll wheels to set the date and time that your event finishes.**

8. **If you have multiple calendars, tap Calendar, and then tap the one in which you want this event to appear.**

9. **Tap Add.** The Calendar app adds the event to the calendar.

The iOS 9 version of Mail includes a feature that recognizes events by analyzing message text. In Figure 10.7, for example, you can see that Mail has underlined the phrase "on October 15, at 6:00PM." Even better, Mail has added a banner to the top of the screen to let you know that it found an event. To add the event to Calendar, tap Add to open the New Event screen, fill in the missing details, then tap Add.

When you add an event in Calendar, the Month view displays a dot underneath the day as a visual reminder that you have something going on that day. Tap the day and Calendar displays a list of all the events you have scheduled. If you have multiple calendars and you want to see all your events, tap Calendars, tap Show All Calendars, and then tap Done.

< Inbox

1 Event found
Thu, Oct 15 at 6:00 pm add...

Paula Fiser
To: Paul McFedries more...

Book launch
Today at 2:46 PM

Hi Paul,

I'm hosting a launch party for John's new book. It's on October 15, at 6:00PM. I hope you can make it.

10.7 The latest version of the Mail app can recognize potential events in message text and asks if you want to add the event to Calendar.

Editing an existing event

Whether you've scheduled an event by hand or synced it from your computer, the event details might change: a new time, a new location, and so on. Whatever the change, you need to edit the event to keep your schedule accurate.

Here are the steps to follow to edit an existing event:

1. **In the Home screen, tap the Calendar icon.** The Calendar app appears.

2. **Tap the date that contains the event you want to edit.**

3. **Tap the event.** You can do this in either Month or Day view. Calendar displays the event info.

4. **Tap Edit.** Your iPhone displays the event data in the Edit screen.

5. **Make your changes to the event.**

6. **Tap Done.** Your iPhone saves your changes and returns you to the event details.

Setting up a repeating event

One of the truly great timesavers in Calendar is the repeat feature. It enables you to set up a single event and then get Calendar to automatically repeat it at a regular interval. For example, if you set up an event for a Friday, you can also set Calendar to automatically repeat it every Friday. You can continue repeating events indefinitely or end them on a specific date.

Follow these steps to configure an existing event to repeat:

1. **In Calendar, tap the date that contains the event you want to edit.**

2. **Tap the event.** Calendar opens the event info.

3. **Tap Edit.** Calendar displays the event data in the Edit screen.

4. **Tap Repeat.** The Repeat screen appears.

5. **Tap the repeat interval you want to use.** Calendar selects the interval and returns you to the Edit screen.

6. **Tap End Repeat.** The End Repeat screen appears.

7. **You have two choices here (either way, tap Edit Event to return to the Edit screen when you're done):**

   - **Set the event to stop repeating on a particular day.** Tap On Date and then use the scroll wheels to set the day, month, and year that you want the final event to occur.

   - **Set the event to repeat indefinitely.** Tap Never.

8. **Tap Done.** Calendar saves the repeat data and returns you to the event details.

Converting an event to an all-day event

Some events don't really have specific times that you can pin down. These include birthdays, anniversaries, sales meetings, trade shows, conferences, and vacations. What all these types of events have in common is that they last all day: in the case of birthdays and anniversaries, literally so; in the case of trade shows and the like, "all day" refers to the entire workday.

Why is this important? Well, suppose you schedule a trade show as a regular event that lasts from 9 a.m. to 5 p.m. When you examine that day in Calendar, you see a big fat block that covers the entire day. If you also want to schedule meetings that occur at the trade show, Calendar lets you do that, but it displays these new events on top of the existing trade show event. This makes the schedule hard to read, so you might miss a meeting.

To solve this problem, you can configure the trade show as an all-day event. Calendar clears it from the regular schedule and displays the event separately near the top of the Day view. Here are the steps to follow:

1. **In Calendar, tap the date that contains the event you want to edit.**

2. **Tap the event.** Calendar opens the event info.

3. **Tap Edit.** Calendar switches to the Edit screen.

4. **Tap the All-day switch to On.**

5. **Tap Done.** Calendar saves the event and returns you to the event details.

Adding an alert to an event

One of the truly useful secrets of stress-free productivity in the modern world is what I call the set-it-and-forget-it school of scheduling. That is, you set up an event electronically and then get the same technology to remind you when the event occurs. That way, your mind doesn't have to waste energy fretting about missing the event because you know your technology has your back.

With your iPhone, the technology of choice for doing this is Calendar and its alert feature. When you add an alert to an event, Calendar automatically displays a reminder of the event, which is a Notification Center banner that pops up on the screen. Your iPhone also vibrates and sounds a few beeps to get your attention. You can choose when the alert triggers (such as a specified number of minutes, hours, or days before the event), and you can even set up a second alert just to be on the safe side.

Caution If you flick the Ring/Silent switch on the side of the iPhone to the Silent setting, remember that you won't hear the Calendar alert chirps. When the alert runs, your iPhone still vibrates and you still see the alert message on-screen.

Follow these steps to set an alert for an event:

1. **In Calendar, tap the date that contains the event you want to edit.**

2. **Tap the event.** Calendar opens the event info.

3. **Tap Edit.** Calendar displays the event data in the Edit screen.

Genius

You can save yourself some time by setting the default alert time for different types of events. Tap Settings in the Home screen, and then tap Mail, Contacts, Calendars. In the Calendars section, tap Default Alert Times, tap the type of alert you want to configure (Birthdays, Events, or All-Day Events), and then tap the default alert interval.

4. **Tap Alert.** The Event Alert screen appears, as shown in Figure 10.8.

5. **Tap the number of minutes, hours, or days before the event you want to see the alert.** If you're editing an all-day event, you can set the alert at 9 a.m. on the day of the event, or one day before, two days before, or a week before the event.

6. **To set up a backup alert, tap Second Alert.** Tap the number of minutes, hours, or days before the event you want to see the second alert, and then tap Done.

7. **Tap Done.** Calendar saves your alert choices and returns you to the event details.

❮ Edit Event	Alert
None	
At time of event	
5 minutes before	
15 minutes before	
30 minutes before	
1 hour before	
2 hours before	
1 day before	
2 days before	
1 week before	

10.8 Use the Event Alert screen to tell Calendar when to remind you about your event.

Genius

You can disable the alert chirps if you find them annoying. On the Home screen, tap Settings, tap Sounds, tap the Calendar Alerts, and then tap None.

Figure 10.9 shows an example of an alert. Tap OK to close the alert, or tap Options to see three more choices: Snooze (redisplay the alert in five minutes), View Event (display the event details), or Close (dismiss the alert).

Radio Interview
Today at 3:30 pm

Close   Options

10.9 Your iPhone displays an alert similar to this to remind you of an upcoming event.

Configuring default alert times

When I add an event to Calendar, I *always* add an alert or two because, it seems to me, that's what the phone is for, at least as far as keeping me on schedule goes. It's takes a few extra steps, but I can't tell you how many appointments and meetings I'd have missed without those alerts.

So it is welcome news, indeed, to know that iOS comes with a setting that enables you to set up a default alert that Calendar adds automatically to each new event. Actually, you can set up three separate default alerts: one each for events, birthdays, and all-day events. Here's how you go about it:

1. **On your iPhone's Home screen, tap Setting to launch the Settings app.**

2. **Tap Mail, Contacts, Calendars.**

3. **Scroll down the Calendars section and tap Default Alert Times.**

4. **For each of the three event types — Birthdays, Events, and All-Day Events — tap the type and then tap the default alert you want to use.**

Note

You might be scratching your head trying to figure out how to set up a "birthday" event in Calendar. The short answer is: You can't! Instead, Calendar gets its birthday info directly from the Contacts app. If you add a Birthday field to a contact, that date appears automatically in Calendar with "*Name*'s Birthday" as an event, where *Name* is the name of the contact.

Controlling events with Siri voice commands

The Siri personal assistant offers a number of voice commands for creating, editing, and querying your events.

To get Siri to schedule an event, you use the following general syntax:

Schedule what with *who* at *when*.

Here, *schedule* can be any of the following:

- "Schedule"
- "Meet"
- "Set up a meeting"
- "New appointment"

The *what* part of the command (which is optional) determines the topic of the event, so it could be something like "lunch" or "budget review" or "dentist"; you can also precede this part with "about" (for example, "about expenses"). The *who* part of the command specifies the person you're meeting with, if anyone, so it can be a contact name or a relationship (such as "my husband" or "Dad"). The *when* part of the command sets the time and date of the event; the time portion can be a specific time such as "3" (meaning 3 p.m.) or "8 a.m." or "noon"; the date portion can be "today" or "tomorrow," a day in the current week (such as "Tuesday" or "Friday"), a relative day (such as "next Monday"), or a specific date (such as "August 23").

Here are some examples:

- "Schedule lunch with Karen tomorrow at noon."
- "Meet with my sister Friday at 4."
- "Set up a meeting about budgeting next Tuesday at 10 a.m."
- "New appointment with Sarah Currid on March 15 at 2:30."

You can also use Siri to modify existing events. For example, you can change the event time by using the verbs "Reschedule" or "Move":

- "Reschedule my meeting with Sarah Currid to 3:30."
- "Move my noon appointment to 1:30."

You can also use the verb "Add" to include another person in a meeting, and the verb "Cancel" to remove a meeting from your schedule:

- "Add Charles Aster to the budgeting meeting."
- "Cancel my lunch with Karen."

Finally, you can query your events to see what's coming up. Here are some examples:

- "When is my next appointment?"
- "When is my meeting with Sarah Currid?"
- "What is on my Calendar tomorrow?"
- "What does the rest of my day look like?"

Handling Microsoft Exchange meeting requests

If you've set up a Microsoft Exchange account in your iPhone, there's a good chance you're already using its push features. That is, the Exchange Server automatically sends incoming email messages to your iPhone, as well as new and changed contacts and calendar data. If someone back at headquarters adds your name to a scheduled meeting, Exchange generates an automatic meeting request, which is an email message that tells you about the meeting and asks if you want to attend.

How will you know? Two ways (see Figure 10.10): First, you see an alert for the invitation; second, the Calendar app's Inbox item in the lower right corner displays a number beside it telling you how many meeting requests you have waiting for you.

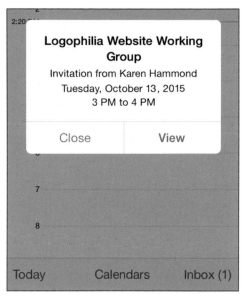

10.10 When a meeting invitation arrives, you see an alert, and the Inbox item in the Calendar menu bar shows you how many meeting requests you have.

Note   If you don't see the Inbox tray icon, then you need to turn on syncing for your Exchange calendar. Open Settings, tap Mail, Contacts, Calendars, then tap your Exchange account. Tap the Calendars switch to the On position and when your iPhone asks what you want to do with the local calendars, tap Keep on My iPhone.

It's best to handle such requests as soon as you can, so here's what you do:

1. **In Calendar, tap Inbox.** Calendar displays your pending meeting requests.

2. **Tap the meeting request to which you want to respond.** Calendar displays the meeting details, as shown in Figure 10.11.

3. **Tap your response:**

- **Accept.** Tap this button to confirm that you can attend the meeting.

- **Maybe.** Tap this button if you're not sure and will decide later.

- **Decline.** Tap this button to confirm that you can't attend the meeting.

Subscribing to a calendar

If you know someone who has published a calendar, you might want to keep track of it within your iPhone Calendar app. You can do that by subscribing to the published calendar. iPhone sets up the published calendar as a separate item in the Calendar app, so you can easily switch between your own calendars and the published calendar.

To pull this off, you need to know the address of the published calendar. This address usually takes the following form: *server*.com/ *calendar*.ics. Here, *server*.com is the address of

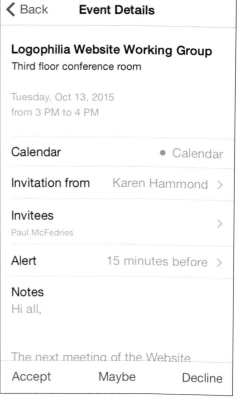

10.11 The details screen for an Exchange meeting request.

the calendar server and *calendar*.ics is the name of the file (which is almost always an iCalendar format file with the extension .ics), preceded (usually) by a folder location.

For calendars published to iCloud, the address always looks like this: ical.icloud.com/ *member*/*calendar*.ics. Here, *member* is the iCloud member name of the person who published the calendar and *calendar* is the name of the file. Here's an example address:

ical.icloud.com/aardvarksorenstam/aardvark.ics

Follow these steps to subscribe to a published calendar:

1. **On the Home screen, tap Settings.** The Settings app appears.

2. **Tap Mail, Contacts, Calendars.** The Mail, Contacts, Calendars screen appears.

3. **Tap Add Account.** The Add Account screen appears.

4. **Tap Other.** Your iPhone displays the Other screen.

5. **Tap Add Subscribed Calendar.** You see the Subscription screen.

6. **Type the calendar address in the Server text box.**

7. **Tap Next.** Your iPhone connects to the calendar.

8. **Tap Save.** Your iPhone adds an account for the subscribed calendar.

To view the subscribed calendar, tap Calendar on the Home screen to open the Calendar app, and then tap Calendars to open the Calendars screen. Your new calendar appears in the Subscribed section. Tap the calendar to view its events.

Creating Reminders

The Calendar app is an excellent tool for tracking appointments, meetings, and other events. By adding an alert to an event, you get a digital tap on the shoulder to remind you when and where your presence is required.

However, our days are littered with tasks that could be called subevents. These are things that need to be done at a certain point during your day but don't rise to the level of full-fledged events: returning a call, taking the laundry out of the dryer, turning off the sprinkler. If you need to be reminded to perform such a subevent, it seems like overkill to crank out an event using the Calendar app.

Fortunately, iOS offers a better solution: the Reminders app. You use this app to create *reminders,* which are simple nudges that tell you to do something, to be somewhere, or whatever. These nudges come in the form of Notification Center banners that appear on your screen at a time you specify or when your iPhone reaches a particular location. If you have an iCloud account, you can sync your reminders between your iPhone, your Mac, your iPad, and any other supported device.

Setting a reminder for a specific time

Here are the steps to follow to set up a reminder that alerts you at a specific time:

1. **On the iPhone Home screen, tap Reminders.** The Reminders app appears.

2. **Tap the list you want to use to store the reminder.**

3. **Tap the first empty line below the list name.** The Reminders app creates a new reminder.

4. **Type the reminder text and then tap the More Info icon (the *i*) that appears on the right side of the new reminder.** The Details screen appears, as shown in Figure 10.12.

5. **Tap the Remind me on a day switch to On.**

6. **Tap the date that appears, and then use the scroll wheels to set the date and time of the reminder.**

7. **Use the Repeat setting to set up a repeat interval for the reminder.**

8. **Use the Priority setting to assign a priority to the reminder: None, Low, Medium, or High.**

9. **Use the Notes text box to add some background text or other information about the reminder.**

10. **Tap Done.** Reminders saves the reminder.

Details	Done
Car license plate renewal	
Remind me on a day	⬤
Alarm	Mon, 15-11-16, 9:00 AM
Repeat	Never ›
Remind me at a location	◯
Priority	None ! !! !!!
List	Reminders ›
Notes	

10.12 Tap More Info to see the full Details screen options.

Setting a reminder for a specific location

Getting an alert at a specific time is the standard way of working with reminders, but the Reminders app supports a second type of criterion: location. That is, when you specify a particular location for a reminder, the app sets up a *geo-fence* — a kind of virtual border — around that location. When your iPhone crosses that geo-fence, the associated reminder appears on your screen. So, for example, if you're on your way to a meeting with a client, you could create a reminder that includes notes about the meeting or the client, and then specify the meeting location as the Remind Me criterion.

Here's how it works:

1. **On the iPhone Home screen, tap Reminders.** The Reminders app appears.

2. **Tap the list you want to use to store the reminder.** If an existing list is displayed and you want to choose another, tap the list name and then tap the list you want to use.

3. **Tap the first empty line below the list name.** The Reminders app creates a new reminder.

4. **Type the reminder text and then tap the More Info icon (the *i*) that appears on the right side of the new reminder.** The Details screen appears.

5. **Tap the Remind me at a location switch to On.** If your iPhone asks whether the Reminders app can use your location, tap Allow.

6. **To choose a location other than your current address, tap Location, use the Search box to specify the address of the location you want to use, and then tap the location when it appears in the search results.**

7. **To have the reminder appear when your iPhone first comes within range of the location, tap When I Arrive.** If you prefer to see the reminder when your iPhone goes out of range of the location, tap When I Leave instead.

8. **Tap Details and then follow Steps 7 to 10 from the previous section to fill in the reminder details.**

Creating a new list

The Reminders app comes with three preset lists that you can use: Reminders, Home, and Work. The default is Reminders, but you can also select a different list if it's more suitable or if you want to keep your personal and business reminders separate. If none of these three prefab lists is exactly right for your needs, feel free to create your own list by following these steps:

1. **If the Reminders app is currently displaying a list, tap the list name.** The Reminders app displays the Lists screen.

2. **Tap New (the + icon in the upper right corner) and then tap List.**

3. **Tap the name of your list.**

4. **Tap Done.** The Reminders app adds the list to the left pane.

Completing a reminder

When a reminder is complete, you don't want it lingering in the Reminders list (or whatever list it's in), cluttering the screen and making it hard to look through your remaining reminders. To avoid that, once the reminder is done, tap the radio button beside it. This tells Reminders that the reminder is complete, and the app immediately moves it to the Completed list.

Deleting a reminder

If you no longer need a reminder, it's a good idea to delete it to keep your reminder lists neat and tidy. To delete a reminder, follow these steps:

1. **In the Reminder app, tap the list that contains the reminder you want to delete.** The Reminders app displays the list's reminders.

2. **Tap Edit.** Reminders places the list into Edit mode.

3. **Tap the red Delete icon to the left of the reminder you want to delete.** Reminders prompts you to delete the reminder.

4. **Tap Delete.** Reminders deletes the reminder.

Setting the default Reminders list

The default list is the one that Reminders uses when you don't specify a particular list when you create a reminder. If you have a particular list you'd prefer to use as the default, follow these steps to set it:

1. **On the Home screen, tap Settings.** The Settings app appears.

2. **Tap Reminders.** The Reminders screen appears.

3. **Tap Default List.** The Default List screen appears.

4. **Tap the list you want to use as the default.**

Setting reminders with Siri voice commands

You can also create reminders via voice using the Siri app. Time-based reminders use the following general syntax:

Remind me to *action* at *when*.

Here, *action* is the task you want to be reminded to perform, and *when* is the date and time you want to be reminded (as described earlier in the chapter where I discuss creating calendar events using Siri). Here are some examples:

- "Remind me to call my wife at 5."
- "Remind me to pick up Greg at the airport tomorrow at noon."
- "Remind me to bring lunch."

Location-based reminders use the following general syntax:

Remind me to *action* when I *location*.

Again, *action* is the task you want to be reminded to perform; *location* is the place around which you want the geo-fence set up (including either "get to" or "leave," depending on whether you want to be reminded coming or going). Here are some examples:

- "Remind me to pick up milk when I leave here."
- "Remind me to call my husband when I get to LaGuardia Airport."
- "Remind me to call my sister when I get home."
- "Remind me to grab my sample case when I arrive at Acme Limited."

For the last of these, you can assume that "Acme Limited" is a company name defined (with an address) in your Contacts list.

Working with Passes

You've probably had the experience of walking into your favorite coffee shop or a movie theater, remembering that you have a loyalty card, gift card, or coupon, and then fumbling around to find it in your purse or wallet. Or, worse, you *forget* you have a card or you leave it at home, so you miss out.

Many merchants are feeling your pain and are doing something about it by creating iOS apps that include gift cards, loyalty cards, coupons, special offers, freebies, and even train or plane boarding passes. These app items usually include bar codes or QR codes, so after you arrive at the destination, the merchant offers a scanner that you can use to scan the code and redeem your card, check in, or whatever. These are great because as long as you have your iPhone (and I know you *always* have your iPhone), you have your cards and passes.

Of course, you still have to fumble about a bit to locate the app, use the app's interface to locate the card or pass, and then place your iPhone into the scanner. And, unfortunately, having the card or pass on your iPhone doesn't guarantee that you'll remember to scan it.

iOS aims to solve all these problems by offering an app called Passbook that acts as a kind of digital wallet to store all the gift cards, loyalty cards, coupons, tickets, special offers, and boarding passes that you've accumulated through your apps.

Passbook offers the following advantages over using merchant apps directly:

- All your passes are stored in one convenient location.

- Passes can have embedded time and location data, so they appear automatically in the Notification Center and the Lock screen when the time is reached or when you arrive at the location.

- Passes are "live" in the sense that if any information changes — for example, your flight's boarding gate gets changed — the pass updates automatically and lets you know about the change.

If you don't have any apps that offer passes, open Passbook and tap the App Store button. This loads the App Store and shows you a list of available apps that offer coupons, passes, store cards, and so on.

Note, however, that when you install any of these apps, they at first show up on the iPhone Home screen as normal. After you use the app at least once, it then appears within the Passbook app.

How Do I Use My iPhone to Navigate My World?

Dedicated GPS devices have become gasp-inducingly popular over the past few years because it's not easy finding your way around in a strange city or an unfamiliar part of town. The old way — deciphering hastily scribbled directions or scratching your head over a possibly out-of-date map — was just too hard and error prone, so having a device tell you where to go (so to speak) was a no-brainer. However, dedicated devices, whether they're music players, ebook readers, or GPS receivers, are going the way of the dodo. They're being replaced by multifunction devices that can play music, read books, and display maps. In this chapter, you take advantage of the multifunction prowess of your iPhone to learn about the amazingly useful Maps app.

Finding Your Way with Maps and GPS

When you're out in the real world trying to navigate your way between the proverbial points A and B, the questions often come thick and fast: "Where am I now?" "Which turn do I take?" "What's the traffic like on the highway?" "Can I even get there from here?" Fortunately, the answers to those and similar questions are now just a few finger taps away. That's because your iPhone comes loaded not only with a way-cool Maps app but also a GPS receiver. Now your iPhone knows exactly where it is (and so, by extension, do you) and it can help you get where you want to go.

To get the Maps app on the job, tap the Maps icon in the iPhone Home screen. Figure 11.1 shows the initial Maps screen. (If you see a dialog letting you know that Maps would like to use your current location, say "But of course!" and tap OK.)

11.1 Use the Maps app to navigate your world.

Searching for a destination

When you want to locate a destination using Maps, the most straightforward method is to search for it:

1. **Tap inside the Search box at the top of the screen.**

2. **Type the name, address, or a keyword or phrase that describes your destination.**

3. **In the on-screen keyboard, tap Search.** Maps locates the destination, moves the map to that area, and drops a pin on the destination, as shown in Figure 11.2.

Now that you have your destination pin-pointed (literally), you can read the map to find your way by looking for street names, local landmarks, nearby major intersections, and so on. (You also can use the Maps app to get specific directions; I show you how that works later in this chapter.) The map is also rotatable so, for example, if you're physically facing east, you can rotate the map so that it also faces east and you can more easily get your bearings. To rotate the map, place two fingers on the screen and rotate either clock-wise or counterclockwise.

Getting info about a destination

Knowing where a destination is located is a good thing, but you might also want to find out more about that destination. Maps has you covered there, as well, because it not only provides you with general info such as a phone number, street address, and website address, but it also ties into Yelp, a service that offers user-generated content — particularly ratings, reviews, and photos — of millions of locations around the world. Tap the destination banner and, as you can see in Figure 11.3, Maps offers tons of data about the destination, including basic info, reviews, and photos.

Directions

Quick Directions

11.2 When you search for a destination, Maps displays a pin to mark its location on the map.

Genius

If you have a Yelp account, you can add your own content about the destination. In the Reviews section, tap Check In to let your Yelp friends know you're at the destination or tap Write a Review to post a review. You can also tap Add Photo to post your own pic of the destination.

Displaying your current location

When you arrive at an unfamiliar shopping mall and you need to get your bearings, your first instinct might be to seek out the nearest mall map and look for the inevitable *You are here* marker. This gives you a sense of your current location with respect to the rest of the mall, so locating Pottery Barn shouldn't be all that hard.

When you arrive at an unfamiliar part of town or a new city, have you ever wished you had something that could provide you with that same *You are here* reference point? If so, you're in luck because you have exactly that waiting for you right in your iPhone. Tap the Tracking icon in the lower left corner of the screen, as pointed out in Figure 11.4. (If this is the first time you've used the Tracking icon, Maps asks for permission to use your current location, so be sure to tap OK.)

That's it! Your iPhone examines GPS coordinates, Wi-Fi hotspots, and nearby cellular towers to plot your current position. When it completes the necessary processing and tri-

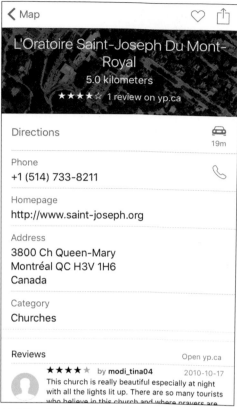

11.3 Tap the Info icon to open the Location screen and gain access to information about the destination as well as Yelp ratings, reviews, and photos.

angulating, your iPhone displays a map of your current city, zooms in on your current area, and then adds a blue dot to the map to pinpoint your current location, as shown in Figure 11.4. Amazingly, if you happen to be in a car, taxi, or other moving vehicle, the blue dot moves in real time.

Seeing what's near you

Knowing where you are is a good thing, but it's even better to know what's nearby. For example, suppose you're in a new city and you're dying for a cup of coffee. You could tap Search in the menu bar, tap the Search box, type something like coffee (or perhaps café or espresso, depending on what you're looking for), and then tap Search. That works, but you might notice something interesting: When you tap inside the Search box, Maps displays icons for a bunch of categories, including Food, Drinks, Shopping, and Fun, as shown in Figure 11.5. Tap a category icon to see its subcategories, as shown in Figure 11.6. Tap one of these icons (such as Coffee Shops) and Maps drops a bunch of pins that correspond to nearby locations that match the subcategory you tapped. Tap a pin to see the name, and tap the banner to see the location's phone number, address, and other info.

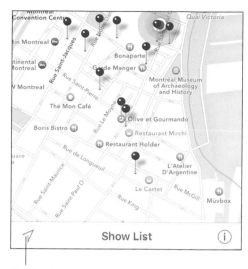

Tracking icon

11.4 Tap the Tracking icon to see your precise location as a blue dot on a map.

Displaying a map of a contact's location

In the old days (that is, a few years ago), if you had a contact located in an unfamiliar part of town or even in another city altogether, visiting that person required a phone call or email asking for directions. You'd then write down the instructions, get written directions via email, or perhaps even get a crudely drawn map faxed to you. Those days, fortunately, are long gone thanks to myriad

11.5 Tap inside the Search box to see these category icons.

online resources that can show you where a particular address is located and even give you driving directions to get there from here (wherever *here* may be).

Even better, your iPhone takes it one step further and integrates with Maps to generate a map of a contact's location based on the person's contact address. So as long as you've tapped in (or synced) a contact's physical address, you can see where he or she is located on the map.

To display a map of a contact's location, follow these steps:

11.6 Tap one of these icons to see nearby locations in that subcategory.

1. **In the Home screen, tap the Contacts icon.** The Contacts app appears.

2. **Tap the contact you want to map.** Your iPhone displays the contact's data.

3. **Tap the address you want to view.** Your iPhone switches to the Maps app and drops a pushpin on the contact's location.

Note
You can also display a map of a contact's location by using the Maps app. In the menu bar, tap the Bookmarks icon (it's on the right side of the Search box). Tap Contacts, and then tap the contact you want to map. The Maps app displays the contact's location.

Mapping an address from an email

Addresses show up in all kinds of email messages these days. Most commonly, folks include their work or home addresses in their email signatures at the bottom of each message. Similarly, if the email is an invitation, your correspondent almost certainly includes the address for the event somewhere in the message.

If you need to know where an address is located, you might think that you need to copy the address from the message and then paste it into the Maps app. Sure, that works, but it's way too much effort! Instead, just do this:

1. **In the Mail app, display the message that includes the address.**

2. **Tap and hold on the address in the message to display a list of actions.** If the address is displayed as a link (that is, underlined in a blue font), it means Mail recognizes it as an address, so you can just tap the address and skip the next step.

3. **Tap Open in Maps.** The Maps app opens and drops a pushpin on the address.

Specifying a location when you don't know the exact address

Sometimes you have only a vague notion of where you want to go. In a new city, for example, you might decide to head downtown and then see if there are any good coffee shops or restaurants. That's fine, but how do you get downtown from your hotel in the suburbs? Your iPhone can give you directions, but it needs to know the endpoint of your journey, and that's precisely the information you don't have. Sounds like a conundrum, for sure, but there's a way to work around it. You can drop a pin on the map in the approximate area where you want to go. The Maps app can then give you directions to the dropped pin.

Here are the steps to follow to drop a pin on a map:

1. **In the Maps app, display a map of the city you want to work with:**

   - If you're in the city now, tap the Tracking icon in the lower left corner of the screen.

   - If you're not in the city, tap Search, tap the Search box, type the name of the city (and perhaps also the name of the state or province), and then tap the Search button.

2. **Use finger flicks to pan the map to the approximate location you want to use as your destination.**

3. **Tap Info (*i*) in the lower right corner of the screen.** The Maps app displays a list of map options.

4. **Tap Drop a Pin.** The Maps app drops a purple pin in the middle of the current map.

5. **Tap and hold the purple pin until it's released, then drag the pin to the location you want.** The Maps app creates a temporary bookmark called Dropped Pin that you can use when you ask the iPhone for directions (as described next).

Getting directions to a location

One possible navigation scenario with the Maps app is to specify a destination (using a contact, an address search, or a dropped pin) and then tap the Tracking icon. This gives you a map that shows both your destination and your current location. You can then eyeball the streets to see how to get from here to there. Depending on how far away the destination is, you may need to zoom out — by pinching the screen or by tapping the screen with two fingers — to see both locations on the map.

"Eyeball the streets"? Ha, how primitive! The Maps app can bring you into the twenty-first century not only by showing you a route to the destination but also by providing you with the distance and time it should take and by giving you street-by-street, turn-by-turn instructions, whether you're driving or walking. It's one of the sweetest features of your iPhone, and it works like so:

1. **Use the Maps app to add a pushpin for your journey's destination.** Use whatever method works best for you: the Contacts list, an address search, a dropped pin, or a bookmark.

2. **Tap Directions in the menu bar (pointed out earlier in Figure 11.2).** The Maps app displays a route that assumes you want to leave from your current location and that you want to drive. If those assumptions apply, skip to Step 7.

Swap icon

11.7 Use the Directions screen to specify the start and end points of your trip, and to swap them.

3. **Tap inside the location box at the top of the screen.** Maps opens the Directions screen, as shown in Figure 11.7.

4. **If you want to use a starting point other than your current location, tap the Start box and then type the address of the location you want to use.**

Genius

Instead of getting directions to the destination, you might need directions *from* the destination. No sweat. When you map the destination, tap the banner, and then tap Directions From Here. If you're already in the Directions screen, tap the Swap icon shown in Figure 11.7. Maps then swaps the locations.

5. **Tap Route.** Maps returns to the route.

6. **Tap the button for the type of directions you want: Drive, Walk, or Transit.** Maps figures out the best routes and then displays them on the map in the Overview screen, which also shows the trip distance and approximate time.

Genius

If you have your destination pinned, you can get immediate directions from your current location to that destination — that is, you can compress Steps 2 to 6 into a single step — by tapping the Quick Directions icon in the information banner (pointed out earlier in Figure 11.2).

7. **Tap the route you prefer to take.**

8. **Tap Start.** The Maps app displays the first leg of the journey.

Maps features turn-by-turn directions for driving and walking. This means that as you approach each turn, Siri tells you what to do next, such as "In 400 feet, turn right onto Main Street." The Maps app also follows along the route, so you can see where you're going and what turn is coming up. You can see your estimated time of arrival, remaining travel time, and distance remaining by tapping the screen.

After tapping the screen, you can also tap Overview to see the entire route. Instead of seeing the directions one step at a time, you might prefer to see them all at once. Tap the screen and then tap the List icon in the middle of the menu bar at the bottom of the screen.

Note
To switch between standard and metric distances, tap Settings, tap Maps, and then tap either In Miles or In Kilometers.

Getting live traffic information

Okay, it's pretty darn amazing that your iPhone can tell you precisely where you are and precisely how to get somewhere else. However, in most cities it's the getting somewhere else part that's the problem. Why? One word: traffic. The Maps app might tell you the trip should take 10 minutes, but that could easily turn into a half-hour or more if you run into a traffic jam.

That's life in the big city, right? Maybe not. If you're on a highway in a major city, the Maps app can most likely supply you with — wait for it — real-time traffic conditions! This is really an amazing tool that can help you avoid traffic messes and find alternative routes to your destination. Maps can also show you traffic construction sites, and it gathers real-time information from Maps users to generate even more accurate traffic data. If you're in the middle of turn-by-turn directions, Maps even recognizes an upcoming traffic delay and offers an alternative route around it!

To see the traffic data, tap the lower right corner of the screen, and then tap Show Traffic. As you can see in Figure 11.8, Maps displays an orange dotted line to indicate traffic slowdowns, a red dashed line to indicate very heavy traffic, and Road Closed icons to indicate route closures.

11.8 For most metropolitan roads and highways, orange dotted lines mean traffic slowdowns and red dashed lines mean stop-and-go traffic.

249

Viewing transit info

If you're trying to get around in an unfamiliar city (or an unfamiliar part of town), some of the most common questions you might asks are, "Where's the nearest subway stop?" and "What streetcar line is this?" The latest version of the Maps app is happy to answer such questions thanks to its new Transit layer that shows information about transit stops and lines. To see this layer, tap the blue More Info icon in the lower right corner, then tap Transit.

Controlling Maps with Siri voice commands

You can use the Siri voice-activated assistant to control Maps with straightforward voice commands. You can display a location, get directions, and even display traffic information. Tap and hold the Home button (or press and hold the Mic button of the iPhone headphones, or the equivalent button on a Bluetooth headset) until Siri appears.

To display a location in Maps via Siri, say "Show *location*" (or "Map *location*" or "Find *location*" or "Where is *location*?"), where *location* is an address, name, or a Maps bookmark. Similarly, to get directions from Siri, say "Directions to *location*," where *location* is an address, name, or a Maps bookmark. To see the current traffic conditions, say "Traffic *location*," where *location* can be a specific place or someplace local, such as "around here" or "nearby." To get your current location, you can say "Where am I?" or "Show my current location."

Genius

Siri generally ignores extra terms you say that aren't relevant to the task at hand. So you can say something like "Give me directions to Hoover Dam" and Siri won't miss a beat. Also, the location you specify can be based on Contacts data, such as "Show my wife's work" or "Directions to my sister's home."

Configuring Location Services

On your iPhone, *location services* refers to the features and technologies that provide apps and system tools with access to location data. This is a handy thing, but it's also something that you need to keep under your control because your location data, particularly your current location, is fundamentally private and shouldn't be given out willy-nilly. Fortunately, your iPhone comes with a few tools for controlling and configuring location services.

Turning off location services

The next couple of sections show you how to turn off location services for individual apps as well as individual system services. That fine-grained control is the best way to handle location services, but there may be times when you prefer a broader approach that turns off location services altogether. For example, if you're heading to a secret rendezvous (how exciting!) and you're bringing your iPhone with you, you might feel more comfortable knowing that no app or service on your iPhone is tracking your whereabouts. On a more mundane level, location services use up battery power, so if your iPhone is getting low or if you just want to maximize the battery (for a long bus ride, for example), then turning off location services completely will help.

Follow these steps to turn off all location services on your iPhone:

1. **On the Home screen, tap Settings.** The Settings app appears.

2. **Tap Privacy.** The Privacy settings appear.

3. **Tap Location Services.** The Location Services settings appear.

4. **Tap the Location Services switch to the Off position.** If you have Find My iPhone activated (see Chapter 2), your iPhone asks you to confirm.

5. **Tap Turn Off.** Your iPhone shuts off all location services.

Controlling app access to GPS

When you open an app that comes with a GPS component, the app displays a dialog like the one shown in Figure 11.9 to ask your permission to use the GPS hardware in your iPhone to determine your current location. Notice that iOS only allows apps to access your location while you use the app. Once you exit the app, it can no longer access your location. Tap Don't Allow if you think that your current location is none of the app's business, or tap Allow if that's just fine with you.

A slightly different scenario is when an app *must* use your location to function. A good example is Foursquare, which requires your location to show you nearby business and to let you "check in" to those places. In this case, iOS automatically gives the app access to your location while you're using the app, but the app might request access to your location even when you're not using it, as shown in Figure 11.10. Again, tap Don't Allow if you think the app is overstepping its bounds, or Allow if it's all good.

Whatever type of permission you choose, after you make your decision, you might change your mind. For example, if you deny your location to an app, that app might lack some crucial functionality. Similarly, if you allow an app to use your location, you might have second thoughts about compromising your privacy.

11.9 When you first launch a GPS-aware app, it asks your permission to access your current location while you use the app.

11.10 An app that must access your location while you use the app might also seek permission to access your location when you're not using it.

Whatever the reason, you can control an app's access to GPS by following these steps:

1. **In your Home screen, tap Settings.** The Settings app appears.

2. **Tap Privacy.** The Privacy settings appear.

3. **Tap Location Services.** The Location Services screen appears.

4. **Configure app access to GPS as follows:**

   - **If you want to deny your current location to all apps, tap the Location Services switch to Off.**

   - **If you want to deny your current location to a specific app, tap the app and then tap Never.**

   - **If you want to allow a specific app to access your current location, tap the app and then tap either While Using the App (the app can only access your location when you use it) or Always (the app can access your location even when you're not using it).**

Enabling or disabling system location services

Your iPhone also provides location services to various internal system services that perform tasks, such as calibrating the iPhone compass, setting the time zone, and serving up iAds that change depending on location data. If you don't want your iPhone providing any of these services, you can turn them off this way:

1. **On the Home screen, tap Settings.** The Settings app appears.

2. **Tap Privacy.** The Privacy screen appears.

3. **Tap Location Services.** The Location Services screen appears.

4. **Tap System Services.** The Settings app displays the System Services screen.

5. **For any system service to which you don't want to provide access to location data, tap its switch to Off.**

Genius

You can enhance your privacy by tapping Frequent Locations and then either tapping Clear History to remove the list of locations you've visited frequently, or by tapping the Frequent Locations switch to Off to tell the iPhone not to save your frequent locations at all.

Sharing Map Data

If you want to show someone where you live, where you work, or where you want to meet, you could just send the address, but that's so last century. The more modern way is to send your friend a digital map that shows the location. With your iPhone this is a snap — you can send a map via email or text message, or post a map on Twitter.

Here are the steps to follow:

1. **Use the Maps app to add a pushpin for the location you want to send.** Use whatever method works best for you: the Contacts list, an address search, a dropped pin, or a bookmark. If you want to send your current location, display it, and then tap the blue dot.

2. **Tap the location banner.** Maps displays the Location screen for the location.

3. **Tap Share.** Maps displays a list of ways to share the map.

4. **Tap the method you want to use to share the map: Message, Mail, Twitter, or Facebook.** The Maps app creates a new email message, text message, tweet, or post that includes a Maps link to the location.

5. **Fill in the rest of your message and then send it.**

Alternatively, if the other person is nearby (that is, within 30 feet or so) and is running iOS 7 or later on an iPhone 5 or later, a fourth-generation iPad or later, an iPad mini, a fifth-generation iPod touch or later, or a Mac running OS X Yosemite, you can use AirDrop to exchange the location wirelessly. Here's how it works:

1. **Use the Maps app to add a pushpin for the location you want to send.** Use whatever method works best for you: the Contacts list, an address search, a dropped pin, or a bookmark. If you want to send your current location, display it, and then tap the blue dot.

2. **Tap the location banner.** Maps displays the Location screen for the location.

3. **Tap Share.** Maps displays a list of ways to share the location.

4. **In the AirDrop section, tap the icon for the person with whom you want to share the location.** The other person sees a dialog asking for permission to share the location, and when she taps Accept, her version of Maps loads and displays the location.

How Do I Manage My Ebook Library?

Physical books are an awesome invention: They're portable, easy to use, and fully showoffable, whether being read on the subway or sitting on a bookshelf at home. Physical books aren't going away anytime soon, but the age of electronic books — ebooks — is upon us. The Amazon Kindle lit a fire under the ebook category, but it's clunky to use and tied to Amazon. Apple filled in these gaps by offering iBooks, an app that's easy to use and supports an open ebook format. The iPhone screen is a bit on the small side, but the Retina display renders text sharply and clearly, so reading books on the iPhone isn't a chore. This chapter introduces you to ebooks on the iPhone.

Getting Your Head around Ebook Formats

If there is one reason why ebooks took a long time to take off (in the same way that, say, digital music now rules the planet), it's because the ebook world started out as hopelessly, head-achingly confusing. At its worst, at least two dozen (yes, two *dozen!*) ebook formats were available, and new formats jumped on the ebook bandwagon with distressing frequency. That was bad enough, but it got worse when you considered that some of these formats required a specific ereading device or program. For example, the Kindle ebook format required either the Kindle ereader or the Kindle app; similarly, the Microsoft LIT format required the Microsoft Reader program. Finally, things turned positively chaotic when you realized that some formats came with built-in restrictions that prevented you from reading ebooks in other devices or programs, or from sharing ebooks with other people.

What the ebook world needed was the simplicity and clarity that comes with having a near-universal ebook format (such as the MP3 format in music). Well, I'm happy to report that one format has emerged from the fray: EPUB. This is a free and open ebook standard created by the International Digital Publishing Forum (IDPF; see www.idpf.org). EPUB files, which use the .epub extension, are supported by most ereader programs and by most ereader devices (with the Amazon Kindle being the very noticeable exception). EPUB is leading the way not only because it's free and nonproprietary but also because it offers quite a few cool features:

- Text is resizable, so you can select the size that's most comfortable for you.
- The layout and formatting of the text are handled by Cascading Style Sheets (CSS), which is an open and well-known standard that makes it easy to alter the look of the text, including changing the font.
- Text is *reflowable,* which means that when you change the text size or the font, the text wraps naturally on the screen to accommodate the new character sizes (as opposed to some ebook formats that simply zoom in or out of the text).
- A single ebook can have alternative versions of the book in the same file.
- Ebooks can include high-resolution images right on the page.
- Publishers can protect book content by adding *digital rights management* (DRM) support. DRM refers to any technology that restricts the usage of content to prevent piracy. Of course, depending on where you fall in the "information wants to be free" spectrum, DRM may not be cool and may not even be considered a feature.

The first bit of good news is that the iBooks app supports the EPUB format, so all the features in the previous list are available in the iBooks app.

Note

For the record, I should also mention that you can use the iBooks app to read books in three other formats: plain text, HTML, and PDF.

The next bit of good news is that iBooks support for EPUB means that a vast universe of public-domain books is available to you. On its own, the Books section of Google Play (https://play.google.com/store/books) offers over a *million* public-domain ebooks. Several other excellent EPUB sites exist on the web, and I tell you about them (as well as how to get them onto your iPhone) a bit later in this chapter.

By definition, public-domain ebooks are DRM-free, and you can use them in any way you see fit. However, a lot of the EPUB books you'll find come with DRM restrictions. In the case of iBooks, the DRM scheme of choice is called FairPlay. This is the DRM technology that Apple used on iTunes for many years. Apple phased out DRM on music a while ago, but still uses it for other content, such as movies, TV shows, and audiobooks.

FairPlay means that many of the ebooks you download through iBooks face the following restrictions:

- You can access your books on a maximum of five computers, each of which must be authorized with your iTunes Store account info.
- You can read your ebooks only on your iPhone, iPad, iPod touch, or a computer that has iTunes installed.

It's crucial to note here two restrictions you'll trip over with DRM-encrusted ebooks:

- FairPlay ebooks do *not* work on other ereader devices that support the EPUB format, including the Kobo Touch and the Barnes & Noble NOOK.
- EPUB-format books that come wrapped in some other DRM scheme do not work on your iPhone.

However, remember that DRM is an optional add-on to the EPUB format. Although it's expected that most publishers will bolt FairPlay DRM onto books they sell in the iBookstore, it's not required, so you should be able to find DRM-free ebooks in the iBookstore (and elsewhere).

Note

If you have an Amazon Kindle, I'm afraid it uses a proprietary ebook format, so Kindle ebooks won't transfer directly to the iBooks app (or any other ereader). However, Amazon does offer a Kindle app for the iPhone. You can use it to download and read any previously purchased Kindle book, although for new Kindle books you must use the Amazon website to send the book to your iPhone.

Syncing Ebooks via iCloud

If you purchase an ebook on your iPad or on your Mac or PC, getting that book onto your iPhone requires a lot of connecting and syncing, which seems a tad primitive in this modern age. However, if you have an iCloud account, you can configure it to automatically download any new ebook purchases directly to your iPhone, all without a cable or your computer's iTunes application in sight.

Here's how to set this up:

1. **On your iPhone, tap Settings in the Home screen.** The Settings app appears.

2. **Tap App and iTunes Stores.**

3. **If you haven't signed in to the iTunes Store, enter your iCloud username and password and then tap Sign In.**

4. **Tap the Books switch to On, as shown in Figure 12.1.**

5. **If you want iCloud to sync ebooks even when you have a cellular-only connection, tap the Use Cellular Data switch to On.**

Now, each time you purchase an ebook via iTunes on another device, that book is sent automatically to the iBooks library on your iPhone, usually within a few seconds.

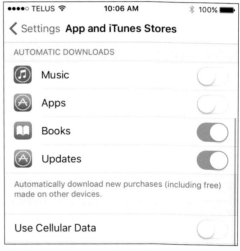

12.1 Tap the Books switch to On to sync ebooks via iCloud.

Managing Your iBooks Library

In this chapter, I concentrate on iBooks, which is the Apple ereader app. However, it's important to stress right off the bat that you're not restricted to using iBooks for reading ebooks on your iPhone. Tons of great ebook apps are available (I mention a few of them at the end of this chapter; see the later section "Reading Other Ebooks"), so feel free to use any or all of them in addition to (or even instead of) iBooks.

The iBooks app combines your ebook library with the iBookstore. Tap the My Books button in the menu bar to see your ebook collection, as shown in Figure 12.2. If you don't see much right now, then it's time to fill that bookcase with your favorite digital reading material. So your first task is to add a few titles to the bookcase, and the next few sections show you how to do just that.

Browsing books in the iBookstore

12.2 The iBooks My Books tab displays your collection of ebooks.

What if you're out and about with your iPhone, you've got a bit of time to kill, and you decide to start a book? That's no problem, because iBooks has a direct link to the iBookstore, the book marketplace run by Apple. Your iPhone can establish a wireless connection to the iBookstore anywhere you have Wi-Fi access or a cellular signal (ideally, at least 3G for faster downloads). You can browse and search the books, read reviews, and purchase any book you want (or grab a title from the large collection of free books). The ebook downloads to your iPhone and adds itself to the iBooks bookcase. You can start reading within seconds!

What about the selection? When Apple announced the iPhone and the iBooks app, it also announced that five major publishers would be stocking the iBookstore: Hachette, HarperCollins, Macmillan, Penguin, and Simon & Schuster. Since then, a number of other publishers have been added, including Random House, the last of the major publishers to sign on. So, along with all those free ebooks, you can rest assured that the iBookstore has an impressive selection.

259

To access the iBookstore, you use the other browse buttons in the menu bar at the bottom of the screen (that is, the buttons other than My Books): Featured, Top Charts, Search, and Purchased. You use these buttons to navigate the iBookstore. Here's a summary of what each browse button does for you:

- **Featured.** Tap this button to display a list of books picked by the iBookstore editors. The list shows each book's cover, title, author, category, star rating, number of reviews, and price. Tap Categories to browse books by subject.

- **Top Charts.** Tap this button to see charts for the top Paid Books and the top Free Books (see Figure 12.3).

- **Search.** Tap this button to run a search on the iBookstore.

- **Purchased.** Tap this button to see a list of the books you've downloaded.

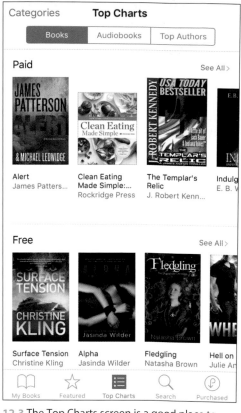

12.3 The Top Charts screen is a good place to begin looking for ebooks for your iPhone.

Note Tap a book to get more detailed information about it. The Info screen that appears is divided into three tabs: The Details tab shows standard book data, such as the title, author, cover, publisher, number of pages, and a description of the book; the Reviews tab offers user ratings and reviews for the book; and the Related tab displays a list of related books.

Adding a PDF attachment to your library

If you receive an email with an attached PDF file, you can open the attachment right from the Mail app. However, the iBooks app now supports PDFs, so if you'd prefer to read the PDF in the friendly confines of iBooks (where you can search the PDF and bookmark your current location), you need to transfer it to your iBooks library. Here's how it's done:

1. **In the Mail app, open the message that contains the PDF attachment.**

2. **Tap and hold the PDF attachment.** Mail displays a menu of commands.

3. **Tap Copy to iBooks.** Your iPhone opens the iBooks app and displays the PDF.

Note

You can also use Safari to open PDF links in iBooks. Open Safari, surf to the PDF page, and watch the download progress. When the download is complete, tap the Open in iBooks button that appears just below the address bar. Note that this button appears for only two or three seconds after the download is complete. If you miss it, tab the Activities icon (the square with the upward-pointing arrow) in Safari's menu bar, then tap Save PDF to iBooks.

Working with collections

iBooks supports both ebooks and PDF documents. In a welcome burst of common sense, the iBooks programmers decided not to combine ebooks and PDFs on the same part of the Bookshelf. Instead, iBooks supports separate library sections called collections, and it comes with four default collections: one for all ebooks (called Books), one for audiobooks (called Audiobooks), one for PDF documents (called PDFs), and one for everything (called All).

You can use the following techniques to work with your iBooks collections:

- **Switching to another collection.** Tap the name of the current collection at the top of the Bookshelf and then tap the name of the collection you want to use.

- **Creating a new collection.** Tap the name of the current collection at the top of the Bookshelf, tap New Collection, type the name of your collection (such as Fiction or Nonfiction), and then tap Done.

- **Moving an item to a different collection.** Tap the Select button, tap the item you want to move, and then tap the Move button. In the list of collections that appears, tap the collection you want to use as the item's new iBooks home.

- **Deleting a collection.** Tap the name of the current collection at the top of the Bookshelf and tap Edit. Next, tap the red Delete icon beside the collection you want to remove and then tap the Delete button that appears. If the collection isn't currently empty, you can either tap Delete Collection and Content or you can tap Delete Collection Only. If you tap the latter, iBooks returns the items in the collection to their original locations (for example, ebooks to the Books collection).

Adding other EPUB ebooks to your library

With the ascendance of the EPUB format, publishers and book packagers are tripping over each other to make their titles EPUB friendly. As a result, the web is awash in EPUB books, so you don't have to get all the ebook content on your iPhone from the iBookstore. Here's a short list of some sites where you can download EPUB files to your computer:

- **epubBooks: www.epubbooks.com.** This is a terrific site for all things related to the EPUB format, and it offers a wide selection of public-domain EPUB books.

- **eBooks.com: www.ebooks.com.** This site has a variety of books in various ebook formats, although most won't work in the iBooks app because most of the EPUB books use the DRM scheme from Adobe. However, you can go to the Advanced Search page (www.ebooks.com/search/advancedsearch.asp) and select "Unencrypted ePub" in the Choose a Format list to see the iBooks-friendly titles that are offered.

- **Feedbooks: www.feedbooks.com.** This site offers public-domain titles in several formats, including EPUB.

- **Books on Google Play: play.google.com/store/books.** This site offers more than a million public-domain titles, many of which are free, plus a lot of current releases that you can buy.

- **ManyBooks: http://manybooks.net.** This site offers a nice collection of free ebooks in a huge variety of formats. When you download a book, be sure to choose the ePub (.epub) format in the Select Format drop-down list.

- **Smashwords: www.smashwords.com.** This intriguing site offers titles by independent and self-published authors. All ebooks are DRM free, and each book is available in the EPUB format.

- **Snee: www.snee.com/epubkidsbooks.** This site offers a lot of children's picture books in the EPUB format.

After you download an EPUB title to your computer, you can import the book into iBooks or iTunes. You do this through the Add to Library dialog:

- **In OS X Mavericks or later.** Open iBooks, choose File ⇨ Add to Library (or press ⌘+Shift+O), locate and click the EPUB file you downloaded, and then click Add. iBooks adds the ebook to the All Books section of the library.

- **In earlier versions of OS X; all versions of Windows.** Open iTunes, choose File ⇨ Add to Library (or press ⌘+O), locate and click the EPUB file you downloaded, and then click Open. iTunes adds the ebook to the Books section of the library.

Editing the iBooks Bookshelf

When you add a book to the iBooks Bookshelf, the app clears a space for the new title on the left side of the top shelf of the bookcase. The rest of the books are shuffled to the right and down.

This is a sensible way to go about things if you read each book as you download it because it means the iBooks Bookshelf displays your books in the order you read them. Of course, life isn't always that orderly, and you might end up reading your ebooks more haphazardly. This means that the order in which the books appear in the Bookshelf won't reflect the order in which you read them.

Similarly, you may have one or more books in your iBooks Bookshelf that you refer to frequently for reference, or because you're reading them piecemeal (such as a book of poetry or a collection of short stories). In that case, it would be better to have such books near the top of the bookcase where they're slightly easier to find and open.

For these and similar Bookshelf maintenance chores, iBooks lets you shuffle the books around to get them into the order you prefer. Here's how it works:

1. **In iBooks, tap My Books.**

2. **To move a book, tap and drag the book cover to the position you prefer.**

3. **If you want to remove a book from your library, tap Select, tap the book's cover to select it (as shown in Figure 12.4), tap Delete, and then tap either Delete This Copy (to remove it from just your iPhone) or Delete From All Devices (to remove it from every device that has a copy).**

12.4 To remove an ebook from your library, you must first select it.

4. **Tap Done.** iBooks closes the library for editing.

Creating a custom ebook cover

If you've obtained any free books from the iBookstore, or if you've downloaded public-domain books to iTunes, you'll no doubt have noticed that many (or, really, most) of these books use generic covers. That's no big deal for a book or two, but it can get monotonous if you have many such books in your iBooks library (as well as making it hard to find the book you want). To work around this, you can create custom book covers from your own photos. Your first task is to convert a photo (or any image) to something that's usable as a book cover. This involves loading the image into your favorite image-editing program and then doing three things:

- **Crop the image so that it's 420 pixels wide and 600 pixels tall.**
- **Use the text tool in the image-editing program to add the book title to the image.**
- **Save the image as a JPEG file.** If the image is already a JPEG, be sure to save it under a different name so you don't overwrite the original file.

Note

Creating a custom ebook cover works only if you're using a version of iTunes that supports ebooks. If you are using OS X Mavericks or later, ebooks are handled by the new iBooks application, which doesn't support custom ebook covers.

Now you're ready to use the new image as a book cover, which you do by importing the cover image into iTunes on your computer:

1. **In iTunes, click the Books category.** iTunes displays your ebooks.
2. **Right-click the book you want to customize, and then click Get Info.** iTunes displays the book's Info dialog.
3. **Click the Artwork tab.** This tab includes a large box for the book cover image.
4. **Use Finder (on a Mac) or Explorer (on a Windows PC) to locate the new cover image.** On a Mac, you can also locate the image in iPhoto.
5. **Click the new image and drop it inside the large box in the Artwork tab.**
6. **Click OK.** iTunes applies the new image as the book's cover.

Reading Ebooks with the iBooks App

If you're a book lover like me, and you have your iBooks Bookshelf groaning under the weight of all your ebooks, you may want to spend some time just looking at all the covers. Or not. If it's the latter, then it's time to get some reading done. The next few sections show you how to control ebooks and modify the display for the best reading experience.

Controlling ebooks on the reading screen

When you're ready to start reading a book using iBooks, getting started couldn't be simpler: Just tap the book you want to read and iBooks opens it.

Here's a list of techniques you can use to control an ebook while reading it:

- To flip to the next page, tap the right side of the screen.

- To flip to the previous page, tap the left side of the screen.

- To "manually" turn a page, flick the page with your finger. Flick left to turn to the next page; flick right to turn to the previous page.

- To access the iBooks controls, tap the middle of the screen. To hide the controls, tap the middle of the screen again.

- To access the book's Table of Contents, display the controls and tap the Contents icon, pointed out in Figure 12.5. You can then tap an item in the Table of Contents to jump to that section of the book.

- To go to a different page in the book, display the controls and tap a dot at the bottom of the screen.

- To search the book, display the controls and tap the Search icon in the upper right corner. Type your search text and tap Search. In the search results that appear, tap a result to display that part of the book.

- To return to the iBooks Bookshelf, display the controls and tap Library in the upper left corner.

Formatting ebook text

I mentioned near the top of the show that the EPUB format supports multiple text sizes and multiple fonts, and that the text reflows seamlessly to accommodate the new text size. The iBooks app takes advantage of these EPUB features, as shown here:

1. **While reading an ebook, tap the middle of the screen to display the controls.**

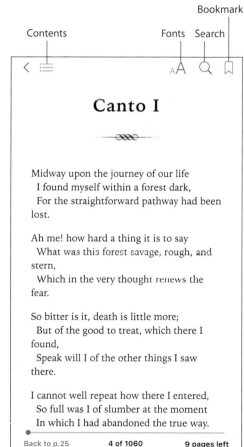

12.5 Tap the middle of the screen to display the controls.

2. **Tap the Fonts icon, pointed out earlier in Figure 12.5.** iBooks displays the Font options, as shown in Figure 12.6.

3. **Tap the larger "A" to increase the text size.** Tap the smaller "A" to reduce the size.

4. **Tap Fonts.** iBooks displays a list of typefaces.

5. **Tap the typeface you want to use.** iBooks reformats the ebook for the new typeface.

6. **To change the colors (such as a sepia background or white text on a black background for night reading), tap the theme you want to use.**

7. **Tap the middle of the screen to hide the controls.**

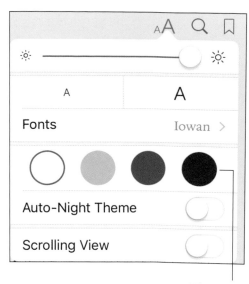

Themes

12.6 Tap the Fonts icon and then tap Fonts to see a list of those that are available.

Adding a bookmark

Reading an ebook with the iBooks app is so pleasurable that you may not want to stop! However, you have to eat at some point, so when it's time to set your book aside, mark your spot with a bookmark:

1. **Display the page where you want to set your bookmark.**

2. **Tap the page.** iBooks displays its controls.

3. **Tap the Bookmark icon, pointed out earlier in Figure 12.5.** iBooks saves your spot by creating a bookmark at the location you chose.

To return to your place, follow these steps:

1. **Tap the page.** iBooks displays the reading controls.

2. **Tap the Contents icon.** iBooks displays the table of contents.

3. **Tap the Bookmarks tab.** iBooks offers up a list of the saved bookmarks.

4. **Tap the bookmark.** iBooks returns you to the bookmarked page.

Looking up a word in the dictionary

While you peruse an ebook, you may come across an unfamiliar word. You can look it up using any of the umpteen online dictionaries, but there's no need for that with iBooks:

1. **Tap and hold the word that has you furrowing your brow.** iBooks displays a set of options.

2. **Tap Define.** The first time you do this, iBooks tells you that it needs to download a dictionary.

3. **Tap Download.** iBooks loads the dictionary, looks up the word, and then displays its definition.

4. **Tap Done to close the definition.**

Highlighting text

If you come across a word, phrase, sentence, paragraph, or section of text that strikes your fancy, there's a good chance you'll want to return to that text later on. The easiest way to do that is to highlight the text. This not only makes the text stick out from the surrounding prose by displaying it with a yellow background, but iBooks also bookmarks it so you can quickly find it again. To do so, use the same steps described earlier for returning to a bookmark.

Follow these steps to highlight text with iBooks:

1. **Tap and hold a word in the text you want to highlight.** iBooks selects the word and displays a set of options. If the word is all you want to highlight, skip to Step 3.

2. **Use the selection controls to expand the selection to include all the text you want to highlight.**

3. **Tap Highlight.** iBooks adds a yellow background to the text and creates a bookmark for it (see Figure 12.7).

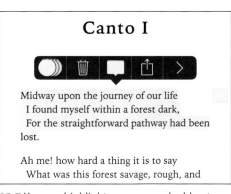

12.7 You can highlight passages and add notes to your ebooks.

Genius

If the yellow highlight background doesn't do it for you, you can change the color. Tap the highlight, tap Colors (the circle icon on the left), and then tap the color you prefer.

Adding a note

Sometimes when you're reading a book, you feel an irresistible urge to provide your own two cents' worth. With a paper book, you can grab the nearest writing implement and jot a margin note, but that's not going to work too well with an ebook. Fortunately, the iBooks programmers have taken pity on inveterate margin writers and provided a Note feature that lets you add your own comments and asides. Even better, iBooks also creates a bookmark for each note, so you can quickly find your additions.

Follow these steps to create a note with iBooks:

1. **Tap and hold a word in the text you want to comment on.** iBooks selects the word and displays a set of options. If the word is all you want to work with, skip to Step 3.

2. **Use the selection controls to expand the selection to include all the text you want to use.**

3. **Tap Note.** iBooks displays a text box that looks like a sticky note.

4. **Type your note.**

5. **Tap Done.** As shown in Figure 12.7, iBooks adds a yellow background to the text, displays a note icon in the margin, and bookmarks it.

Reading Other Ebooks

In this chapter, I focus on the iBooks app, mostly because it's an excellent app that's optimized for the iPhone and integrates seamlessly with iTunes. But the iPhone is arguably the best ereader available today, so it seems a shame to ignore the massive universe of ebooks that aren't iBooks-compatible. If you want to turn your iPhone into an ultimate ereader that's capable of reading practically *any* ebook in practically *any* format, then just head for the App Store and install the appropriate ereader apps.

A complete list of ereader apps would extend for pages, so I'll just hit the highlights here:

- **eBookMobi.** This powerful app (it costs $2.29) supports an amazing variety of ebook formats, including EPUB, PDF, and Mobipocket.

- **eReader.** This app supports the ereader format.

- **i2Reader.** This app supports EPUB books and PDF documents.

- **iSilo.** This app (which costs $11.99) supports the iSilo and Palm Doc formats.

- **Kindle.** The Amazon Kindle app is the way to go if you want to read Kindle ebooks on your iPhone.

- **Kobo Reading App.** This app is supplied by the same folks who make the Kobo ereader, and it supports both EPUB books and PDF documents.

How Do I Keep My Life in Sync with iCloud?

When you go online, you take your life along with you, of course, so your online world becomes a natural extension of your real world. However, just because it's online doesn't mean the digital version of your life is any less busy, chaotic, or complex than the rest of your life. The Apple iCloud service is designed to ease some of that chaos and complexity by automatically syncing your most important data — your email, contacts, calendars, photos, notes, and bookmarks. Although the syncing may be automatic, setting up is not, unfortunately. This chapter shows you what to do.

Understanding iCloud

These days, the primary source of online chaos and confusion is the ongoing proliferation of services and sites that demand your time and attention. What started with web-based email has grown to a website, a blog, a photo-sharing site, online bookmarks, and perhaps a few social networking sites, just to consume those last few precious moments of leisure time. You might be sitting in a chair, but you're being run ragged anyway!

A great way to simplify your online life is to get a free iCloud account. You get a one-stop web shop that includes email, an address book, a calendar, and 5GB of online file storage. (If you want more storage, you can get 50GB for $0.99 a month, 200GB for $2.99 a month, or 1TB for $9.99 a month.)

The web applications that make up iCloud — Mail, Contacts, Calendar, Photos, iCloud Drive, Find My iPhone, Notes, Reminders, Pages, Numbers, and Keynote — are certainly useful and are surprisingly functional for online applications. However, the big news with iCloud is the "cloud" part of the name. This means that your data, particularly your email accounts, contacts, calendars, and bookmarks, is stored on a bunch of icloud.com networked servers that Apple collectively calls the cloud. When you log in to your iCloud account at icloud.com, you use the web applications to interact with that data.

That's pretty mundane stuff, right? What's revolutionary here is that you can let the cloud know about all the other devices in your life: your Mac, your home computer, your work PC, your notebook, your iPad, and, of course, your iPhone. If you sign in to your iCloud account and, say, add a new appointment, the cloud takes that appointment and immediately sends the data to all your devices. Fire up your Mac, open Calendar, and the appointment's there; switch to your Windows PC, click the Outlook Calendar folder, and the appointment's there; tap Calendar on your iPhone Home screen and, yup, the appointment's there, too.

This works if you change data on any of your devices. Move an email message to another folder on your Mac, and the same message is moved to the same folder on the other devices and on your iCloud account; modify a contact on your Windows PC, and the changes also propagate everywhere else. In each case, the new or changed data is sent to the cloud, which then sends the data to each device, usually in a matter of seconds.

Note

If you've used email, contacts, and calendars in a company that runs Microsoft Exchange Server, then you're no doubt used to push technology because Exchange has done that for a while through ActiveSync (a feature that your iPhone supports, by the way). iCloud push is a step up, however, because you don't need a behemoth corporate server to make it happen. Apple calls iCloud "Exchange for the rest of us."

With iCloud, you never have to worry about entering the same information into all your devices. With iCloud, you won't miss an important meeting because you forgot to enter it into the calendar on your work computer. With iCloud, you can never forget data when you're traveling because you have up-to-the-moment data with you at all times. iCloud practically organizes your life for you; all you have to do is show up.

Understanding iCloud Device Support

iCloud promises to simplify your online life, but the first step to that simpler existence is to configure iCloud on all the devices that you want to keep in sync. The next few sections show you how to configure iCloud on various devices, but it's important to understand exactly what devices can do the iCloud thing. Here's a summary:

- **iPhone (3Gs or later), iPad, and iPod touch (3rd generation or later).** iCloud works with any of these devices as long as they're running version 5.1.1 or later of iOS. However, Apple recommends devices running at least iOS 8.3, which requires an iPhone 4s or later, an iPad 2 or later, or a 5th generation iPod touch.

- **Mac.** Many iCloud features work with a minimum of OS X Lion (10.7.5), but Apple recommends running OS X El Capitan (10.11) or later. To access the iCloud web applications, you should be using Safari 8 or later, Chrome 28 or later, or Firefox 22 or later.

- **Windows.** Any Windows 7, 8, or 8.1 version works with iCloud. To access the iCloud web applications, you need at least Internet Explorer 9, but Apple recommends Internet Explorer 10 or later. As I write this, iCloud doesn't support Windows 10, but most of the apps work fine, even if you use the Microsoft Edge browser. Other recommended browsers are Safari 8 or later, Firefox 22 or later, or Chrome 28 or later. For push email, contacts, and calendars, you need Outlook 2007 or later.

Configuring iCloud on Your iPhone

iCloud is designed particularly with the iPhone in mind, because it's when you're on the town or on the road that you need data pushed to you. To ensure your iPhone works seamlessly with your iCloud data, you need to add your iCloud account and configure the iCloud sync settings on your iPhone.

Setting up your iCloud account on your iPhone

Start by setting up your iCloud account on your iPhone:

1. **On the Home screen, tap Settings.** Your iPhone opens the Settings app.

2. **Tap Mail, Contacts, Calendars.** The Mail, Contacts, Calendars screen appears.

3. **Tap Add Account.** The Add Account screen appears.

4. **Tap the iCloud logo.** Your iPhone displays the iCloud screen, as shown in Figure 13.1.

5. **Tap the Apple ID text box and enter your iCloud email address.**

6. **Tap the Password text box and enter your iCloud password.**

7. **Tap Next.** Your iPhone verifies the account info and then asks what type of data you want pushed to your iPhone, as shown in Figure 13.2.

8. **If there are any data types you don't want pushed to your iPhone, tap the corresponding switch to Off.**

9. **Tap Save.** Your iPhone returns you to the Mail settings screen with your iCloud account added to the Accounts list.

13.1 Use the iCloud screen to configure your iCloud account on your iPhone.

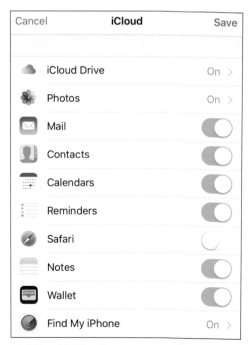

13.2 Use this iCloud screen to specify the types of data you want iCloud to push to your iPhone.

Setting up iCloud synchronization on your iPhone

No matter where you are, iCloud ensures that your email messages, contacts, and calendars get pushed to your iPhone and remain fully synced with all your other devices. Your iPhone comes with this push feature turned on, but if you want to double-check this or if you want to turn off push to concentrate on something else, you can configure the setting by following these steps:

1. **In the Home Screen, tap Settings.** The Settings app appears.

2. **Tap iCloud.** Settings displays the iCloud screen, as shown in Figure 13.3.

3. **If there are any data types you don't want pushed to your iPhone, tap the corresponding switch to Off.**

Setting up and using Family Sharing

iCloud means you have easy access to *your* email, photos, reminders, notes, and more.

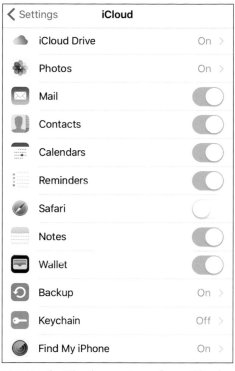

13.3 Use the iCloud screen to configure iCloud synchronization on your iPhone.

Similarly, if your spouse or kids also have iCloud accounts, then they have easy access to *their* personal content. What's wrong with this picture? Right: Despite being a family, no one has access to anyone else's cloud data. You can't see your spouse's reminders; he or she can't see your photos; none of you can see your kids' calendars.

This has long been a major drawback with iCloud because the only way to work around it was to share an account. Now, however, iOS offers Family Sharing, an iCloud feature that allows up to six family members to share each other's content, including photos, calendars, and reminders. And if purchases are made through the App Store, iTunes Store, or iBookstore using a single credit card, then each family member also gets access to purchased apps, songs, movies, TV shows, and ebooks.

Assuming you'll be the Family Organizer (that is, the person who'll be setting up and maintaining Family Sharing), follow these steps to get things started:

1. **Tap Settings to launch the Settings app.**

2. **Tap iCloud.** The iCloud settings appear.

3. **Tap Set Up Family Sharing.** iCloud displays an overview of Family Sharing.

4. **Tap Get Started.** iCloud explains your duties as the Family Organizer.

5. **Tap Continue.** iCloud explains how purchases made with your Apple ID will be shared with other family members.

6. **Tap Continue.** iCloud shows you the payment method that will be used for all Family Sharing purchases. (If you have multiple payment methods, you can change the default method a bit later in this process.)

⟨ iCloud	**Family**

FAMILY MEMBERS

Paul McFedries (Me)
Organizer   ⟩

Add Family Member...

Family members share music, movies, apps, photos, location, and more. Learn more...

SHARED PAYMENT METHOD

VISA   **Visa (•••• 9999)**
Expires 2018-11

Purchases initiated by family members will be billed to this payment method. Change it in iTunes & App Store Settings.

13.4 As the Family Organizer, you use this screen to add family members and set the default payment method.

7. **Tap Continue.** iCloud asks if you want to share your location with your family.

8. **Tap Share Your Location.** If you prefer not to share your location, tap Not Now, instead. The Family Sharing screen appears, as shown in Figure 13.4.

9. **Tap Add Family Member then type the name or email address of the family member you want to add.** If the person has an iCloud account, iCloud asks how you want the family member to confirm.

10. **Tap Ask *Name* to Enter Password (where *Name* is the family member's first name) and then type the password for that person's iCloud account.** If you don't know the password, tap Send an Invitation, instead.

11. **If you have multiple payment methods set up, tap the existing method shown under Shared Payment Method and then tap the payment you want to use for Family Sharing.**

Setting up iCloud Keychain

A *keychain* is a master list of usernames and passwords that a system stores for easy access by an authorized user. iCloud Keychain is a special type of keychain that stores website passwords auto-generated by Safari. This means that you don't have to remember these passwords because Safari can automatically retrieve them from your iCloud account. Even better, any other iOS device or Mac that uses the same iCloud account has access to the same keychain, so your website passwords also work on those devices.

Follow these steps to set up your iCloud Keychain on your iPhone:

1. **In the Home Screen, tap Settings.** The Settings app appears.

2. **Tap iCloud to open the iCloud settings.**

3. **Tap Keychain.**

4. **Tap the iCloud Keychain switch to On.** Settings prompts you to enter your iCloud password.

5. **Type the password and then tap OK.** iCloud sets up keychain access, which usually takes a few moments.

6. **Allow your iPhone to use your iCloud Keychain:**

   - **If you're already using iCloud Keychain on another device,** that device prompts you to allow your iPhone to access the iCloud Keychain, as shown in Figure 13.5 (this is an OS X notification). In this case, you'd click View, type your iCloud password, and then click Allow. If you need access to the Keychain sooner, use your iPhone to tap Approve with Security Code and then type the code that you entered when you originally set up iCloud Keychain. You'll also need to enter a verification code that gets sent to your phone via text message.

   - **If you're not using iCloud Keychain on any other device or an iCloud security code,** iCloud asks if you want to use your phone's existing passcode. Tap Use Passcode (or tap Create Different Code if you want to use something else, although why complicate things?), tap the passcode, then enter a phone where verification text messages can be sent. After you enter your iCloud password, you're set to go.

13.5 If you have already set up iCloud Keychain on another device (such as a Mac, as shown here), use that device to approve your iPhone.

Managing your iCloud storage

I mentioned earlier that your iCloud account comes with 5GB of storage free. That storage is used for your iCloud Photo Library, device backups, email, and app documents and data. If you find that you're running low on storage space, follow these steps to remove data and free up some cloud headroom:

1. **In the Home Screen, tap Settings.** The Settings app appears.

2. **Tap iCloud to open the iCloud settings.**

3. **Tap Storage.** The Storage screen tells you your total storage and how much is available.

4. **Tap Manage Storage.** The Manage Storage screen appears and displays a list of the items in your iCloud storage as well as how much space each item takes up, as shown in Figure 13.6.

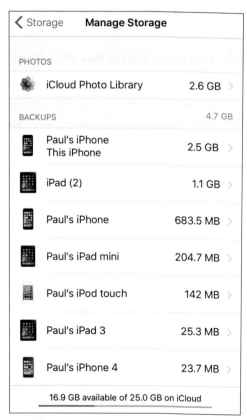

13.6 The Manage Storage screen shows you how much space each item takes up.

5. **To remove data from iCloud, tap an item and then use the following techniques:**

   - **Your iPhone backups.** Tap Delete Backup to remove the current backup.

   - **Other device backups.** Tap Delete Backup to remove the current backup.

   - **Documents.** Tap Edit, tap the red Delete icon to the left of the document you want to remove, tap the Delete button that appears, then tap Delete to confirm.

Changing your iCloud storage plan

If, despite your best management efforts, you find that you're still getting low on iCloud storage, then you should consider changing your storage plan to give yourself more cloud real estate. See "Understanding iCloud," earlier in this chapter, to learn what it will cost you to get more storage. Once you know what you want, follow these steps to upgrade:

1. **Tap Settings to display the Settings app.**

2. **Tap iCloud to open the iCloud settings.**

3. **Tap Storage.** The Storage screen appears.

4. **Tap Change Storage Plan.** The Buy More Storage screen appears.

5. **Tap the storage plan you want to use and then tap Buy.** iCloud prompts you for your password.

6. **Type your password, tap OK, then tap OK again when iCloud tells you the purchase is complete.**

Note

If you find that you're not using the extra storage, you can downgrade to a cheaper plan (or even down to the free 5GB). Tap Settings, iCloud, Storage, then Change Storage Plan. Tap Downgrade Options, tap the new plan you want to use, then tap Done.

Upgrading to iCloud Drive

Regular iCloud storage includes backups and email, as well as the documents and data used by individual apps. That's a good feature, but it's limited because it means you can access those documents and the app data only by using the associated apps. In other words, there is no "folder" on iCloud that you can view to see your saved documents and data.

If you'd prefer to see such a folder, as well as use iCloud to save a wider variety of documents and data, then you should consider upgrading to iCloud Drive, which provides all those features and even enables you to access your cloud data from any Mac or PC.

Here are the steps to follow to set up iCloud Drive on your iPhone:

1. **Tap Settings to display the Settings app.**

2. **Tap iCloud to open the iCloud settings.**

3. **Tap iCloud Drive.** The iCloud Drive overview appears.

4. **Tap the iCloud Drive switch to On.** iCloud turns on iCloud Drive and then displays a list of apps that can use iCloud Drive, as shown in Figure 13.7.

5. **For each app that you don't want to store documents in iCloud Drive, tap the app's switch to Off.**

6. **If you don't want your iPhone to use a cellular connection to transfer data to and from iCloud Drive, tap the Use Cellular Data switch to Off.**

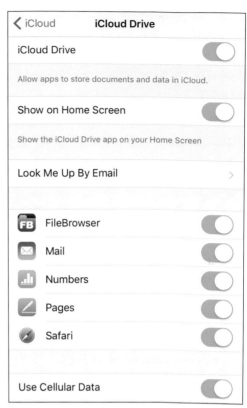

13.7 Once you turn on iCloud Drive, you see a list of apps that can use the service to store documents.

Using the iCloud Drive app

You might have noticed in Figure 13.7 that the iCloud Drive screen includes a Show on Home Screen switch. When this switch is On, your iPhone's Home screen sprouts a new app called iCloud Drive, that gives you access to your iCloud Drive folders and documents directly from your iPhone.

When you open iCloud Drive, as shown in Figure 13.8, you see a screen that shows your folders — usually one for each app that you've used to access iCloud Drive — and perhaps a document or three.

iCloud Drive is a straightforward app with a limited set of features, including the following:

- **Tap a folder to see its contents.**
- **Tap a document to download it to your iPhone and view it.**
- **Create a folder by opening an existing folder (or just using the iCloud Drive main folder), tapping Select, and then tapping New Folder**
- **Sort a folder's contents by tapping a sort tab: Date, Name, or Tags.**
- **Move a document or a folder by tapping Select, tapping the document or folder, and then tapping Move.**
- **Delete a document or a folder by tapping Select, tapping the document or folder, and then tapping Delete.**

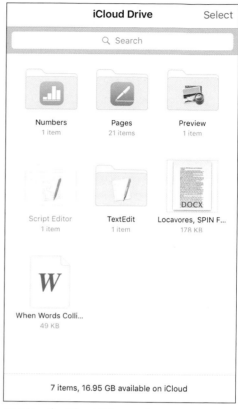

13.8 Use the iCloud Drive app to access your iCloud Drive folders and documents directly from your iPhone.

Configuring iCloud on Your Mac

If you want to keep your Mac in sync with the iCloud push services, you need to add your iCloud account to the Mail application and configure iCloud synchronization on your Mac.

Setting up an iCloud account on your Mac

Here are the steps to follow to get your iCloud account into the Mail application:

1. **In the Dock, click the Mail icon.** The Mail application appears.

2. **In OS X Mavericks or later, choose Mail ⇨ Add Account.** In earlier versions of OS X, choose File ⇨ Add Account, instead. Mail displays the Add Account dialog.

3. **Select the iCloud option and click Continue.** The iCloud dialog appears.

4. **Type your Apple ID address and password.**

5. **Click Sign In.** Mail verifies the account info and displays the account summary screen.

6. **Select the check box beside each type of data you want to set up.**

7. **Click Add Account.** Mail adds the iCloud account.

Setting up iCloud synchronization on your Mac

Macs were made to sync with iCloud, so this process should be a no-brainer. To ensure that is the case, you need to configure your Mac to make sure iCloud sync is activated, and that your email accounts, contacts, and calendars are part of the sync process. Follow these steps to set your preferences:

1. **Click the System Preferences icon in the Dock.** Your Mac opens the System Preferences window.

2. **Click the iCloud icon.** The first time you do this, your Mac prompts you to sign in to iCloud.

3. **Type your iCloud email address and password, and then click Sign In.** If this is the first time you've launched the iCloud preferences, you run through a few dialogs to set your initial preferences. When that's done, you end up at the iCloud preferences window.

4. **Select the check box beside each data item you want to sync with your iCloud account (see Figure 13.9).**

5. **Click the Close button.** Your Mac is now ready for iCloud syncing.

13.9 Select the check box beside each item you want to sync.

Configuring iCloud on Your Windows PC

iCloud is happy to push data to your Windows PC. However, unlike with a Mac, your Windows machine wouldn't know iCloud if it tripped over it. To get Windows hip to the iCloud thing, you need to do two things:

- **Download and install the latest version of iTunes.**

- **Download and install the iCloud Control Panel for Windows, which you can find at http://support.apple.com/kb/DL1455.**

With that done, you can now configure iCloud to work with your Windows PC by following these steps:

1. **On the Windows PC that you want to configure to work with iCloud, open the Control Panel window:**

   - **Windows 8 and later.** Press Windows Logo+X and then click Control Panel.

   - **Earlier versions of Windows.** Choose Start ➪ Control Panel.

2. **Double-click the iCloud icon.** If you don't see this icon, first open the Network and Internet category. The iCloud dialog box appears.

3. **Use the Apple ID text box to type your iCloud address.**

4. **Use the Password text box to type your iCloud password.**

5. **Click Sign In.** Windows signs in to your account and then displays the iCloud Control Panel, as shown in Figure 13.10.

6. **Select the check box beside each type of data you want to sync.**

7. **Click Apply.**

13.10 Use the iCloud Control Panel to set up your Windows PC to work with iCloud.

How Do I Fix My iPhone?

The good news about iPhone problems — whether they're problems with iPhone software or with the actual iPhone — is that they're relatively rare. On the hardware side, although the iPhone is a sophisticated device that's really a small computer (not just a fancy phone), it's far less complex than a full-blown computer, and so much less likely to go south on you. On the software side (and to a lesser extent on the accessories side), app developers (and accessory manufacturers) only have to build their products to work with a single device made by a single company. This really simplifies things, and the result is fewer problems. Not, however, zero problems. Even the iPhone sometimes behaves strangely or not at all. This chapter gives you some general troubleshooting techniques for iPhone woes and also tackles a few specific problems.

General Techniques for Troubleshooting Your iPhone

If your iPhone is behaving oddly or erratically, it's possible that a specific component inside the phone is the cause. In that case, you don't have much choice but to ship your iPhone back to Apple for repairs. Fortunately, however, most glitches are temporary and can often be fixed by using one or more of the following techniques:

- **Restart your iPhone.** By far the most common solution to an iPhone problem is to shut it down and then restart it. By rebooting the iPhone, you reload the entire system, which is often enough to solve many problems. You restart your iPhone by pressing and holding the Sleep/Wake button for a few seconds until you see the Slide to Power Off screen (at which point you can release the button). Drag the Slide to Power Off slider to the right to start the shutdown. When the screen goes completely black, your iPhone is off. To restart, press and hold the Sleep/Wake button until you see the Apple logo and then release the button.

- **Reboot your iPhone hardware.** When you restart your iPhone by pressing and holding Sleep/Wake for a while, what you're really doing is rebooting the system software. If that still doesn't solve the problem, you might need to reboot the iPhone hardware as well. To do that, press and hold down the Sleep/Wake and Home buttons. Keep them pressed until you see the Apple logo (it takes about 8 seconds or so), which indicates a successful restart.

Genius

The hardware reboot is also the way to go if your iPhone is *really* stuck and holding down just the Sleep/Wake button doesn't do anything.

- **Recharge your iPhone.** It's possible that your iPhone just has a battery that's completely discharged. Connect your iPhone to your computer or to the dock. If it powers up and you see the battery logo (this might take a minute or two), then it's charging just fine and will be back on its feet in a while.

- **Shut down a stuck app.** If your iPhone is frozen because an app has gone haywire, you can usually get it back in the saddle by forcing the app to quit. Press and hold the Sleep/Wake button until you see the Slide to Power Off screen; then press and hold the Home button for about 6 seconds. Your iPhone shuts down the app and returns you to the

Home screen. If an app is frozen but your iPhone still works fine otherwise, double-press the Home button to display the multitasking bar, scroll right or left as needed to bring the app's thumbnail screen into view, then drag the app thumbnail up to the top of the screen. Your iPhone sends the thumbnail off the screen and shuts down the app.

- **Check for iPhone software updates.** If Apple knows about the problem you're having, it will fix it and then make the patch available in a software update. I tell you how to update your iPhone a bit later in this chapter.

- **Check for app updates.** It's possible that a bug in an app is causing your woes, so you can often solve such problems by updating the app. Fortunately, app updates are automatic in iOS (since version 7), so this should never be much of a problem. To confirm that your apps are updating automatically, open Settings, tap iTunes & App Store, and make sure the Updates switch is On.

- **Erase and restore your content and settings.** This may seem like drastic advice, but it's possible to use iTunes to perform a complete backup of everything on your iPhone. You can then reset the iPhone to its original, pristine state, and then restore the backup. I show you how to back up your iPhone in Chapter 2, and I explain the rather lengthy restore process later in this chapter.

- **Reset your settings.** Sometimes your iPhone goes down for the count because its settings have become corrupted. In that case, you can fix the problem by restoring the iPhone to its original settings. If iTunes doesn't recognize your iPhone, then the restore option is out. However, you can still reset the settings on the iPhone. Tap Settings in the Home screen, tap General, tap Reset, and then tap Reset All Settings. When your iPhone asks you to confirm, tap Reset All Settings.

Genius

If resetting your iPhone doesn't get the job done, it could be some recalcitrant bit of content that's causing the problem. In that case, tap Settings in the Home screen, tap General, tap Reset, and then tap Erase All Content and Settings. When your iPhone asks you to confirm, tap Erase iPhone.

Troubleshooting connected devices

There are only a few ways that you can connect devices to your iPhone: using the headset jack, the Lightning connector, or Bluetooth. Although the number of devices you can connect is relatively limited, that doesn't mean you might never have problems with those devices.

If you're having trouble with a device attached to your iPhone, the good news is that a fair chunk of those problems have a relatively limited set of causes. You may be able to get the device back on its feet by attempting a few tried-and-true remedies. If it's not immediately obvious what the problem is, then your hardware troubleshooting routine should always start with these very basic techniques:

- **Check connections, power switches, and so on.** Some of the most common (and most embarrassing) causes of hardware problems are the simple physical things, so make sure that a device is turned on and check that cable connections are secure. For example, if you can't access the Internet through the Wi-Fi connection on your iPhone, make sure your network's router is turned on. Also make sure that the cable between your router and the ISP's modem is properly connected.

- **Replace the batteries.** Wireless devices such as headsets really chew through batteries, so if such a device is working intermittently (or not at all), always try replacing the batteries to see if that solves the problem.

- **Turn the device off and then on again.** You *power cycle* a device by turning it off, waiting a few seconds for its innards to stop spinning, and then turning it back on. You'd be amazed how often this simple procedure can get a device back up and running. For a device that doesn't have an On/Off switch, try either unplugging it from the power outlet or removing and replacing the batteries.

- **Reset the device's default settings.** If you can configure a device, then perhaps some new setting is causing the problem. If you recently made a change, try returning the setting back to its original value. If that doesn't do the trick, most configurable devices have some kind of Restore Default Settings option that enables you to quickly return them to their factory settings.

- **Upgrade the device's firmware.** Some devices come with *firmware* — a small program that runs inside the device and controls its internal functions. For example, all routers have firmware. Check with the manufacturer to see if a new version exists. If it does, download the new version and then see the device's manual to learn how to upgrade the firmware.

Updating software

The iPhone software should check for available updates from time to time when you connect it to your computer, provided the computer has an Internet connection. This is another good reason to sync your iPhone regularly. The problem is, you might hear about an important update that adds a feature you're really looking forward to or perhaps fixes a gaping security hole. What do you do if iTunes isn't scheduled to check for an update for a few days? In that case, you take matters into your own hands and check for updates yourself.

You can check for updates right on your iPhone by following these steps:

1. **On the Home screen, tap Settings.** The Settings app appears.

2. **Tap General.** Your iPhone displays the General options screen.

3. **Tap Software Update.** Your iPhone begins checking for available updates. If you see the message "Your software is up to date," then you can move on to bigger and better things.

4. **If an update is available, tap Download and Install.** Your iPhone downloads the update and then proceeds with the installation, which takes a few minutes.

Caution Your iPhone only goes through with the update if it has more than 50 percent battery life through the entire update operation. To ensure the update is a success, either plug your iPhone into an AC outlet or only run the update when the battery is fully charged.

Here's the iTunes route:

1. **Connect your iPhone to your computer.** iTunes opens and connects to your iPhone.

2. **Click your iPhone in the Devices list.**

3. **Click the Summary tab.**

4. **Click Check for Update.** iTunes connects to the Apple servers to see if any iPhone updates are available. If an update exists, you see the iPhone Software Update dialog, which offers a description of the update.

5. **Click Next.** iTunes displays the Software License Agreement.

6. **Click Agree.** iTunes downloads the software update and installs it.

Restoring data and settings

Sometimes your iPhone goes down for the count because its settings have become corrupted. In that case, you can attempt to fix the problem by restoring iPhone to its original settings. The best way to go about this is to use the Restore feature in iTunes because that enables you to make a backup of your settings. However, it does mean that your iPhone must be able to connect to your computer and be visible in iTunes.

If that's not the case, see the instructions for resetting in Chapter 2. Otherwise, follow these steps to restore your iPhone:

1. **On your iPhone, turn off Find My iPhone, if it's turned on.** You do this by opening Settings, tapping iCloud, tapping Find My iPhone, tapping the Find My iPhone switch to Off, and then entering your Apple password.

2. **Connect your iPhone to your computer.**

3. **In iTunes, click your iPhone in the Devices list.**

4. **Click Sync.** This ensures that iTunes backs up your iPhone and has copies of all the data from your iPhone.

Caution
If you have confidential or sensitive data on your iPhone, that data becomes part of the backup files and could be viewed by some snoop. To prevent this, select the Summary tab's Encrypt iPhone backup check box, and then use the Set password dialog to specify your decryption password. Then click Back Up Now.

5. **Click the Summary tab.**

6. **Click Restore iPhone.** iTunes asks you to confirm you want to restore.

7. **Click Restore.** iTunes downloads the software and restores the original software and settings. When your iPhone restarts, iTunes connects to it and might ask you to enter your Apple ID credentials. After you've done that, iTunes displays the Welcome to Your New iPhone screen, as shown in Figure 14.1.

14.1 When your factory-fresh iPhone restarts, use iTunes to restore your settings and data.

8. **Select the Restore from this backup option.**

9. **If you happen to have more than one iPhone backed up, use the list to choose yours.**

10. **Click Continue.** iTunes restores your backed-up data, restarts your iPhone, and syncs it.

11. **Go through the tabs and check the sync settings to make sure they're set up the way you want.**

12. **If you made any changes to the settings, click Apply.** This ensures that your iPhone has all its data restored.

Putting your iPhone in Device Firmware Upgrade mode

In some rare cases, your iPhone goes utterly haywire, where not only does iTunes not recognize the device, but even completely resetting it doesn't solve the problem. (This sort of scenario occurs most often if you've tried something naughty, such as jailbreaking your iPhone.) If this happens, you can still recover everything, but you have to do it using a special hardware mode called Device Firmware Upgrade (DFU). This mode essentially bypasses the current OS installed on the phone (which is good because in this scenario your current OS is toast) and tells iTunes to install a factory-fresh version of the OS. You can then restore your stuff as described in the previous section.

Follow these steps to put your iPhone into DFU mode:

1. **Turn off your iPhone.**

2. **Connect your iPhone to your Mac or Windows PC.**

3. **Launch iTunes.**

4. **Press and hold down the Sleep/Wake and Home buttons for exactly 10 seconds.**

5. **After 10 seconds, release the Sleep/Wake button, but continue to hold down the Home button for another 10 seconds.**

6. **After 10 seconds, release the Home button.** iTunes now recognizes your iPhone and displays the dialog shown in Figure 14.2.

7. **Click OK.**

8. **Click Restore iPhone.** iTunes asks you to confirm, as shown in Figure 14.3.

9. **Click Restore and Update.** iTunes restores your iPhone to the factory state.

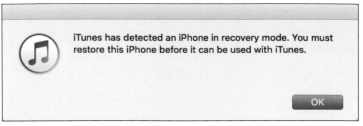

iTunes has detected an iPhone in recovery mode. You must restore this iPhone before it can be used with iTunes.

OK

14.2 When you boot your iPhone in DFU mode, iTunes recognizes the phone and displays this dialog to remind you to restore it.

Are you sure you want to restore the iPhone "iPhone" to its factory settings? All of your media and other data will be erased, and the newest version of the iPhone software will be installed.

iTunes will verify the restore with Apple. After this process is complete, you will have the option to restore your contacts, calendars, text messages and other settings.

Cancel   Restore and Update

14.3 iTunes asks you to confirm that you want to revert to the iPhone factory settings.

Taking Care of the iPhone Battery

Your iPhone comes with a large lithium-ion battery. Apple claims that the iPhone 6s Plus gives you up to 16 days of standby time, 24 hours of talk time on a 3G network, 12 hours of Internet use on an LTE, 3G, or Wi-Fi connection, 80 hours of audio playback, and 14 hours of video playback. For the iPhone 6s, the corresponding numbers are 10 days standby, 14 hours talk, 10 hours Internet use (11 hours on Wi-Fi), 50 hours audio, and 11 hours video.) Those are all impressive times, although you should count on getting less in the real world.

Sending in Your iPhone for Repairs

To have your iPhone repaired, you can either take it to an Apple Store or send it in. Visit www.apple.com/support and follow the prompts to find out how to send in your iPhone for repairs. Remember that the memory comes back wiped, so be sure to sync with iTunes, if you can. Also, don't forget to remove your SIM card before you send it in.

The biggest downside to the iPhone battery is that it's not, in Apple parlance, *user-installable*. If your battery dies, you have no choice but to return it to Apple to get it replaced. This is all the more reason to take care of your battery and try to maximize its life.

Tracking battery use

Your iPhone doesn't give a ton of battery data, but you can monitor both the total usage time (this includes all activities: calling, surfing, playing media, and so on) and standby time (time when your iPhone was in sleep mode). Also, one of the nice features in iOS is a breakdown of recent (the last three hours) battery usage by app, so you can see which apps have been draining your battery. Follow these steps to track your iPhone battery use:

1. **On the Home screen, tap Settings.** The Settings app appears.

2. **Tap Battery.** Your iPhone displays the Battery screen.

14.4 The new Battery Usage screen breaks down recent battery usage by app.

3. **Tap the Battery Percentage switch to On.** Your iPhone shows you the percentage of battery life left in the status bar beside the battery icon (see Figure 14.1).

4. **Use the Battery Usage section to view recent usage by app, as shown in Figure 14.4.**

Note

If you don't want to clutter the status bar with the battery percentage, you can examine the Usage and Standby values that appear in the Usage screen instead. As your battery runs down, check the Usage screen periodically to get a sense of your iPhone battery use.

Tips for extending battery life

Reducing battery consumption as much as possible on the iPhone not only extends the time between charges but also extends the overall life of your battery. The Battery Usage screen usually offers a suggestion or two for extending battery life, but here are a few suggestions you're not likely to see on that screen:

- **Turn off Background App Refresh.** Some apps update their content even when you're not using them, and this handy feature is called Background App Refresh. Handy, yes, but also a major battery hog, so turn off this feature when you need to go easy on the juice. Open Settings, tap General, tap Background App Refresh, and then tap the Background App Refresh switch to Off. As an alternative, consider leaving that switch on but turning off Background App Refresh for individual apps (particularly active apps such as Facebook and Gmail).

- **Turn on Low Power mode.** This mode (it's new in iOS 9) saves battery life by turning off Background App Refresh, Mail push, and automatic content and app downloads, disabling a few visual effects, and dimming the screen. iOS asks if you want to switch to Lower Power mode when the battery level falls to 20 percent, as shown in Figure 14.5. (This message also appears when the level falls to 10 percent.) Tap Low Power Mode to activate this feature. To activate Low Power Mode full-time, open Settings, tap Battery, tap the Low Power Mode switch to On, and then tap Continue. Note that you can tell when this feature is active by looking at the battery icon, which turns yellow during Low Power mode.

14.5 When your iPhone's battery level falls to 20 percent, iOS asks if you want to switch to Low Power mode.

Note

With Low Power mode on, Settings automatically configures your iPhone to auto-lock in 30 seconds *and* it disables the Auto-Lock setting.

Dim the screen. The touchscreen drains a lot of battery power, so dimming it reduces the amount of power used. On the Home screen, tap Settings, tap Display & Brightness, and then drag the Brightness slider to the left to dim the screen.

Cycle the battery. All lithium-based batteries slowly lose their charging capacity over time. If you can run your iPhone on batteries for 4 hours today, later on you'll only be able to run it for 3 hours on a full charge. You can't stop this process, but you can delay it significantly by periodically cycling the iPhone battery. *Cycling* — also called *reconditioning* or *recalibrating* — a battery means letting it completely discharge and then fully recharging it again. To maintain optimal performance, you should cycle your iPhone battery every one or two months.

Note Paradoxically, the less you use your iPhone, the *more* often you should cycle its battery. If you often go several days or a week or two (I can't imagine!) without using your iPhone, then you should cycle its battery at least once a month.

Slow the auto-check on your email. Having your email frequently poll the server for new messages eats up your battery. Set it to check every hour or, ideally, set it to Manual check if you can. To do this, tap Settings; tap Mail, Contacts, Calendars; tap Fetch New Data; and then in the Fetch section, tap either Hourly or Manual.

Turn off push. If you have an iCloud or Exchange account, consider turning off the push feature to save battery power. Tap Settings; tap Mail, Contacts, Calendars; and then tap Fetch New Data. In the Fetch New Data screen, tap the Push switch to Off, and in the Fetch section, tap Manually.

Minimize your tasks. If you won't be able to charge your iPhone for a while, avoid background chores, such as playing music, or secondary chores, such as organizing your contacts. If your only goal is to read all your email, stick to that until it's done because you don't know how much time you have.

Put your iPhone into sleep mode manually, if necessary. If you are interrupted — for example, the pizza delivery guy shows up on time — don't wait for your iPhone to put itself to sleep because those few minutes use precious battery time. Instead, put your iPhone to sleep manually right away by pressing the Sleep/Wake button.

Avoid temperature extremes. Exposing your iPhone to extremely hot or cold temperatures reduces the long-term effectiveness of the battery. Try to keep your iPhone at a reasonable temperature.

- **Turn off Wi-Fi if you don't need it.** When Wi-Fi is on, it regularly checks for available wireless networks, which drains the battery. If you don't need to connect to a wireless network, turn off Wi-Fi to conserve energy. Tap Settings, tap Wi-Fi, and then tap the Wi-Fi switch to Off.

- **Turn off cellular data if you don't need it.** Your iPhone constantly looks for nearby cellular towers to maintain the signal, which can use up battery power in a hurry. If you're surfing on a Wi-Fi network, you don't need cellular data, so turn it off. Tap Settings, tap Cellular, and then tap the Cellular Data switch to Off.

- **Turn off GPS if you don't need it.** When GPS is on, the receiver exchanges data with the GPS system regularly, which uses up battery power. If you don't need the GPS feature for the time being, turn off the GPS antenna. Tap Settings, tap Privacy, tap Location Services, and then tap the Location Services switch to Off.

- **Turn off Bluetooth if you don't need it.** When Bluetooth is running, it constantly checks for nearby Bluetooth devices, and this drains the battery. If you aren't using any Bluetooth devices, turn off Bluetooth to save energy. Tap Settings, tap Bluetooth, and then tap the Bluetooth switch to Off.

Genius

If you don't need all four of the iPhone antennae for a while, a faster way to turn them off is to switch your iPhone to Airplane mode. Either tap Settings and then tap the Airplane Mode switch to On, or swipe up from the bottom to reveal the Control Center and then tap the Airplane Mode icon.

Solving Specific Problems

The generic troubleshooting and repair techniques that you've seen so far can solve all kinds of problems. However, there are always specific problems that require specific solutions. The rest of this chapter takes you through a few of the most common of these problems.

The iPhone screen won't respond to taps

Every now and then, your iPhone might freeze and no amount of tapping, swiping, or threatening will get the phone to respond. The most likely problem is that the touchscreen has become temporarily stuck. To fix that, press the Sleep/Wake button to put the iPhone to sleep, press Sleep/Wake again to wake the iPhone, and then drag Slide to Unlock. In most cases, you should now be able to resume normal iPhone operations.

If that doesn't work, then it's possible that the app you're using has crashed, so you need to shut it down as I described earlier in the "General Techniques for Troubleshooting Your iPhone" section.

Your battery won't charge

If you find that your battery won't charge, here are some possible solutions:

- **If the iPhone is plugged in to a computer to charge via the USB port, it may be that the computer has gone into standby.** Waking the computer should solve the problem.

- **The USB port might not be transferring enough power.** For example, the USB ports on most keyboards and hubs don't offer much in the way of power. If you have your iPhone plugged in to a USB port on a keyboard or hub, plug it in to a USB port on your Mac or PC.

- **Attach the USB cable to the USB power adapter, and then plug the adapter in to an AC outlet.**

- **Double-check all connections to make sure everything is plugged in properly.**

- **Try another Lightning cable if you have one.**

If you can't seem to locate the problem after these steps, you may need to send your iPhone in for service.

You have trouble accessing a Wi-Fi network

Wireless networking adds a whole new set of potential snags to your troubleshooting chores because of problems such as interference and device ranges. Here's a list of a few troubleshooting items that you should check to solve any wireless connectivity problems you're having with your iPhone:

- **Make sure the Wi-Fi antenna is on.** Tap Settings, tap Wi-Fi, and then tap the Wi-Fi switch to On.

- **Make sure the iPhone isn't in Airplane mode.** Tap Settings and then tap the Airplane Mode switch to Off.

- **Check the connection.** The iPhone has a tendency to disconnect from a nearby Wi-Fi network for no apparent reason. Tap Settings. If the Wi-Fi setting shows as Not Connected, tap Wi-Fi, and then tap your network in the list.

- **Renew the lease.** When you connect to a Wi-Fi network, the access point gives your iPhone a Dynamic Host Control Protocol (DHCP) lease that allows it to access the net-work. You can often solve connectivity problems by renewing that lease. Tap Settings, tap Wi-Fi, and then tap the blue More Info icon to the right of the connected Wi-Fi network. Tap the DHCP tab, and then tap the Renew Lease button, shown in Figure 14.6.

- **Reconnect to the network.** You can often solve Wi-Fi network woes by disconnecting from the network and then reconnecting. Tap Settings, tap Wi-Fi, and then tap the blue More Info icon to the right of the connected Wi-Fi network. Tap the Forget This Network button to disconnect, and then reconnect to the same network.

- **Reset the network settings on your iPhone.** This removes all stored network data and resets everything to the factory state, which might solve the problem. Tap Settings, tap General, tap Reset, and then tap Reset Network Settings. When your iPhone asks you to confirm, tap Reset Network Settings.

‹ Wi-Fi	**LogophiliaB**	
Forget This Network		
IP ADDRESS		
DHCP	BootP	Static
IP Address		192.168.2.68
Subnet Mask		255.255.0.0
Router		192.168.2.1
DNS		192.168.2.1
Search Domains	no-domain-set-bellcanada	
Client ID		
Renew Lease		

14.6 Open the connected Wi-Fi network settings, and then tap Renew Lease to get a fresh lease on your Wi-Fi life.

- **Reboot and power cycle devices.** Reset your hardware by performing the following tasks, in order: Restart your iPhone, reboot your iPhone hardware, power cycle the wireless access point, and power cycle the broadband modem.

- **Look for interference.** Devices such as baby monitors and cordless phones that use the 2.4 GHz radio frequency (RF) band can play havoc with wireless signals. Try either moving or turning off such devices if they're near your iPhone or wireless access point.

- **Check your range.** If you're getting no signal or a weak signal, your iPhone could be too far away from the access point. You usually can't get much farther than about 230 feet (for an 802.11n Wi-Fi network; 115 feet for 802.11a/b/g networks) away from an access point before the signal begins to degrade. Either move closer to the access point or, if it has one, turn on the access point's range booster. You could also install a wireless range extender.

- **Update the wireless access point firmware.** The wireless access point firmware is the internal program that the access point uses to perform its various chores. Wireless access point manufacturers frequently update their firmware to fix bugs, so you should see if an updated version of the firmware is available. See your device documentation to learn how this works.

- **Reset the router.** As a last resort, reset the router to its default factory settings (see the device documentation to learn how to do this). Note that if you do this, you need to set up your network from scratch.

Caution

You should keep your iPhone and wireless access point well away from microwave ovens, which can jam wireless signals.

iTunes doesn't see your iPhone

When you connect your iPhone to your computer, iTunes should start and you should see the iPhone in the Devices list. If iTunes doesn't start when you connect your iPhone, or if iTunes is already running but the iPhone doesn't appear in the Devices list, it means that iTunes doesn't recognize your iPhone. Here are some possible fixes:

- **Check the connections.** Make sure the USB connector and the Lightning connector are fully seated.

- **Try a different USB port.** The port you're using might not work, so try another one. If you're using a port on a USB hub, try using one of the computer's built-in USB ports.

- **Restart your iPhone.** Press and hold the Sleep/Wake button for a few seconds until the iPhone shuts down. Press and hold Sleep/Wake again until you see the Apple logo.

- **Restart your computer.** This should reset the computer's USB ports, which might solve the problem.

- **Check your iTunes version.** You need at least iTunes version 12 to work with iOS 9.0.

- **Check your operating system version.** On a Mac, your iPhone requires OS X Lion (10.7.5) or later. On a Windows PC, your iPhone requires Windows 7 or later.

iTunes won't sync your iPhone

If iTunes sees your iPhone, but you can't get it to sync, you probably have to adjust some settings. See Chapter 7 for some troubleshooting ideas related to syncing. Another possibility is that your iPhone is currently locked. That's not usually a problem for iTunes, but it sometimes gets confused by a locked iPhone. The easy remedy is to unplug the iPhone, unlock it, and then plug it in again.

You have trouble syncing music or videos

You may run into a problem syncing your music or videos to your iPhone. The most likely culprit here is that your files are in a format that the iPhone can't read, such as WMA, MPEG-1, or MPEG-2. First, convert the files to a format that the iPhone does understand using converter software. Then put them back on iTunes and try to sync again. This should solve the problem.

iPhone-supported audio formats include AAC, Protected AAC, HE-AAC, MP3, MP3 VBR, Audible (formats 2, 3, and 4, Audible Enhanced Audio, AAX, and AAX+), Apple Lossless, AIFF, and WAV. iPhone-supported video formats include H.264, MPEG-4, and Motion JPEG.

You can't get your iPhone serial number

There are times when you might need the serial number of your iPhone. For example, if you contact Apple support, it asks you for your iPhone serial number.

Under normal circumstances, you follow these steps to get the serial number:

1. **Connect your iPhone to your computer.**
2. **In iTunes, click the iPhone in the Devices list.**
3. **Click the Summary tab.**
4. **Read the Serial Number value.**

If iTunes doesn't recognize your iPhone, you may still be able to get the serial number by following these steps:

1. **Connect your iPhone to your computer.**
2. **In iTunes, choose iTunes ➪ Preferences (Mac) or Edit ➪ Preferences (Windows).** The iTunes preferences appear.

3. **Click the Devices tab.**

4. **Hover the mouse over a backup of your iPhone.** As you can see in Figure 14.7, iTunes displays a message that includes the phone's serial number.

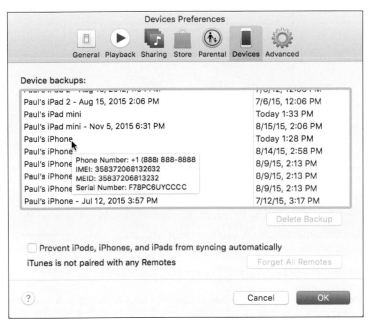

14.7 Hover the mouse pointer over a backup of your iPhone to get your serial number.

If you can't boot your iPhone, if iTunes doesn't recognize your iPhone, or you don't have a backup of your iPhone, you can still get the serial number. Shut down your iPhone, remove the SIM card tray, and then read the serial number that's printed on the side of the SIM tray.

An app is taking up a large amount of space

The iPhone is so useful and so much fun, it's easy to forget that it has limitations, especially when it comes to storage. This is particularly true if you have a 16GB model, but even a big 32GB iPhone can fill up in a hurry if you stuff it with movies, TV shows, and tons of magazine subscriptions.

You can tell how much free space your iPhone has left either by connecting it to iTunes or by tapping Settings, then General, and then Storage & iCloud Usage. The Storage & iCloud Usage screen not only shows you how much storage space you have available but also lets you tap Manage Storage in the Storage section to see how much space each app is using, as shown in Figure 14.8.

If you see that your iPhone is running low on space, check the apps to see if any of them are taking up more than their fair share of hard drive real estate. If you see a hard drive hog, you have two ways to delete its data and give your iPhone some room to breathe:

- **Third-party apps.** For an app you picked up via the App Store, tap the app, tap Delete App, and then tap Delete App when your iPhone asks you to confirm.

- **Built-in apps.** For an app that came with your iPhone (such as Music or Video), tap the app to display a list of the data it's storing on your iPhone, and then tap Edit. This puts the list in Edit mode, as shown in Figure 14.9. To remove an item, tap the red Delete button to the left of the item, and then tap the Delete button that appears.

Back	Storage	
Used		3.1 GB
Available		8.6 GB
Dictionary		219 MB >
Facebook		137 MB >
Spotify		136 MB >
Kindle		115 MB >
Evernote		113 MB >
Chrome		108 MB >
Flickr		101 MB >
Readability		99.1 MB >

14.8 The Storage screen tells you how much space each app is taking up.

	Music	Done
MUSIC		27.6 MB
All Songs		27.6 MB
ARTISTS		27.6 MB
The Black Keys 3 albums		27.6 MB

14.9 You can free up storage space by deleting individual items from some of the built-in apps.

Glossary

3D Touch On the iPhone 6s or 6s Plus, a light press on a screen object (such as a Home screen icon) activates that object's Peek feature, which either gives you a sneak peek of the object or displays commands that you can run on the object. If you then release the screen, iOS takes you back to where you were. Otherwise, a slightly harder press on the screen object activates the object's Pop feature, which takes you into the object's app.

3G A third-generation cellular network that includes the *HSPA*, *HSPA+*, and *DC-HSDPA* standards. It is supported in iPhone 3G and later models for data delivery over the cellular network.

4G See *LTE*.

802.11 See *Wi-Fi*.

Accelerometer The component inside the iPhone that senses the phone's orientation in space and adjusts the display accordingly (such as switching Safari from portrait mode to landscape mode).

access point A networking device that enables two or more devices to connect over a Wi-Fi network and to access a shared Internet connection.

Activation lock An iOS security feature that prevents anyone from activating your iPhone without knowing your Apple ID and password.

AirDrop A service that enables your iPhone to share information such as links, photos, and maps wirelessly via a Bluetooth connection.

Airplane mode An operational mode that turns off the transceivers for the phone, Wi-Fi, and Bluetooth features of an iPhone, which puts the phone in compliance with federal aviation regulations.

AirPlay A wireless technology that enables you to stream iPhone video or audio to an Apple TV device and so see or hear that media on your TV or audio receiver.

AirPrint A wireless technology that enables you to send a web page, email message, or other text from your iPhone to a printer.

alert A notification message that pops up on your iPhone screen and must be dealt with before you can resume what you were doing.

app An application that is designed for and runs on a specific device (such as an iPhone) or a set of related devices (such as an iPhone, iPad, and iPod touch).

Apple Pay An iPhone 6 or later feature that uses Near-Field Communications (NFC) to enable you to pay for items in a store by placing your finger on the Touch ID sensor and holding your phone near the store's contactless reader.

authentication See *SMTP authentication*.

Auto-Capitalization A keyboard feature that automatically activates the Shift key after you tap a sentence-ending character such as a period or question mark.

Auto-Correction A keyboard feature that automatically corrects errors as you type.

Background App Refresh An iOS feature that enables apps to update content even when you are not using them.

badge A small red icon that appears in the upper right corner of an app's icon to let you know that some new activity or data awaits you on the app.

banner A notification message that appears at the top of the iPhone screen but lets you keep working.

Bluetooth A wireless networking technology that enables you to exchange data between two devices using radio frequencies when the devices are within range of each other (usually within about 33 feet/10 meters).

bookmark An Internet site saved in Safari so that you can access it quickly in future browsing sessions.

burst mode A Camera app feature that takes photos at 10 frames per second when you tap and hold the Shutter button.

character preview A feature that briefly displays a pop-up that shows the keyboard character you are tapping.

cloud The collection of icloud.com servers that store your iCloud data and push any new data to your iPhone, Mac, or Windows PC.

Continuity A set of features that enables you to switch seamlessly between your iPhone and your Mac.

Control Center A configuration screen that enables you to control settings such as Airplane mode, Wi-Fi, Bluetooth, brightness, and volume. Swipe up from the bottom of the screen to display the Control Center interface.

crop To remove unneeded or distracting elements from a photo.

cycling Letting the iPhone battery completely discharge and then fully recharging it again.

data roaming A cell phone feature that enables you to make calls and perform other activities, such as checking for email, when you're outside of your provider's normal coverage area.

DC-HSPDA The Dual-Carrier High Speed Downlink Packet Access cellular transmission standard, which supports theoretical maximum download speeds of 42 Mbps.

desktop version A version of a web page designed to be viewed using a desktop computer.

digital rights management Technology that restricts the usage of content to prevent piracy.

discoverable A term to describe a device that has its Bluetooth feature turned on so that other Bluetooth devices can connect to it.

double-tap To use a fingertip to quickly press and release the iPhone screen twice.

DRM See *digital rights management*.

EDGE (Enhanced Data rates for GSM [Global System for Mobile communication] Evolution) A cellular network that's older and slower than 3G, although still supported by the iPhone.

emoji A character that uses an icon to represent an emotional state or a symbol.

event An appointment or meeting that you've scheduled in your iPhone Calendar.

Family Sharing An iCloud feature that enables up to six family members to share photos, calendars, and other iCloud content, as well as apps, media, and books purchased with a single credit card.

filter A special effect applied to a photo.

flick To quickly and briefly drag a finger across the iPhone screen.

FM transmitter A device that sends the output of an iPhone to an FM radio frequency, which you then play through your car stereo.

geo-fence A virtual, GPS-based perimeter around a location that, when crossed by your iPhone, can be used to trigger a reminder.

geotagging Using the iPhone's built-in GPS sensor to add location data to each photo, which enables you to organize your photos by location.

GPS (Global Positioning System) A satellite-based navigation system that uses wireless signals from a GPS receiver — such as the one in the iPhone — to accurately determine the receiver's current position.

group A collection of cards in the Contacts app.

Handoff A feature that enables you to begin an email message or text message on your phone and then continue it on your Mac.

headset A combination of headphones for listening and a microphone for talking.

High Dynamic Range A Camera app feature that enables you to take a photo of a high-contrast scene by adjusting the exposure in different areas, especially by underexposing extremely bright areas and overexposing extremely dark areas.

Home screen The main screen on your iPhone, which you access by pressing the Home button.

Home Sharing An iTunes feature that enables you to share the iTunes library on your Mac or PC with your iPhone.

HSPA The High Speed Packet Access cellular transmission standard, which supports theoretical maximum download speeds of 3.1 Mbps and is supported by the iPhone 5 and later.

HSPA+ The Evolved High Speed Packet Access cellular transmission standard, which supports theoretical maximum download speeds of 21 Mbps and is supported by the iPhone 5 and later.

iCloud Drive An online storage system that comes as part of an iCloud account.

image stabilization A Camera app feature that helps create a sharp, stable image by taking multiple shots at the same time and combining them automatically. The iSight camera in the iPhone 6 and later also features optical image stabilization, which uses the iPhone gyroscope and motion chip to precisely adjust the lens to compensate for hand shake.

IMAP (Internet Message Access Protocol) A type of email account where incoming messages, as well as copies of messages you send, remain on the server.

Internet tethering See *tethering*.

keychain A list of saved passwords on a Mac or on iCloud.

Live Photos Takes a series of still images for 1.5 seconds before and after you press the Shutter button. The result is a special animated JPEG image that, when pressed using 3D Touch, displays these images sequentially, resulting in what appears to be a three-second video clip. This feature requires the iPhone 6s or 6s Plus.

location services The features and technologies that provide apps and system tools with access to location data.

Low Power mode A battery-saving mode that kicks in automatically at 20 percent battery power and reduces power consumption by turning off certain features and effects.

LTE The Long-Term Evolution cellular transmission standard, which supports theoretical maximum download speeds of 73 Mbps. LTE does not meet the full specifications of the 4G standard, so it is referred to as "3.9G."

magnetometer A device that measures the direction and intensity of a magnetic field.

Mbps Megabits per second, or millions of bits per second; a unit of data transmission speed.

memory effect The process where a battery loses capacity over time if you repeatedly recharge it without first fully discharging it.

mirroring Displaying your iPhone screen on your TV.

multitouch A touchscreen technology that can detect and interpret two or more simultaneous touches, such as two-finger taps, spreads, and pinches.

notification Data that an app sends to let you know that the app has had recent activity for you to check out.

pair To connect one Bluetooth device with another by entering a passkey.

pan To slide a photo or other image up, down, left, or right.

Panorama A Camera app mode that enables you to take a wide-angle photo by sweeping the iPhone horizontally across the scene you want to capture.

passcode A six- or four-digit code, or a custom numeric or alphanumeric code, used to secure or lock an iPhone.

Peek See *3D Touch*.

personal hotspot An iPhone that is used as a kind of Internet gateway device where you share the Internet connection of the iPhone with one or more other devices, either directly via a USB cable or wirelessly via Wi-Fi or Bluetooth.

pinch To move two fingers closer together on the iPhone screen. See also *spread*.

playlist A collection of songs that you create using iTunes.

Pop See *3D Touch*.

POP (Post Office Protocol) A type of email account where incoming messages are stored temporarily on the provider's mail server until you connect to the server. The messages are then downloaded to your iPhone and removed from the server. See also *IMAP*.

power cycle To turn a device off, wait a few seconds for its inner components to stop processing, and then turn it on again.

predictive typing An iPhone keyboard feature that attempts to predict words as you type.

preferences The options, settings, and other data that you've configured for your Mac via System Preferences.

private browsing A web-browsing mode where Safari doesn't add sites to the History list, doesn't store site data in the cache, and doesn't save searches and passwords.

push To send data immediately without being prompted.

Reader A Safari feature that removes ads and other distractions from a web page.

ringtone A sound that plays when an incoming call is received.

RSS (Real Simple Syndication) A special file that contains the most recent posts added to a blog or similar website.

side switch The sliding switch that appears on the side of your iPhone, beside the volume rockers.

silent mode An operational state where the iPhone plays no sounds except alerts set with the Clock application.

slide To drag a finger across the iPhone screen.

smartphone A cell phone that also performs other tasks, such as accessing the Internet and managing contacts and appointments.

SMTP (Simple Mail Transport Protocol) The set of protocols that determines how email messages are addressed and sent.

SMTP authentication The requirement that you must log on to a provider's SMTP server to confirm that you're the person sending an email.

SMTP server The server that an Internet service provider uses to process outgoing email messages.

spread To move two fingers apart on the iPhone screen. See also *pinch*.

SSID (Service Set Identifier) The name that identifies a network to Wi-Fi devices.

swipe To briefly slide a finger left, right, up, or down on the iPhone screen.

synchronization A process that ensures that data on your computer (such as contacts, email accounts, and events) is the same as the data on your iPhone.

tap To use a fingertip to quickly press and release the iPhone screen.

tethering On a device such as an iPad, Mac, or Windows PC, using the Internet connection of an iPhone when the iPhone is configured as a *personal hotspot*.

text shortcut A short sequence of characters that represents a longer phrase.

Time Lapse A Camera app mode that takes a video of a scene by automatically snapping a picture approximately every second.

Touch ID Using your fingerprint to identify yourself to your iPhone and to apps that support this feature.

touchscreen A screen that responds to touches, such as finger taps and finger slides.

transceiver A device that transmits and receives wireless signals.

trim To edit the start and end points of a video recording or voice memo.

two-fingered tap To use two fingertips to quickly press and release the iPhone screen.

user-installable A component that an end user can remove and replace.

vCard A file that contains a person's contact information.

wallpaper The background image you see when you unlock your iPhone.

web clip A Home screen icon that serves as a link to a web page and preserves the scroll position and zoom level on that page.

Wi-Fi A wireless networking standard that enables wireless devices to transmit data and communicate with other devices using radio frequency signals beamed from one device to another.

Index

formats
    ebooks, 256–258
    recording, 198
formatting
    ebook text in iBooks, 265–266
    email text, 131–132
forwarding incoming calls, 87
4G. See LTE
Frequent Locations, clearing, 252
front microphone, 10
front-facing camera, 10, 176

G

GarageBand, creating ringtones with, 166–168
general techniques, troubleshooting
    about, 288–289
    connected devices, 289–290
    Device Firmware Upgrade mode, 293–294
    restoring data and settings, 291–293
    updating software, 290–291
Genius setting, 172
geo-fence, 308
geotagging, 177
gestures, maintaining email messages with, 135–136
getting started
    Control Center, 18–19
    Home button, 4
    physical features, 8–11
    Ring/Silent switch, 7–8
    Sleep/Wake button, 4–7
    touchscreen, 12–18
    volume controls, 8
Google
    email, 120
    popularity of, 115
GPS. See also Maps app
    controlling app access to, 251–252
    defined, 308
    disabling, 298
group, 308

H

H.264 video, 196
Handoff feature, 81, 308
hardware, rebooting, 288
headset jack, 9, 308
headsets, answering incoming calls while listening
    to music on, 162

hidden Wi-Fi networks, 59–60
High Dynamic Range (HDR), shooting photos in,
    180–181
High Quality on Cellular setting, 173
high-definition (HD) video recording capabilities, 197
highlighting text in iBooks, 267
History list
    about, 106–107
    deleting, 111
holding calls, 88
Home button, 4
Home screen
    customizing
        adding Safari web clips, 24
        creating app folders, 22–24
        resetting default layout, 25
    defined, 308
Home Sharing, 308
Home-click speed, changing, 54
hotspots, connecting to Wi-Fi, 64
HSPA/HSPA+ (High Speed Packet Access) networks,
    76, 308
HTML (Hypertext Markup Language), 134
Hypertext Markup Language (HTML), 134

I

i2Reader app, 268
iBooks app
    ebook formats, 256–258
    managing library
        about, 259
        adding EPUB books to, 262
        adding PDF attachments to, 260–261
        browsing books in iBookstore, 259–260
        collections, 261
        creating custom ebook covers, 263–264
        editing iBooks Bookshelf, 263
    reading ebooks with
        about, 264
        adding bookmarks, 266
        adding notes, 268
        controlling ebooks on reading screen, 264–265
        formatting ebook text, 265–266
        highlighting text, 267
        looking up words in dictionary, 267
    syncing ebooks with iCloud, 258
iBooks Bookshelf, editing, 263
iBookstore, browsing books in, 259–260